Dis-Positions: Troubling Methods and Theory in STS

Series Editors: **Mike Michael**, University of Exeter and **Alex Wilkie**, Goldsmiths, University of London

---

Turning the mirror on science and technology studies (STS), this pioneering book series explores the pivotal changes in the discipline. It occupies a unique position in the field as a platform for adventurous projects that redraw the disciplinary boundaries of STS.

Find out more at
bristoluniversitypress.co.uk/dis-positions

International advisory board

Itty Abraham, National University of Singapore
Ben Anderson, Durham University, UK
Casper Bruun-Jensen, Kyoto University, Japan
Nerea Calvillo, University of Warwick, UK
Tomás Sánchez Criado, Humboldt University of Berlin, Germany
Didier Debaise, Université Libre de Bruxelles, Belgium
Marisol de la Cadena, University of California, Davis, US
Carl DiSalvo, Georgia Tech, US
Miquel Domènech, Autonomous University of Barcelona, Spain
Ignacio Farías, Humboldt University of Berlin, Germany
Michael Guggenheim, Goldsmiths, University of London, UK
Michael Halewood, University of Essex, UK
Gay Hawkins, Western Sydney University, Australia
Christopher M. Kelty, University of California, Los Angeles, US
Daniel López Gómez, Open University of Catalonia, Spain
Celia Lury, University of Warwick, UK
Patrice Maniglier, Paris Nanterre University, France
Noortje Marres, University of Warwick, UK
Amade M'charek, University of Amsterdam, Netherlands
Atsuro Morita, Osaka University, Japan
Fabian Muniesa, Paris Mines School, France
Dimitris Papadopoulos, University of California, Santa Cruz, US
Kavita Philip, University of British Columbia, Canada
Maria Puig de la Bellacasa, University of California, Santa Cruz, US
Kane Race, University of Sydney, Australia
Israel Rodríguez Giralt, Open University of Catalonia, Spain
Martin Savransky, Goldsmiths, University of London, UK
Melanie Sehgal, University of Wuppertal, Germany
Manuel Tironi, Pontifical Catholic University of Chile, Chile
Martin Tironi, Pontifical Catholic University of Chile, Chile

Find out more at
bristoluniversitypress.co.uk/dis-positions

MORE-THAN-HUMAN AESTHETICS

Venturing Beyond the Bifurcation of Nature

Edited by
Melanie Sehgal and Alex Wilkie

First published in Great Britain in 2025 by

Bristol University Press
University of Bristol
1-9 Old Park Hill
Bristol
BS2 8BB
UK
t: +44 (0)117 374 6645
e: bup-info@bristol.ac.uk

Details of international sales and distribution partners are available at bristoluniversitypress.co.uk

© Bristol University Press 2025

British Library Cataloguing in Publication Data
A catalogue record for this book is available from the British Library

ISBN 978-1-5292-2778-9 hardcover
ISBN 978-1-5292-2779-6 paperback
ISBN 978-1-5292-2780-2 ePub
ISBN 978-1-5292-2781-9 ePdf

The right of Melanie Sehgal and Alex Wilkie to be identified as editors of this work has been asserted by them in accordance with the Copyright, Designs and Patents Act 1988.

All rights reserved: no part of this publication may be reproduced, stored in a retrieval system, or transmitted in any form or by any means, electronic, mechanical, photocopying, recording, or otherwise without the prior permission of Bristol University Press.

Every reasonable effort has been made to obtain permission to reproduce copyrighted material. If, however, anyone knows of an oversight, please contact the publisher.

The statements and opinions contained within this publication are solely those of the editors and contributors and not of the University of Bristol or Bristol University Press. The University of Bristol and Bristol University Press disclaim responsibility for any injury to persons or property resulting from any material published in this publication.

Bristol University Press works to counter discrimination on grounds of gender, race, disability, age and sexuality.

Cover design: Andrew Corbett and Alex Wilkie
Front cover image: Alex Wilkie

Contents

Notes on Contributors   vii
Acknowledgements   xi
Dis-Positions Series Preface   xii

1   Beyond the Bifurcation of Nature: Tracing More-Than-   1
     Human Aesthetics in Times of Socio-Ecological Crisis
     Melanie Sehgal and Alex Wilkie

PART I   **Feeling and Experiencing**

2   Whitehead, Dewey, Metaphysics, Aesthetics, Experience   29
     and Our World(s)
     Michael Halewood

3   Eternal Objects of Nuclear Waste Futures   42
     Thomas P. Keating

4   Geo-Narrativity: Anthropocene, Aesthetics, Forensics   57
     Alexander Damianos

5   Race and Reality: Towards a Social Aesthetics of Race   71
     Michael L. Thomas

PART II   **Problematizing and (Re)Valuing**

6   A New Taste for Life? Value Ecologies and the   89
     Aesthetics of the Outside
     Martin Savransky

7   Variations on the Great Refusal via Dante and Whitehead   104
     Cécile Malaspina

8   Aesthetic Axiology: Amanda Piña's *Climatic*   120
     Dances/Danzas Climáticas
     Maximilian Haas

PART III   **Infecting and Caring**

9   To Err is More Than More-Than-Human: Patient   139
     Safety and the Aesthetics of a Never Event
     Alex Wilkie

| 10 | Machinic Highs and Pathic Patchworks of Addicted Systems
Matthew Fuller and Andrew Goffey | 153 |
| 11 | On the Aesthetics of Care/Care of Aesthetics in Social Scientific Research
Mike Michael | 172 |

PART IV (Un)Learning and Luring

12	An Ethology of Abstractions: Learning How to Cultivate Our Modes of Thought with Stengers *Didier Debaise*	189
13	Back to the Classroom: What Whitehead Took from Art, and What a New Aesthetic Paradigm Can Take from Whitehead *Nicholas Gaskill*	205
14	Schools of Feeling: Unlearning the Bifurcation of Nature Through Aesthetic Education *Melanie Sehgal*	221

Index   238

Notes on Contributors

Alexander Damianos is Lecturer in law at the University of Kent. He holds a PhD in law from the London School of Economics and Political Science, where he also completed an MSc in Law, Anthropology and Society. He completed a post-doc in the Department of Science and Technology Studies at the University of Leiden and had been a researcher at Studio Olafur Eliasson. He is currently working on his first monograph, an ethnographic study of the Anthropocene Working Group's ongoing formalization effort.

Didier Debaise is a permanent researcher at the Fonds National de la Recherche Scientifique and Professor at Université Libre de Bruxelles, where he teaches contemporary philosophy. He co-founded, with Maria Puig de la Bellacasa, Isabelle Stengers and Nathalie Trussart the Groupe d'études constructivistes and is the director of two collections with Presses du réel. Didier's main areas of research include speculative philosophy, the invention of the concept of Nature, new forms of perspectivisms and the links between American pragmatism and French contemporary philosophy. He has published two books on Whitehead's philosophy (*Speculative Empiricism. Revisiting Whitehead*, Edinburgh University Press, 2017 and *Nature as Event. The Lure of the Possible*, Duke University Press, 2017), edited volumes on pragmatism (Vie et experimentation, Vrin, 2019) and the history of contemporary metaphysics (*Philosophie des Possessions*, Presses du réel, 2011), and he has recently published two edited collections, one with Stengers on William James and a second on a metaphysics of perspectivism.

Matthew Fuller is a cultural theorist who works on art, science, politics and aesthetics. His books include *How to Sleep: The Art, Biology and Culture of Unconsciousness* (Bloomsbury, 2018); *How to Be a Geek: Essays on the Culture of Software* (Polity, 2017); with Olga Goriunova, *Bleak Joys: Aesthetics of Ecology and Impossibility* (University of Minnesota Press, 2019); and with Eyal Weizman, *Investigative Aesthetics: Conflicts and Commons in the Politics of Truth* (Verso, 2021). He is Professor of Cultural Studies at Goldsmiths, University of London.

Nicholas Gaskill is Associate Professor of American Literature at the University of Oxford and tutorial fellow at Oriel College. He is the author of *Chromographia: American Literature and the Modernization of Color* (University of Minnesota Press, 2018) and co-editor, with A.J. Nocek, of *The Lure of Whitehead* (University of Minnesota Press, 2014). In 2023, along with Kate Stanley, he edited a special section of *Publications of the Modern Language Association* titled 'Aesthetic Education: A Twenty-First-Century Primer'. His current projects include an analysis of intensity as an aesthetic category and a study of pragmatist experiments in aesthetic education.

Andrew Goffey is Associate Professor in Critical Theory and Cultural Studies and the Director of the Centre for Critical Theory at the University of Nottingham. He is the author, with Matthew Fuller, of *Evil Media* (MIT Press, 2012), the editor, with Éric Alliez, of *The Guattari Effect* (Bloomsbury, 2011) and, with Roland Faber, of *The Allure of Things* (Bloomsbury, 2013). He has published widely on philosophy, technology and culture; he is the translator of numerous works of French philosophy and co-edits the journal *Computational Culture*.

Maximilian Haas is a performance and dance theorist, dramaturge and Visiting Professor of Theatre Studies at the Berlin University of the Arts. He received his PhD from the Academy of Media Arts, Cologne, and his research interests include dramaturgy in contemporary dance and theatre, aesthetics of performative arts, methodology and epistemology of artistic research, ecology and sustainable modes of production, science, animal and environmental studies. His recent publications include *Animals on Stage: An Aesthetic Ecology of Performance* (Kadmos, 2018), and *How to Relate: Knowledge Arts Practices* (Transcript, 2021). Haas has worked as a curator at organizations such as HAU Hebbel am Ufer, Berliner Festspiele and the Volksbühne. With Margarita Tsomou, he curates the series *Burning Futures: On Ecologies of Existence* at HAU.

Michael Halewood is Professor of Social Theory at the University of Essex. His work tries to explore certain problems which inhabit and inhibit philosophy and sociology. He often uses the thought of Alfred North Whitehead to help him. His books include *Language and Process: Words, Whitehead and the World* (Edinburgh University Press, 2020); *A.N. Whitehead and Social Theory* (Anthem, 2011) and *Rethinking the Social Through Durkheim, Marx, Weber and Whitehead* (Anthem, 2014).

Thomas P. Keating is a researcher in Technology and Social Change at Linköping University, Sweden. His research intersects cultural geography and process philosophies, and he engages with problems involving human–technology relationships. He has recently published on Gilbert Simondon (*Progress in Human Geography*), geophilosophies (*Subjectivity*), speculative empiricism (*Theory, Culture and Society*), and has co-edited a collection on *Speculative Geographies* (Palgrave Macmillan). Currently, he is writing a Key Information File – commissioned by Svensk Kärnbränslehantering Aktiebolag – that aims to communicate memory of nuclear waste repositories in Sweden 100,000 years into the future.

Cécile Malaspina is Directrice de Programme at the Collège International de Philosophie, Paris, and was a member of its executive board and scientific committee from 2019 to 2022. She programmes Art and Curatorial Practice for the New Centre for Research and Practice. Based at King's College London, where she is a Visiting Research Fellow, she is the author of *An Epistemology of Noise* (Bloomsbury, 2018) and principal translator of Gilbert Simondon's *On the Mode of Existence of Technical Objects* (Univocal, 2016). Cécile is a member of the editorial boards of *Angelaki: Journal of the Theoretical Humanities, Copy Press*, and guest editor at *Nature: Humanities and Social Sciences Communications*.

Mike Michael is a sociologist of science and technology, and Professor in the Department of Social and Political Science, Philosophy and Anthropology at the University of Exeter. His research interests have touched upon the relation of everyday life to technoscience, the use of design to develop a 'speculative methodology', and the role of aesthetics and affect in the making of publics. Recent publications include (co-authored with Andy Boucher et al) *Energy Babble: Entangling Design and STS* (Mattering Press, 2018), *Actor-Network Theory: Trials, Trails and Translations* (Sage, 2017), and *The Research Event: Towards Prospective Methodologies in Sociology* (Routledge, 2021).

Martin Savransky is Reader in the Department of Sociology at Goldsmiths, University of London, where he convenes the MA in Ecology, Culture and Society. His work combines philosophy and the social sciences, post-colonial thought and the environmental humanities to activate fugitive and speculative methodologies of life on unstable ecological terrain. He is the author of *Around the Day in Eighty Worlds: Politics of the Pluriverse* (Duke University Press, 2021) and *The Adventure of Relevance: An Ethics of Social Inquiry* (Palgrave, 2016), and co-editor of *After Progress* (Sage, 2022) and of *Speculative Research: The Lure of Possible Futures* (Routledge, 2017).

Melanie Sehgal is Director of Research at the Institut für Grundlagenforschung zur Philosophiegeschichte at Bergische Universität Wuppertal. Her work is situated at the crossroads of process philosophy, the environmental humanities, science and technology studies, aesthetics and the history and historiography of philosophy. She is the author of *A Situated Metaphysics. Empiricism and Speculation in William James and Alfred North Whitehead*

(Konstanz University Press, 2016) and various articles on process philosophy, aesthetics, transdisciplinary practices and on what she calls the 'arts of the Anthropocene', techniques for composing worlds beyond modern habits of demarcation.

Michael L. Thomas is Assistant Professor of Philosophy in Critical Cultural Theory at the University of Amsterdam working in Social Aesthetics and the Philosophy of Race. He was formerly a Humboldt Foundation Research Fellow at the JFK Institute for North American Studies at the Freie Universität Berlin and Assistant Professor of Philosophy and Coordinator of Africana Studies at Susquehanna University. He has published work in philosophy and literature, social theory, the philosophy of race and North American studies.

Alex Wilkie is Professor of Design and Societies at Goldsmiths, University of London. His interests are located at various articulations between design, more-than-human computer interaction and science and technology studies. Here, his research explores aesthetics, speculative thought and practices, climate change and the environment, public engagement with science and technology, healthcare as well as practice-research and inventive methods. Recent publications include *Speculative Research: The Lure of Possible Futures* (Routledge, 2017) and *Inventing the Social* (Mattering Press, 2018).

Acknowledgements

This volume has taken more time to come into being than anticipated, having been impacted, like other adventures, by COVID-19, but emerging with the elation of life's creation as well as confronting mortality and adversity, including an incident that figures in this book. We are delighted that the book has now materialized and are immensely grateful to the contributing authors for their patience, perseverance and continued enthusiasm for the project. The origins of the book lie in a meeting between the editors on 21 February 2018 after Melanie Sehgal delivered a talk as part of the Pluralistic Variations Lecture Series, hosted by the Unit of Play at the Department of Sociology, Goldsmiths, University of London. For instigating this meeting and appreciating the link between our shared interests in the work of A.N. Whitehead and generalized aesthetics, we would like to express our warm thanks to Martin Savransky. An online workshop titled 'Adventures in aesthetics: rethinking aesthetics beyond the bifurcation of nature' was convened in summer 2020, supported by the Centre for Invention and Social Process (CISP), also at the Department of Sociology, Goldsmiths. Here, we would like to thank the Directors of CISP, Michael Guggenheim and Marsha Rosengarten (alongside Alex Wilkie) for supporting the event as well as the workshop participants, particularly those whose work now features in this volume.

We would like to extend our thanks to Mike Michael in his capacity, alongside Alex Wilkie, as Dis-Positions series editor for his invaluable advice on developing this project on aesthetics, turning this into a book and welcoming it as the second in the series. At Bristol University Press, Paul Stevens supported the proposition of the book from the very beginning and helped nurture it through its early stages, while Georgina Bolwell, Bahar Celik Muller, Ellen Mitchell and Kelly Winter provided helpful production guidance and support.

Dis-Positions Series Preface

The aim of the Dis-Positions book series is to bring together recent work in the emerging intersections of such disciplines as sociology, anthropology, history, geography, design and philosophy, not least as they bear on the broad field of science and technology studies (STS). Conversely, if STS is undergoing major shifts in how it engages with 'the social' and the question of 'societies', it raises vital matters of concern for these various disciplines and their inter-connections. Dis-Positions thus provides a platform on which varieties of generative mutualities across these areas of scholarship can be presented.

In this respect, Dis-Positions is undergirded by a desire to promote novel fields of inquiry, adventurous theoretical and empirical projects, and inventive methodological practices. It seeks to encourage authors to address live debates while drawing on and interrogating developments across academic areas, in the process disturbing and repatterning STS. In pursuing this ethos, Dis-Positions comprises a consolidated, rigorous and proactive space through which creative and critical new perspectives in STS and beyond can find a voice. Under this rubric fall discussions of the post-human, post-colonial, affective and aesthetic; methodological inventions that incorporate speculative, engaged, entangled and socio-material practices; empirical novelty that ranges from emergent technoscientific innovations to reformulations of the ordinary; and conceptually creative and critical developments that capture processual and pluralistic thought, extensions of assemblage and practice theories, and the turns to affect and post-performativity.

We are delighted to have the volume *More-Than-Human Aesthetics: Venturing Beyond the Bifurcation of Nature* as the second publication in the Dis-Positions series. Edited by Melanie Sehgal and Alex Wilkie, this innovative collection introduces a Whiteheadian version of aesthetics into our thinking about a range of topics that are central to STS and to the social sciences (broadly defined) in general. Taking as a starting point the argument that the aesthetic today manifests as a fundamental dimension in the world, the volume asks in what ways feeling and being – modes of sensibility – are able to survive within, or adapt to, the unfolding socio-ecological crisis. Here, aesthetics is no longer a marker of a phenomenological engagement with an art object, nor a projection of human values on a mute world, instantiating the 'bifurcation of nature'. Rather, aesthetics is decidedly more-than-human, encompassing the circulations and resonances of feeling that trouble such easy distinctions as the human and the non-human.

This basic insight is deployed in various ways by the contributors to *More-Than-Human Aesthetics* to rethink approaches to what has been called the Anthropocene. As such, chapters variously extend the parameters of a generalized aesthetics, interject a more-than-human aesthetics to challenge the typical forms of scientific practice and environmental knowledge production; apply Whiteheadian aesthetics to illuminate the micro-processes and patterns of care and non-care in such domains as social media apps, clinical malpractice and social scientific methodology; and explore how reformed aesthetic pedagogies can lay the foundation for alternative reconfigurations of various constituencies' relations with nature and the environment in their emergent guises. Pivotal across the volume is a thorough immersion in the empirical: the authors' arguments grapple with, and emerge from, their entanglement in their case studies. In this respect, the volume is aesthetically self-exemplifying insofar as author and world are mutually constitutive; that is, they share in the flow of feeling.

The editors have managed to bring together a range of chapters which contextualize this via an introduction that situates more-than-human aesthetics in relation to broader discussions of aesthetics (and the links to metaphysics and ontology), to disciplinary traditions that draw on aesthetics (substantively and methodologically), and to the multitude of environmental concerns currently faced. Taken as whole, *More-Than-Human Aesthetics: Venturing Beyond the Bifurcation of Nature* serves as a profound provocation for re-imagining how academic thought and practice might be conducted under conditions of socio-ecological crisis. On this score, it fits perfectly into the Dis-Positions series.

Mike Michael, University of Exeter
Alex Wilkie, Goldsmiths, University of London

1

Beyond the Bifurcation of Nature: Tracing More-Than-Human Aesthetics in Times of Socio-Ecological Crisis

Melanie Sehgal and Alex Wilkie

Aesthetics in times of socio-ecological crisis

Intense hues of red, orange and pink diffuse across the sky. A spectacular sunset unfolds; beautiful, perhaps sublime to the human observer. The hues that make for dramatic and spectacular sunsets are induced by aerosols, fine particles in the atmosphere, changing the way rays of light are scattered and, as a result, shifting the colours from bluish and purple hues to red ones. These aerosols are products of pollution, mainly through the combustion of fossil fuels. It seems as if sunsets have become even more spectacular and, to most human eyes, more beautiful through air pollution. Vast and complex infrastructures of meteorological and environmental sensors enmesh the earth, sensitive to and sensing, among other factors, climatic changes in temperature and carbon dioxide concentrations: sensors which resource any number of knowledge practices. Earth is simultaneously rendered as both an 'object' of knowledge, computational modelling and intervention and as an immense centre of experiences, feelings and sensitivities. In conflict and war zones, machine vision technologies, algorithmically trained to detect and identify targets, ruthlessly enact violence, death and destruction through computational sensing. Here, military and security forces, along with ever-more sophisticated ordnance, wreak more-than-human havoc on adversaries, civilians and the environment alike, all of whom sense, register and suffer the violence wrought. Various ensembles of digital platforms involving computational interactivity, artificial intelligences resourced by (and resourcing) ever-growing data sets continually territorialize new domains and registers of activity and feeling, sensitized to and bringing into being novel and intensive forms of algorithmic surveillance, predictive consumption and political calculus. In the Chilean district of Puchuncaví, an industrialized and highly toxic environment, much like other industrial and post-industrial settings, tomato farmers endlessly clean chemical ash from their crops. Here, tending and caring mark ways of coping and living with toxicity, techniques for conserving feeling and acting in a world where states and biochemical industries literally fumigate feeling.[1]

Intensely polluted sunsets, climate sensitivity, algorithmically enabled conflict, surveillance capitalism and contaminated conditions of existence are not, however, exceptions, but rather variations of living in times of socio-ecological crisis where sensing and feeling are writ large and placed centre stage. Thus, these vignettes serve to highlight the starting point of this volume: the sense that there is a proliferation of aesthetics beyond the narrow confines of sectors specifically dedicated to it in the arts and humanities. They show that aesthetics is at play in all manner of human and more-than-human processes of becoming sensitive and sensitized, as well as in processes of becoming numbed and anaesthetized in encounters of creation, perishing and change. Rather than being a supplementary dimension of values, the beautiful or the sublime added by human observers, the aesthetic today manifests as a fundamental and critically important dimension in fashioning, cultivating and sustaining more-than-human worlds. At the same time, these examples dramatize that the way we have come to think of the aesthetic, its place(s), practices and manifestations, no longer holds in a world marked by the consequences of extractivist practices and ecological destruction made possible by technoscientific deliverance.

In this volume, we wager that the changes that life on this planet is currently undergoing, call them, after Crutzen and Stoermer (2000), Anthropocene or not, put aesthetics centre stage. Which ways of feeling and being, which modes of sensibility, get to survive and continue or evolve their modes of existence? In the face of the mass extinction event currently under way, many ways of feeling and being in the world are irretrievably lost (Van Dooren, 2014). Our present moment is marked by an unprecedented loss in sensibility while new exploits of technological feeling (see Goffey and Fuller, Chapter 10, this volume) are incessantly produced, compounding the losses. But how can we account for these changes when our modes of sensibility and representation have evolved in relation to entirely different worlds, when they are even built into our very senses? If the Anthropocene is principally an aesthetic event, as Heather Davis and Etienne Turpin (2015: 11) have argued, how can we conceptualize this version of aesthetics, especially given that our conceptual apparatuses concerning aesthetics are geared towards the appreciation of works of art and culture alone? How can we account for the fact that aesthetics no longer pertains to the worlds of humans but to being writ large?

In light of these issues that mark our present, the contributions in this volume spring from a shared sense that rethinking aesthetics is urgently needed today. In a world out of joint, the conceptual apparatus inherited from Western modernity no longer seems to provide suitable instruments to grasp the current predicament. This, we contend, particularly concerns the grammar and vocabulary of aesthetics. While aesthetic questions may seem frivolous in the face of the magnitude and seriousness of contemporary issues, we wager that this assessment is precisely part of the problem. It is only within the frame of thought of Western modernity that the realm of aesthetics has been relayed to the margins, even if these are honorific, in the first place. It is only within this frame of thought that the aesthetic has been conceptualized as a specific kind of feeling, attributed to specific actors in specific situations and settings vis-à-vis specific objects, epitomized in the human 'subject', or viewer, in front of an artwork installed in a gallery or museum.

In the 1980s, at the dawn of the ecological crisis, Félix Guattari was already stressing the necessity to reconceptualize aesthetics beyond its modern compartmentalization. He proposed (1995) a 'new aesthetic paradigm' that transversally cuts across what he termed the three ecologies: the environmental, the social and the psychical, thus largely transcending the anthropocentric and the realm of the arts and taking in worlds marked by developments in technoscience and extractivist modes of production alike. Guattari reminds us that the relegation of the aesthetic to a special realm of society happened only very late in Western history. Hence, speculatively, it is by no means the only way of negotiating heterogenous modes of existence. If today it is hard to imagine other ways of doing and thinking the aesthetic, it is only because 'this sectorisation of modes of valorisation is now so deeply rooted in the cognitive apprehension of our era' (Guattari, 1995: 99) that it is difficult to imagine otherwise. In this volume, we start from the intuition that the philosophy of Alfred North Whitehead might provide the tools to imagine and conceptualize aesthetics beyond the modes of valorization that have come to define our present. On the one hand, Whitehead provides a reading of his own present – and the implicit habits of thought that structure it – that strikes us as pertinent in order to understand our own epoch and the habits of thought – and feeling – that have come to shape it and the place afforded to aesthetics. On the other hand, his process philosophy equips us with tools to reconceptualize the place and the contours of aesthetics beyond the frameworks of modernity. For both Whitehead and Guattari, the realm of the aesthetic, even if it, in principle, rests on the same plane as other modes of expression, takes on a privileged position with which to rethink contemporary modes of thought. The realm of aesthetics transversally (re)conceived promises to provide a lever in order to unhinge modern habits of thought and their modes of compartmentalizing reality. But why aesthetics? Where does the particular importance of aesthetics come from, and does it still hold today, at the beginning of the 21st century?

Aesthetics and the bifurcation of nature

Whitehead's diagnosis of a 'bifurcation of nature' in modern thought – formulated at the beginning of the 20th century, long before Guattari wrote *Chaosmosis*, and with concerns other than that of environmental destruction in mind – provides a possible answer. By 'bifurcation of nature' Whitehead (1967b: 54, 2004: 30) referred to an implicit incoherent fault at the heart of the modern conception of nature. Within the corpus of modern philosophy ranging from Newton to Kant, the concept of nature, Whitehead notes, is at once thought of as 'bare nature', modelled on a materialistic understanding of the physical world that functions causally, and a 'nature as perceived' – with its qualities, values and meaning apprehended by a human subject – without providing a possibility to relate or connect these two concepts of nature.[2] To this day, endless debates about the relation between body and mind, primary and secondary qualities or first and second nature testify to this impossibility, birthing further bifurcations such as the distinction between nature and culture, fact and fiction, subject and object, sex and gender. Whitehead's critique concerns the fact that these

> two systems of reality (...) are real in different senses. One reality would be the entities such as electrons which are the study of speculative physics. This would be the reality which is there for knowledge; although on this theory it is never known. For what is known is the other sort of reality, which is the byplay of the mind. Thus there would be two natures, one is the conjecture and the other is the dream. Whitehead (2004: 30)

How did this bifurcation come about? How did such an incoherence take hold, particularly in a culture of thought that prides itself upon its rational procedures? And what does aesthetics have to do with it? Whitehead points out that the concept of nature 'bifurcates' into two mutually incompatible concepts – causal nature and apparent nature – when a materialistic understanding of nature, generated within the framework of classical physics, is misunderstood as representing nature at large and in consequence is generalized beyond its domain. Instead of denoting a particular degree of abstraction – pertaining to the realm of moving bodies as they form the object of classical physics – this conception of nature is mistaken as an adequate description of reality as such and, more precisely, of reality in its most concrete instance.[3] Whitehead (1967b: 49) identifies a fundamental presupposition that is operative within this culture of thought: nature, in its most concrete instance, is thought of as matter 'simply located' in time and space. Its relations, becoming or values, in Whitehead's words, are not essential to what it is; no 'reference to other regions of space-time' is required for the explanation of what it is. Nature is 'merely' matter. Nature bifurcates because we, as humans, want to exclude ourselves from such a description – in contrast, we are free, follow purposes and hold values. Moreover, in this frame of thought, we endow an essentially valueless world with our own values, colours and emotions. Whitehead describes this 'second nature' as a 'dream' because its relation to 'reality', or first nature, is unclear as this first nature is simply a 'conjecture', never known as such. Not only does it become difficult if not impossible, within the materialist scheme, to negotiate the relation between these two realms, but more fundamentally for our context, aesthetics gets boxed into the realm of second nature: of added values to a valueless world, of human dreams untethered to reality.

Thus, a historical hypothesis linking the bifurcation of nature to the 'invention of modern science' lies at the basis of Whitehead's reading of modernity. However, it is the astonishing success, persistence and ruthless productivity of Newtonian physics that explains the generalization of a materialist understanding of nature beyond its remit. Whitehead's concern, therefore, is directed towards the philosophical interpretation of the materialistic doctrine: its interpretation as what is the most concrete aspect of nature and its consequent generalization beyond the domain of classical physics. It is in this sense, for Whitehead, that the bifurcation of nature marks a defeat for philosophy (though certainly not for physics or the sciences more widely) because it would have been the job of philosophy to single out and criticize such fallacious ways of thinking rather than reifying them. In Whitehead's reading, modern philosophy rightly rejects the materialist doctrine as an adequate description of the mind (the subjective), but it implicitly accepts it as an adequate description of nature because it retreats from the realm of nature altogether. In this way, scientific materialism, with its notions of bare facts and bare matter, remains undisputed; it is simply supplemented by the realm of subjectivity.

The discipline of aesthetics, as formed in the 18th century, can be read as a reaction to this conundrum and as an exemplary epistemological realm where this reification took hold. Alexander Gottlieb von Baumgarten, who coined the term 'aesthetics', deriving it from the Greek 'aisthanomai' and replacing older theories of the beautiful by a theory of sensuous perception (Townsend, 1998: 669), insisted on the importance of the senses as a mode of knowledge production in their own right. He was thereby carving out a space for other kinds of knowledge practices next to, albeit inferior to, those of the materialist sciences, precisely by leaving the latter's epistemological claims firmly intact. One could say, then, that since the 18th century and the 'event' of modern science, the ways in which the aesthetic has been conceived have largely mirrored the ordering of science founded on the bifurcation of nature (Sehgal, 2018). In other words, whereas science and scientific practices have forcefully mobilized themselves around 'bare nature' independent of 'culture' and the 'social', aesthetic thinking has also colluded in, and is a product of, this opposition, concerning itself with the experiencing subject, artistic expression and the creation of values. However, based as they are on the assumption of a bifurcated notion of nature, such values can only be conceived of as an added, but ultimately inessential, layer to reality. The bifurcation of nature thus extends far beyond specialized discussions of philosophy. For Whitehead, these discussions reflect a wider culture of thought, which they make explicit or even solidify, but to whose poisons they find no antidote.

These poisons become palpable when the experiential consequences of the bifurcation of nature are taken into consideration. Here, we must first note that the theory of the bifurcation of nature is simply inconsistent with experience: few things or beings behave in the same way as polished billiard balls rolling down an inclined plane. Hence, they are impossible to adequately describe in materialist terms. More gravely, the problem is that everything that does not fit into the materialist scheme is, in consequence, denied the status of existence proper, and thus explained away, disfigured as merely illusory, merely subjective, merely psychological, merely aesthetic, pitting experience against reality: 'you might experience the beauty of the glowing sunset, but *actually* it is only the outcome of a particular play of atoms that cause certain neurological reactions in the brain – the perception of beauty is a mere byplay of the mind, merely a subjective illusion'. Here, the anaesthetic dimension of the habit of letting nature bifurcate becomes fully obvious: if something that is in fact part of experience, part of reality, is explained away as merely illusionary and subjective, experience ends up being impoverished, stripped of its very qualities and values. We end up experiencing less than what is given in experience when 'apparent nature' – that which is experienced – is excluded from reality proper. Even if, within the 'cosmology of the moderns' (Debaise, 2017: 41), the aesthetic seems to be given a central and honorific place – museums are constructed, artists are celebrated for their genius and their artworks fetishized – this marked position only hides the fact that it is premised on a fundamental structural devaluation of the aesthetic as secondary and non-essential.[4] In sum, with the concept of the bifurcation of nature, Whitehead diagnoses the invention of the modern concept of nature through experimental science and philosophy as *the* fundamental operation shaping and configuring the dominant contemporary – or 'modern' – experience of reality and the experiential, epistemic and political operations that ensue far beyond the realm of science or philosophy. The habit of letting nature bifurcate all but defines the experience of the moderns.

The bifurcation of nature can therefore be called a cosmology, or metaphysics, of the moderns, rendering a particular culture of thought (Halewood, 2011; Sehgal, 2016). But it is not an explicit worldview or philosophy. In concert with Debaise (2017) we want to emphasize its implicit and, most importantly, essentially operative, machinic character. The bifurcation of nature involves undergirding operations or movements of thought that translate into action and may even stem from action such as experimental dispositives (Sehgal, Chapter 14, this volume). It is fed by what Debaise (2021: 314) calls 'predatory abstractions' that *repeatedly* let nature bifurcate into two separate and generalizable realms where one can be approved and authorized to the detriment of the other, which is disqualified. Within the realm of contemporary knowledge practices, notable cases in point are the science wars or two cultures of thought and, more generally, any form of scientism which tries to remedy the inconsistencies brought on by the incoherent concept of nature by generalizing their side and explaining everything through their lens. Despite this attention to the politics of modern knowledge practices, little or no attention has been paid to its corollary for aesthetic reasoning, practices and processes.[5] It is this we wish to address and remedy in this volume.

Generalization and inversion: towards a metaphysics of more-than-human aesthetic experience

Addressing the place of aesthetics within the cosmology of the moderns does not imply criticizing aesthetics at large or suggesting that, by being irredeemably marked by the bifurcation of nature, the realm of the aesthetic has become superfluous. Rather, we are insisting on rethinking the very nature of aesthetics and its modes of conceptualization beyond modern confines. This implies untethering aesthetics from the assumptions guiding modern philosophy's engagement with it, predicated as they are on a bifurcated notion of nature. Undoing these assumptions comprises two interrelated movements of thought. First, a new aesthetic paradigm, which, rather than bifurcating reality into two realms and allocating aesthetics to only one half of it, *generalizes* aesthetics across the entire realm of being, viewing it as fundamental to the feeling and experience of all actors, entities and phenomena (Dewey, 2005; Shaviro, 2009; Sehgal, 2018: 118). Thus, instead of understanding aesthetics as an added layer to (human) being, we propose to understand aesthetics as immanent to all processes and all kinds of existence. Second, an *inversion* of modern aesthetics, which builds upon the general inversion of Kant's philosophy that Whitehead's 'philosophy of organism' undertakes, replacing Kant's Critique of Pure Reason by a 'Critique of Pure

Feeling' (1978: 113). While Kant, according to Whitehead (1978: 156), is to be credited for the introduction of 'the conception of an act of experience as a constructive functioning', he is quick to point out that Kant got the order in which experience is constructed wrong. Rather than conceptualizing experience as 'a process from subjectivity to apparent objectivity' (Whitehead, 1978: 156), and in so doing starting from the subject as given as Kant does, Whitehead insists that the inverse is true: subjective experience starts from a world posited as given, as a datum or object, and subsequently, through an act of appropriation, turns objectivity into subjective experience. In order to grasp the full force of these two movements of thought, it is necessary to unpack the specific notion of experience that a Whiteheadian, more-than-human aesthetics mobilizes.

A new more-than-human aesthetic paradigm relies on a notion of experience which can be traced back to 19th-century physiology and psychology. Its importance for philosophy was grasped by William James, who ventured to chart the emerging field of experimental psychology in his monumental *The Principles of Psychology* (1890/1981) and drew philosophical conclusions of this work in his *Essays in Radical Empiricism* (1912/1976). Equally, John Dewey (1896) stressed the importance of the 'reflex arc concept' for philosophy as well as the import of Darwinism in order to rethink cherished theorems and implicit – but not experientially warranted – assumptions about the nature of experience in philosophy. It was 19th-century experimental physiology which, according to Whitehead, 'put mind back into nature' (1967b: 148), countering the habit of letting nature bifurcate which was rampant within the philosophical discourse on experience. What does this conception of experience entail and how does it circumvent letting nature bifurcate into two irreconcilable realms? What import does it have for rethinking aesthetics?

Here, two interconnected points are key. They concern, first, the primacy of feeling over cognitive processes and, second, the fact that experience is conceptualized without recourse to a transcendental structure or an experiencing human subject. In *The Principles of Psychology* James famously describes experience as a 'stream'.[6] This stream starts out from an experience which is impossible to either locate in a subject which experiences or in an object experienced. Take an unknown taste: 'it is simply that taste', James (1981: 262) insists, neither locatable 'in' the subject nor 'in' the object. He stresses the fact that, psychologically speaking, experience does not come personified: personhood cannot be presupposed. Instead, its constitution requires explanation by psychology. Rather than starting from a dualism of mind and body, subject and world, James (1976) starts from a 'world of pure experience' that the various streams of thought set in motion. This process engenders bodily feeling, but such feeling still does not distinguish between its object and its subject. Knowledge about what it is that has been felt and even reflection upon it come after the fact of feeling. Thus, knowledge happens, when it does, within continuity to feeling. It begins with a vague 'knowledge by acquaintance' and only then, potentially, moves towards a more reflexive form of knowledge that James terms 'knowledge about' (1981). The experiencing self emerges out of and through its experiences, through its processes of feeling. The self, then, is essentially characterized by its possessive structure, grasping what is there to be experienced as datum, welcoming and rejecting elements of it. Experience, therefore, is a process of selection and interpretation, aesthetic processes par excellence, and it is by means of these processes that the self is constituted in the first place. It does not pre-exist or give rise to experience.[7]

What seems like a minor technical issue – the critique of a certain notion of nature in a particular tradition of thought – becomes the lever for a whole new way of thinking which unfastens cherished certainties of modern thought. It leads Whitehead to construct a metaphysics in which the concept of nature does not bifurcate (Stengers, 2011), a metaphysics of experience in which the Jamesian notion of experience is generalized (Sehgal, 2016). In this metaphysics, aesthetics holds *the* central place (Shaviro, 2009: 74). Thus, for Whitehead, the whole universe is relationally formed through aesthetic processes of feeling and grasping, for which he coins the strange term 'prehension' (dropping the cognitivist and humanistic prefixes from terms such as apprehension or comprehension – see Wilkie, Chapter 9, this volume for an extended discussion of prehension). Whitehead, in this way, develops a relational and processual cosmology at the core of which are what he calls 'actual entities', 'drops of experience, complex and interdependent' (1978: 11), thus avoiding the assumption of simple localization. The fact that 'the final facts are, all alike, actual entities' underscores that Whitehead is not starting from a bifurcated notion of reality but rather from a plane of immanence. This, however, implies that terms such as experience, feeling or subject no longer refer to the human alone. Rather, Whitehead's use of terms such as feeling, experience and subject is technical to indicate its metaphysical extension: feeling, experience and even subjectivity pertain to all being(s).[8]

It is therefore possible to speak of a 'generalization of aesthetic concerns' (Sehgal, 2018) at the core of Whitehead's metaphysics as the aesthetic is no longer confined to the human who adds aesthetic value to an essentially valueless world. The very process of being is described by Whitehead as an aesthetic process: the process of concrescence undergone by each actual entity in its very own and singular constitution is a process of patterning, intensification, of building contrasts and creating rhythms, culminating in its 'satisfaction'. Hence, Steven Shaviro (2009: 66) concludes that for Whitehead the 'immanent criterion for order can only be an aesthetic one'. It is from here that Whitehead's own claim that 'Beauty is a wider, and more fundamental notion than Truth' (1967a: 265) takes on full significance. Aesthetics and ontology are intimately aligned and take precedence over epistemology, which cedes its modern status as first philosophy.

Specifying and singularizing aesthetics

If we are to trace the importance of aesthetics in today's world marked by science and technology as well as the accelerating environmental crisis, however, this metaphysical definition of aesthetics, albeit fruitful and coherent theoretically, needs specifying as it risks becoming too broad. Generalizing and inverting aesthetics is a necessary precondition in order to avoid a bifurcated view of the aesthetic, but it is only the precondition to ask the next question: what singularizes the aesthetic when it is understood as transversally cutting across every domain of experience, be it human or not? The metaphysical generalization precisely opens up the space to inquire into the specificities of the aesthetic, transversally conceived. In this volume, we attempt such a specification by looking at the way in which aesthetics operates beyond its modern confines in worlds distinguished by crisis in naturecultures and technoscientific deliverance.

It is time, then, to switch register and turn towards empirical manifestations of aesthetics in the sense that we have fleshed out, for it is only if the conceptualization of aesthetics that we propose here reverberates in the world and engenders novel insights that it is worth the effort of pursuing it in the first place. Here, we might follow a suggestion and path forged by John Dewey. In *Art as Experience* (2005: 9), Dewey stresses the importance 'of recovering the continuity of esthetic experience with normal processes of living'. Therefore, one cannot start with the realm of the arts, narrowly conceived, and one has to abandon any idea of what would, a priori, constitute an aesthetic object as Dewey (2005: 9) clarifies: 'Even a crude experience, if authentically an experience, is more fit to give a clue to the intrinsic nature of esthetic experience than is an object already set apart from any other mode of experience'. Whitehead takes a similar path (see Gaskill, Chapter 13, this volume) when he uses the example of the factory – usually considered an anathema to aesthetics – to reconceive aesthetic experience beyond the bifurcation of nature. Nevertheless, hasn't such a generalization of aesthetics, beyond preconceived realms of the arts towards society at large, already been realized? We might reasonably assume that social and cultural research, where the aestheticization of everyday life has long been a central preoccupation, has already done so. If, however, the aim of sociocultural research has been to extend the social analysis of aesthetics beyond the arts – placing it at the centre of debates concerning the very nature of sociality in modernity and so-called postmodernity, such as processes of urban culture, consumption or social class – there remains in such accounts a bifurcated aesthetics prioritizing and dramatizing the experiencing (and typically consuming) human subject.[9] Likewise, anthropological accounts of non-Western aesthetics preoccupied with, for instance, seemingly axiomatic cultural or period-specific aesthetics, linguistic and symbolic models of aesthetic communication (Coote and Shelton, 1992) or indexical abductive agency (Gell, 1998) present versions of aesthetics that are variously upshots of some manner of bifurcation, firmly embedded in the idiom of subject–object relations, socio-cultural appreciation and consumption as well as the nature and efficacy of the arts. Thus, despite a seeming 'pluralization' of aesthetics across various domains of sociality[10] – beginning with classical and modern socio-cultural engagements with urban culture, from the Frankfurt to the Chicago School to the analysis of social class and the attainment and deployment of 'social capital' (Bourdieu, 1984) and to post-modern approaches where, for instance, persons engage in interpretivist aesthetics involving individual non-cognitive reflexive understanding (Lash and Urry, 1994) – there persists a bifurcated aesthetic subject and corresponding object. Furthermore, efforts to break with Kantian and Humean aesthetics, whether 'contextual aesthetics' (Eaton, 1999) or 'social aesthetics' (Born et al, 2017), simply amend bifurcated aesthetics as situated pleasure and judgements of taste (still in the arts), regardless of whether it is attributed to individuals or social collectives.[11] Second, and mindful of Dewey's guidance to seek out the aesthetic in 'crude' experience, accounts of aesthetic objects in social and cultural research operate to arouse and excite aesthetic experience in the subject. Consequently, aesthetics remains trapped in the anthropocentric idiom of bifurcated subject–object dynamics. Thus, even Alfred Gell's (1998: 31) notable observation that the Asmat shields of southwest New Guinea, used by headhunters to render fear and terror, arguably recapitulates dominant Western anthropological perspectives, where persons are staged as central actors whose experiences are stirred by artefacts designed to render affects. At first glance, socio-cultural preoccupations with aesthetics may appear to be the evident places to begin to be sensitized to and appreciate generalized aesthetics across different domains and territories of experience. On closer inspection, however, such accounts remain largely grounded in modern bifurcated aesthetics, where human subjective experience is placed centre stage and, at best, merely furnishes the non-human with human values and qualities.

To become substantively sensitized to a singularized and generalized aesthetics, where experience transversally cuts across domains of existence, we propose turning to the aftermath of the aforementioned science wars. It is precisely here where 'nature' and the non-human have been contested and rescued, with great empirical force, from maltreatment as mute and valueless resources to be harnessed and exploited by the practices and forces of technoscience, including, but not limited to, capitalism, colonialism and resource extraction. Since ecological crises necessarily dramatize and place centre stage the more-than-human, particularly entities and phenomena shaped and wrought into being by science and technology, we can look to the broad and disparate field of science and technology studies (STS) and its longstanding engagements with the predatory abstraction of objectivity, the fabrication of facts, contested knowledges about naturecultures and the power dynamics of technoscience. Here, accounts of scientists' and engineers' knowledge and material practices have unmistakably revealed the necessary involvement of non-humans, to echo Sandra Harding (1986: 146), as 'active participants in the determination of their own futures'. Certainly, kinds of aesthetics may be discerned in the concrete milieus of technoscience, where nature is permitted to speak, knowledge fashioned, socio-technical effects accomplished and realities strengthened. This may be by way of sociological and anthropological accounts of scientists' material ethnomethods in laboratory settings, visualization practices or their rhetorical strategies for organizing beliefs, accounting for action and negotiating facts.[12] Such interplays of humans and non-humans help to raise awareness of certain aesthetic dimensions involving the more-than-human as lively actors in routine technoscientific practices; however, experience and feelings remain skewed towards human-centred ambitions and interests.[13] Nevertheless, this question of scientists' and engineers' instrumental *interests* opens another way of appreciating, detecting and singularizing generalized aesthetics in technoscience.[14]

If an initial achievement of constructivist and feminist studies of science and technology was to establish the role of practitioners' functional purposes and reasoning in the production of truth claims and objectivity in processes of invention and validation, a subsequent accomplishment has been to illuminate how interests operate as affective and animating forces, articulating humans and non-humans in strongly political and ethical matters of concern and care. What interests relay is how technoscientific practices cannot be reduced to passionless discovery and the possession of knowledge of a bare nature 'out there' but operate, rather, as situated practices and processes that are implicated in and concerned with the becoming of phenomena as primarily aesthetic rather than epistemic processes. In short, modern science is anything but dislocated, dispassionate and disinterested. We can, however, go a step further here, given how stabilized matters of fact become rearticulated as troubling matters of concern – such as chlorofluorocarbons (CFCs) depleting the ozone layer, forever chemicals (PFAS) harming more-than-human life or harvested data resourcing chatbots – where novel entities and phenomena necessitate new modes of feeling, sensing and qualification to both render them knowable and grant them legitimate agency as consequential issues and actors in the modification of our and other's 'cosmograms' (Tresch, 2005). In so doing, we expand on Isabelle Stengers' (2000: 9) observation that interests serve to both explain the diversity and ordering of purposes, conduct and reasoning *and* function ontologically to distribute relational agency across more-than-human assemblages. Here, interests serve in the aesthetic concrescence of issues as matters of concern as they enter into and modify collective life that not only require new institutional arrangements and new political protocols (Latour, 2007: 819) but also demand new techniques of prehension and feeling as well as care for the novel values that ensue (see Savransky, Chapter 6, this volume). The question of *care* also entails the diligence required to maintain those feelings and experiences that are necessary more-than-human constituents of liveable worlds to which our fortunes are bound. For Maria Puig de la Bellacasa (2017: 32), aesthetics can be understood as one of three core dimensions of a non-anthropocentric care, alongside labour and ethico-politics, not least in how objects as 'things' are staged as matters of concern and represented as lively ensembles or collectives.[15] In this move to care, agnostic interests are replaced with an engaged concern for troubling technoscientific issues that are animated by affective charge. Likewise, the knowledge politics brought about by science and technology and carefully rendered by scholars in STS are redramatized as a transversal, generalized or, better yet, distributed aesthetic politics that must resist bifurcating the entanglement of affects, worries and troubles from the vibrant and lively existence of things as matters of care and concern.[16]

So, how, then, to pragmatically proceed with generalized aesthetics as an impassioned adventure for researchers and practitioners who are not indifferent to the concerns and matters of care that environmental crisis and collapse present us with and that co-emerge in our work? This volume offers some tentative starting points, in concert with those who we see as engaged in attuning to the obligations and demands brought into relief by generalized and transversal aesthetics, as already outlined. In the latter stages of his career, Bruno Latour developed a manifest interest in aesthetics, not least through his engagement with the aesthetic implications of the bifurcation of nature (2008), the work of philosopher Étienne Souriau, and his involvement with the médialab at SciencesPo, where, among other things, he began to explicate (2016) three aesthetics (of science, of politics and of arts) that he viewed as necessary to render 'us publically [sic] sensitive to the New Climate Regime'.[17] From the perspective of ethological more-than-human relations, Vinciane Despret provides parables as to how to become impassioned in becoming-with the researched and how passions set the 'conditions' and not the 'results' of scientific knowledge, echoing geneticist Barbara McClintock's sensitivity to and affective relations with maize cytogenetics.[18] To craft situated knowledges (Haraway, 1988) is to feel for and with phenomena that coalesce locally in practice. As Savransky (2021: 11), citing Despret (2016), points out, non-humans, such as animals, endure their own problems, which typically find expression outside human discourse and experience and thus may not 'concern thought or knowledge at all'. Problems are felt and experienced before and whether or not being known. Accordingly, acts of experience precede and set the parameters for knowing, objectivity and truth claims and, perhaps more baldly, processes of individuation are recast as intrinsically aesthetic and not dependent on or determined by human presence. To this end, we researchers must learn to re-passion our knowledge that will, in turn, provide more partial, more objective and more robust worlds that maintain our and other's 'withness' with and in the world (Despret, 2004: 131), rather than reproduce dispassionate knowledge that persistently bifurcates and abstracts bodies and minds, subjects and objects, persons and nature.

Situating and re-passioning knowledge also calls to mind activist inquiry, starting with feminist scholars of technoscience 'coming to terms' with the implications of a successor science and overhauled 'objectivity' (Haraway, 1988: 575) to more recent efforts, in STS, environmental humanities and design, to create interventionist approaches to investigation as a response to the demands of the Anthropocene and decolonization (for example, Bastian et al, 2016). Drawing on activist struggles in Latin America, Arturo Escobar (2020) argues, that '(w)e must sentipensar (feel-think) new notions about what is real and thus what is possible ... that suggest a way of knowing that does not separate thinking from feeling, reason from emotion, knowledge from caring'.[19] The investigative aesthetics (Fuller and Weizman, 2021) of Forensic Architecture show how transversal aesthetics and empirical social research can combine to intervene in concrete truth politics and conflict, thereby overhauling the stale and limited repertoires of empirical technologies (qualitative interviews, focus groups etc) of socio-cultural research. Furthermore, interdisciplinary engagements between design and STS (for example, Wilkie, 2016; Marres et al, 2018) explore the repercussions of the insight that the social is not merely 'performed' but 'invented' in the course of material and technological research practices through architecture, interaction and participatory design, providing ways to rethink aesthetic relations between humans and the more-than-human through associations with air (Calvillo González, 2018), energy demand reduction (Wilkie and Michael, 2018) and noise pollution (Nold, 2018).

Feeling for and feeling with more-than-human others raises the methodological challenge of how to gain practical and empirical access to affects and experiences. In the final chapter of *Spinoza: Practical Philosophy*, Deleuze (1988) offers a concise definition of affect where he assigns the listing of affects as a pragmatic approach to understanding a 'body' and its aesthetic capacities. The example he provides is that of the tick, defined by the biologist Jakob Johann von Uexküll as a synthesis of light, smell and heat affects. This evokes Whitehead's aesthetic ontology (see Debaise, 2017: 58), where 'subjects' are understood as centres of experience, all of which express in various ways and to various degrees. Both Deleuze and Whitehead's aesthetic ensembles involve conjunctive multiplicities of affect or experience, the complexity of which depends on, or rather defines, the body/subject, where a tick is a relatively simple body and a person a far more complex centre of experience. Accordingly, aesthetic and affective experience assemble on one or more complexes of experiential loci. Perhaps unsurprisingly, given both Deleuze and Whitehead's influence on ANT, identifying and indexing the capacities of actors is offered as a practical technique for researchers investigating technoscience (see, for instance, Latour, 2005b). Focussing on indexing feeling and experience, rather than capacities, may also serve as one way to empirically explore aesthetic processes and become sensitive to the detection of expressive phenomena.

Returning to the arts? The efficacy of aesthetic figures

Sketching a new aesthetic paradigm predicated on a more-than-human ontology developed with the philosophy of Whitehead has led us away, in the first instance, from the arts. This does not imply, however, that the arts are to be abandoned in a new aesthetic disposition. Indeed, one might even wager that today a generalized aesthetic paradigm is more apt for grasping contemporary artistic practices that increasingly combine aesthetic creation, research and political intervention while eschewing modern conceptions of the artist as genius and sole creator. Once we have side-stepped modern assumptions about aesthetics, the question of the arts re-imposes itself. It points to the importance of considering the arts as but one vector for feeling and thinking with a generalized notion of the aesthetic, including the concomitant tools and techniques to do so (see Haas, Chapter 8; Gaskill, Chapter 13; and Sehgal, Chapter 14, this volume).

In gesturing towards the way a more-than-human aesthetic paradigm necessarily turns the gaze back towards the researcher and their affectual involvement in the research process, we might finally turn to the efficacy of conceptual personae and aesthetic figures: concepts, or certain kinds of abstractions, that render us sensitive to the experience and feeling of more-than-human others while retaining awareness of and receptivity to our own embodied and grounded positionality and becoming through research practices. If indexing feeling and experience, as previously mentioned, provide empirical entry-points to aesthetic processes, then personae and figures offer a way to conceptually appreciate and attune to the possibilities of aesthetic existence and values that are fundamental to the immanent becoming of all entities and phenomena. In *What is Philosophy?* Deleuze and Guattari (1994: 65) distinguish between *conceptual personae* and *aesthetic figures*, where the former refers to the ability of concepts to occasion 'thought-beings' that resource creative reasoning, while the latter designates processes of experience that operate on and in (political) compositions. If conceptual personae, such as cyborgs, coyotes and tricksters (Haraway, 1985), diplomats or idiots (Stengers, 2005) exceed common-sensical understanding, then aesthetic figures have the power to go beyond customary or mundane experience, affect, and objects of perception and make perceptible, or propose, new compositions and formations of existence that bear new modes of relevance, be they parasites (Serres, 1982), shamans (Viveiros de Castro, 2014), witches (Pignarre and Stengers, 2011: xviii) or fugitives (Moten, 2018).[20] Accordingly, we can appreciate how Stengers' conceptual persona of the idiot impacts on thought by demanding a greater ideational creativity through its nonsensical nature that prompts both a slowing down and a questioning of the philosopher's or practitioner's authority and confidence to believe they 'possess the meaning of what they know' (Stengers, 2005: 995). Furthermore, we can also recognize how the idiot, predisposed to questions of knowledge, also acts to open up affective dimensions through the tremendous threat they pose to habitual thoughts and practices and to thinking per se. It is under such circumstances that we can begin to appreciate aesthetic figures, which operate to remonstrate against the exclusion of aesthetics from knowledge practices, and to occasion sensibility and attunement to the speculative possibilities of more-than-human aesthetic values and practices of existence. The aesthetic figure of the poet, for instance, draws on Whitehead's (1967b: 77) invocation of 18th-century Romantic poets, in particular Wordsworth and Shelley, which bears witness to the narrowness of the scientific-materialist scheme, insisting on the fact that 'something important had been left out' of the modern account of nature. Against the abstractions of science and philosophy, Whitehead points out, the Romantic poets insist on their experiencing nature as fundamentally related and with inherent value 'for its own sake'. Aesthetic figures, such as the poet, demand that we acknowledge the complex richness of the empirical in all its heterogenous, unfolding and aesthetic complexity and, crucially, that empirical questions are prefaced by aesthetic concerns: what we know and *can know* requires the semblance of what we feel, or, rather, we must *feel and* experience something before we can know it (Wilkie and Michael, 2023). Poetry in particular holds promise for Whitehead as it conjoins intuition into the nature of things with a practice of skilful linguistic expression. Aesthetic figures demand that we grasp the worrying and disturbing novelty and dimensionality of things brought about by and rendered differently by ecological crises. Given this, our wager is that grasping and working with the demands and obligations of more-than-human distributions of feeling, as set out here, are necessary for a more just (symmetrical) environmental politics of liveable worlds.

The structure of the book

In this volume we aim to give shape and depth to a more-than-human aesthetics by paying due attention to the conceptual and the empirical processes and practices involved in venturing into this new territory. The contributions collected here transversally cut across various disciplines and fields, objects and practices, including biomedicine and healthcare, capitalism and race, dance, design research, education, geology, metaphysics, activism, human–computer interaction (HCI) and software design. As such, this volume provides tentative vectors of aesthetic exploration in the realms of technoscience, contested knowledges, creative practices and politics in a planet in distress. We have organized the volume along a set of four transversal registers that cross the established borders of the modern constitution and point to sensitizations and attendant modes of feeling, thinking and understanding.

Part I, 'Feeling and Experiencing', opens in Chapter 2 with Michael Halewood, who expands on core aspects of a generalized aesthetics and considers the milieus in which capitalism is 'imbued', the feelings and experiences it engenders and those that are being destroyed or lost. Consequently, aesthetic devastation (the loss of feeling and experiences) coincides with the material loss and destruction (species for instance) occasioned by socio-ecological crisis. In Chapter 3, Thomas P. Keating turns our attention to a specific environmental problem, namely the storage of nuclear waste and the speculative aesthetics required for communicating nuclear memory. Here, generalized aesthetics offers new ways to entertain 'possible nuclear waste futures'. Alexander Damianos, in Chapter 4, thinks through the work of the Anthropocene Working Group (AWG) in view of formulating a 'forensic aesthetics'. This not only highlights the aesthetic dimensions of the production of geological knowledge as a form of storytelling or through bringing into being novel entities such as the 'technofossil', but it also brings to the fore the quality of landscapes themselves as not only geological but aesthetic agents whose feelings and experiences, in particular those of ecological disruption, are relayed and woven into narratives by geologists. Michael L. Thomas conjoins Whitehead with Black Studies and the Philosophy of Race in Chapter 5 to develop a social aesthetics of race. This allows him to exhibit the 'function of race as a predatory abstraction, which bifurcates human societies between worlds of colour' but also highlights the aesthetic nature of theory itself: rather than being merely propositional, a social aesthetics of race works towards the transformation and thickening of experience, countering modern predatory abstractions such as race.

In Part II, 'Problematizing and (Re)Valuing', each chapter variously considers the demands of and for aesthetic values occasioned by ways of thinking, knowledge and performative practices. Martin Savransky's contribution in Chapter 6 enjoins us to reclaim aesthetic values from the modern historicity of *aesthesis*, which has operated so ruthlessly to anaesthetize and destroy feeling and experience through the alliance of capitalism, colonialism and extractivism that has engendered socio-ecological disaster. For Savransky, one judicious response to the disqualification and destruction of value is to nourish senses by experimenting with aesthetic events that express new values and modes of existence. In Chapter 7, Cécile Malaspina traces the resonances between Dante and Whitehead in their use of the phrase 'the great refusal', which Whitehead employed in the context of his critique of the bifurcation of nature as well as the 'prosperous middle classes ... who placed an excessive value upon placidity of existence [refusing] to face the necessities for social [and] for intellectual reform' in *Science and the Modern World* (1967b: 207). This too involves acknowledging and addressing the 'great refusal' or the anesthetisation of scientific events, or rather appealing against the dissociation or disqualification of the aesthetic dimensions of scientific events and their accomplishments. Thinking with Amanda Piña's contemporary dance piece *Climatic Dances/Danzas Climaticas*, Maximilian Haas considers in Chapter 8 how the proposition of generalized aesthetics invites experimentations with aesthetic practices that may yield novel values. Thus, contemporary dance becomes a research format through which audiences, publics and dancers alike can become sensitized to the losses of bio- and cultural diversity brought about by climate change wherein the 'stage' literally dramatizes ecological experiences.

The chapters that comprise Part III, 'Infecting and Caring', address both the care and callousness that variously illuminate how aesthetics opens new ways of appreciating the anaesthetized experience of a patient safety event, the machinic demands placed on the users of social media apps and the socio-material care involved in conducting practice-based design research. In his auto-ethnographic account of a serious patient safety incident, a 'never event' in National Health Service (NHS) jargon, Alex Wilkie presents in Chapter 9 an aesthetic analysis of clinical error through the Whiteheadian concepts of positive and negative prehensions. Motivating this is the sentiment that experimentation in response-ability is required to prevent or mitigate harmful and life-threatening events and the violence of aesthetic abstraction enacted through patient safety protocols and evidence-based medicine. For Andrew Goffey and Matthew Fuller (Chapter 10), user interface design elicits compulsive dependency on social media through techniques such as gamification and, in so doing, territorializes new moments for transient engagement, 'machinic highs', and psychotic unmediated experience. This provides a cautionary tale about the nature of these new 'machinic environments' where feeling and experience are designed precisely to supress and impede thought and cognition. Mike Michael's discussion of the care enacted as part of the design and deployment, among research participants, of experimental interactive devices in the field of HCI considers the heterogenous aesthetic compossibility of those socio-material elements that compose the 'research event'. The chapter opens up a way of appreciating and describing the fine-graining of 'fitting and harmonization' that takes place in knowledge practices, signalling one way that practitioners may appreciate aesthetics as part of their knowledge practices.

In the final section, Part IV, '(Un)Learning and Luring', the three constituent chapters inquire into the challenge of generalized aesthetics for pedagogies, perhaps necessary for becoming sensitized to novel modes of feeling and the nature of immanent values occasioned therein. For Didier Debaise (Chapter 11), drawing on Isabelle Stengers, abstraction is radically recognized as 'one of the deepest modalities of the aesthetic' and not in contradistinction to it. This necessarily involves cultivating our modes of abstraction as an 'art of possibilities' that is fully embedded in experiencing rather than extracting feeling and experience into the cognitive. In highlighting aspects of aesthetics in the work of Whitehead and Dewey, Nicholas Gaskill (Chapter 13) draws on Whitehead's engagement with art to consider how aesthetic abstractions might be cultivated and, in so doing, how it might be possible to escape the rigid disciplinary entrapments of thought and practice. Not only are aesthetic abstractions part of what makes us human, they may also be necessary tools in the pedagogical equipment required in order to rise to the challenges of the climate and socio-ecological crisis. Also speaking to Whitehead's commentaries on disciplinary rigidity, the apotheosis of which is the modern university, Melanie Sehgal reflects in Chapter 14 on the role a more-than-human, or non-bifurcated, aesthetic education might play in 'unlearning' modern habits of thought. Drawing on examples where students' senses and sense-practices were nurtured and trained, Sehgal invites us to consider the concrete settings where modern habits might be unlearned and new modes of feeling fostered.

One might employ the Whiteheadian term 'adventure' to signal that the task at hand is uncertain and risky, involving yet-to-be-felt problems, articulated questions and omissions. The success of an adventure, as Whitehead reminds us, is not a given. It derives its importance from the fact that opening to new ways of feeling and perceiving – and in so doing, changing modern habits of thought – has become an urgent task. Our wager is that the limits of Western modernity have become clearly palpable and there is acute need to place aesthetics at the very epicentre of experimentation in knowledge practices.

Notes

[1] See (Liboiron et al, 2018).
[2] See Debaise (2017) for an extended discussion of the bifurcation of nature which makes possible the operations that produce the 'cosmology of the moderns' as well as Sehgal in Chapter 14 of this volume.

3   This, Whitehead remarks, implies committing what he calls 'a fallacy of misplaced concreteness' (1967b: 52), an error in reasoning that consists in mistaking the abstract for the concrete.

4   As Debaise (2017: 7) points out, the cosmology of the bifurcation of nature includes Cartesian dualism as but one reductive symptom of its processes of differentiating reality into two distinct realms.

5   There have been several efforts to develop A.N. Whitehead's philosophy of aesthetics and aesthetic experience, starting with Susanne K. Langer's (1953) work (see: Sherburne, 1963, Richardson, 2006, Shaviro, 2009, Dadejík et al, 2021). These have either outlined a Whiteheadian aesthetic from within the conceptual cosmos of Whitehead or have traced its import in the realm of the arts and aesthetics narrowly construed. While acknowledging the importance and validity of these projects, our own has been to develop a more-than-human, generalized aesthetics that operates without the assumption of a bifurcated notion of nature and, crucially, tests such a conception of aesthetics within fields beyond those that already designated as aesthetic, particularly those engaging with the current socio-ecological crises.

6   James (1981: 175) coins the term 'stream of thought' while stressing the fact that 'thought' is here used on a par with feeling, without implying cognitive faculties. His struggle with the language available to him in this paragraph is highly significant because, similar to Whitehead, James problematizes the fact that language itself makes metaphysical assumptions (such as a bifurcated notion of nature) not warranted by experience.

7   David Lapoujade describes this self as a 'cogito proprement jamesien, fondé sur une relation indirecte d'interprétation' (Lapoujade 1999, 22f.). The importance of possession has been taken up by Debaise (2011).

8   Whitehead (1978: 5) explicitly discusses his method of generalization, sidestepping unilateral generalizations from one field only (resulting in physicalisms, sociologisms, biologisms etc), using the metaphor of an aeroplane that takes off from a particular ground of observation, lifts into the 'thin air of imaginative generalization' in which novel abstractions are formed, then lands in a different empirical field in which these abstractions are tested and adapted. Whitehead chose to work with psychological concepts (such as feeling, prehension etc) for the pragmatic reason that it is here that relationality and process have become theorized within modern philosophy (Sehgal, 2016).

9   This is starkly apparent in, for instance, Thomas Osborne's (1997) anthropocentric discussion of 'aesthetically oriented social theory', though his notion of *problematics of freedom* that orients towards a critical sociology of freedom might, in the context of our discussion, be aptly reinterpreted as flight towards a critical more-than-human sociology.

10 Disappointingly, Wolfgang Welsch's attempts to move 'beyond' art and pluralize aesthetics (see for instance: 1995, 1996) simply distributes the attribution of aesthetics across different domains of socio-cultural life while retaining people as the foci of aesthetic processes.

11 A notable exception being Antoine Hennion's (2016, originally published in French in 1993) sociology of mediation that brought the insights of actor-network theory (ANT) to bear on music and the arts more generally with a relational model of aesthetics that treats human and non-human agency symmetrically.

12 Versions of aesthetics observed in scientific practice typically feature characterizations of scientists' bifurcated criteria of beauty (for example, McAllister, 1996) as, for instance, an aspect of their visualization techniques (Lynch and Edgerton Jr., 1987). Nonetheless, Lorraine Daston and Peter Galison (2007) provide a historical analysis of the production of scientific objectivity where different technologies of visualization and their corresponding epistemics of vision offer different models of objectivity and aesthetic relation between the arts and sciences. See Gilbert and Mulkay (1984) for a foundational account of how biochemists construct and manage their beliefs and accounts of social action involving humour, which produce certain affects and feelings during routine laboratory work. Accounts of scientific

visualization, notably formative ANT perspectives in laboratory studies, show how certain aesthetic distributions, transformations and displacements of agency take place through inscription devices (Latour and Woolgar, 1979) that transform laboratory materials (such as chemicals and rats) and scientific objects into immutable mobiles (such as figures and illustrations (see Latour, 1986: 18), or reified and malleable abstractions.

[13] This echoes criticisms of ANT's early treatment of non-humans as the subalterns of the managerial (Star, 1991) or Machiavellian (Law, 1994, de Laet and Mol, 2000) agendas of male engineers and scientists, such as Rudolf Diesel (Latour, 1987) or Louis Pasteur (Latour, 1988), who are ultimately responsible for marshalling and managing the constituent elements of an actor-network. In addressing this weakness, Emilie Gomart and Antoine Hennion (1991) describe how music listeners and drug users perform an aesthetic agency of 'active passion' by attaching and submitting to the agency of music or drugs rather than exhibiting purposeful and rational action, through which they emerge and are expressed as *superjects*, to use Whiteheadian terminology. See Wilkie (2010) for an ethnographic account of users as more-than-human ensembles involving interplays of aesthetic experience and expression, occasioned in user-centred design practices.

[14] See Woolgar (1981) for an overview of interests (and symmetry) as an explanatory resource operating in the social contents of science.

[15] Latour's (2005a: 13) notion of 'thing' recasts stabilized (scientific and technical) objects and facts as lively and unsettled issues, which provokes 'questions of style'. Here, aesthetics, portrayed as the staging of objectivity and facts, is respecified as an 'aesthetics of matters of concern' (Latour, 2008: 47) that must *matter* (make a difference in the pragmatist sense) to those implicated and affected in issues and controversies and whose identity and requirements are all rendered durable in the process. The image of aesthetics as 'staging' echoes notions associated with ANT, such as 'script' (Akrich, 1992) and 'mise-en-scène' (Callon, 1999), where the role, identity and arrangement of actors constituting the disposition of a fact, issue or technical artefact are demarcated.

[16] The notion of distributed aesthetics evokes Jaques Rancière's (2004: 13) distribution of the sensible as 'a delimitation of [14] [sic] spaces and times, of the visible and the invisible, of speech and noise, that simultaneously determines the place and the stakes of politics as a form of experience'. Rancière's aesthetics, however, remains a resolutely anthropocentric topology of feeling in stark contrast to the more-than-human distributions of feeling we discuss here.

[17] For Latour (2011), Souriau's (2015) notion of 'instauration' resonates with Whitehead's bifurcation of nature, not least in how the artist and artwork elaborate one another.

[18] See Evelyn Fox Keller's (1983) biography of Barbara McClintock's intimate relationship with corn and the science of cytology and genetics.

[19] Escobar (2020: 161) attributes Orlando Fals Borda (1984) with first publicizing the terms *sentipensar* and *sentipensamiento* to describe riverine and coastal communities' aesthetic techniques for living in Columbia.

[20] See Blencowe (2016) for an exploration of anti-fascist and anti-capitalist aesthetics of hope using aesthetics figures in a themed section in GeoHumanities (Brigstocke and Noorani, 2016) on aesthetic attunement and more-than-human agency. Stengers (2008) provides a discussion of witches as aesthetic figures that operate to render ways of connecting with novel and urgent phenomena and power.

References

Akrich, M. (1992) 'The de-scription of technical objects', in W. Bijker and J. Law (eds), *Shaping Technology/Building Society: Studies in Sociotechnical Change*, Cambridge, MA: MIT Press, pp 205–24.

Bastian, M., Jones, O., Moore, N. and Roe, E. (2016) *Participatory Research in More-Than-Human Worlds,* London and New York: Routledge.

Blencowe, C. (2016) 'Ecological attunement in a theological key: Adventures in antifascist aesthetics', *GeoHumanities,* 2(1): 24–41.

Born, G., Lewis, E. and Straw, W. (2017) *Improvisation and Social Aesthetics,* Durham, NC and London: Duke University Press.

Bourdieu, P. (1984) *Distinction: A Social Critique of the Judgement of Taste,* Cambridge, MA: Harvard University Press.

Brigstocke, J. and Noorani, T. (2016) 'Posthuman attunements: Aesthetics, authority and the arts of creative listening', *GeoHumanities,* 2(1): 1–7.

Callon, M. (1999) 'Ni intellectuel engagé, ni intellectuel dégagé: la double stratégie de l'attachement et du détachement', *Sociologie du travail,* 41(1): 65–78.

Calvillo González, N. (2018) 'Inviting atmospheres to the architecture table', in N. Marres, M. Guggenheim and A. Wilkie (eds), *Inventing the Social,* Manchester, Mattering Press, pp 41–64.

Coote, J. and Shelton, A. (1992) *Anthropology, Art, And Aesthetics,* Oxford and New York: Oxford University Press.

Crutzen, P.J. and Stoermer, E.F. (2000) 'The "Anthropocene"', *Global Change Newsletter,* (41): 17–18.

Dadejík, O., Kaplický, M., Ševčík, M. and Zuska, V. (2021) *Process and Aesthetics: An Outline of Whiteheadian Aesthetics and Beyond,* Prague: Karolinum Press.

Daston, L. and Galison, P. (2007) *Objectivity,* New York and London: Zone.

Davis, H. and Turpin, E. (2015) 'Art & Death: Lives between the fifth assessment & the sixth extinction', in H. Davis and E. Turpin (eds), *Art in the Anthropocene: Encounters among Aesthetics, Politics, Environments and Epistemologies,* London: Open Humanities Press, pp 3–30.

de la Bellacasa, M.P. (2017) *Matters of Care: Speculative Ethics in More Than Human Worlds,* Minneapolis, MN and London: University of Minnesota Press.

de Laet, M. and Mol, A. (2000) 'The Zimbabwe bush pump: Mechanics of a fluid technology', *Social Studies of Science,* 30(2): 225–63.

Debaise, D. (2011) *Philosophie des possessions,* Dijon: Les presses du réel.

Debaise, D. (2017) *Nature as Event: The Lure of the Possible,* Durham, NC: Duke University Press.

Debaise, D. and Keating, T.P. (2021) 'Speculative empiricism, nature and the question of predatory abstractions: A conversation with Didier Debaise', *Theory, Culture & Society,* 38(7–8): 309–23.

Deleuze, G. (1988) *Spinoza: Practical Philosophy,* San Francisco, CA: City Lights Books.

Deleuze, G. and Guattari, F. (1994) *What is Philosophy?* London and New York: Verso Books.

Despret, V. (2004) 'The body we care for: Figures of anthropo-zoo-genesis', *Body & Society*, 10(2–3): 111–34.

Despret, V. (2016) *What Would Animals Say if We Asked the Right Questions?*, Minneapolis, MN: University of Minnesota Press.

Dewey, J. (1896) 'The reflex arc concept in psychology', *Psychological review*, 3(4): 357.

Dewey, J. (2005) *Art as Experience*, New York: Perigree Books.

Eaton, M.M. (1999) 'Kantian and contextual beauty', *The Journal of Aesthetics and Art Criticism*, 57(1): 11–15.

Escobar, A. (2020) *Pluriversal Politics: The Real and the Possible*, Durham, NC and London: Duke University Press.

Fals Borda, O. (1984) *Resistencia en el San Jorge*, Bogotá: Carlos Valencia Editores.

Fuller, M. and Weizman, E. (2021) *Investigative Aesthetics: Conflicts and Commons in the Politics of Truth*, London and New York: Verso Books.

Gell, A. (1998) *Art and Agency: An Anthropological Theory*, New York and Oxford: Oxford University Press.

Gilbert, G.N. and Mulkay, M. (1984) *Opening Pandora's Box: A Sociological Analysis of Scientists' Discourse*, Cambridge: Cambridge University Press.

Gomart, E. and Hennion, A. (1991) 'A sociology of attachment: Music amateurs, drug users', in J. Law (ed), *Sociology of Monsters: Essays on Power, Technology and Domination*, London and New York: Routledge, p 273.

Guattari, F. (1995) *Chaosmosis: An Ethico-aesthetic Paradigm*, Bloomington, IN: Indiana University Press.

Halewood, M. (2011) *A.N. Whitehead and Social Theory: Tracing a Culture of Thought*, London, New York and Delhi: Anthem Press.

Haraway, D.J. (1985) 'Manifesto for cyborgs: Science, technology, and socialist feminism in the 1980s', *Socialist Review*, 80: 65–108.

Haraway, D.J. (1988) 'Situated knowledges: The science question in feminism and the privilege of partial perspective', *Feminist Studies*, 14(3): 575–99.

Harding, S.G. (1986) *The Science Question in Feminism*, Ithaca, NY: Cornell University Press.

Hennion, A. (2016) *The Passion for Music: A Sociology of Mediation*, Abingdon and New York: Routledge.

James, W. (1976) *Essays in Radical Empiricism*, Cambridge, MA and London: Harvard University Press.

James, W. (1981) *The Principles of Psychology*, Cambridge, MA and London: Harvard University Press.

Keller, E.F. (1983) *A Feeling for the Organism: The Life and Work of Barbara McClintock*, New York: W.H. Freeman and Company.

Langer, S.K. (1953) *Feeling and Form: A Theory of Art Developed from Philosophy in a New Key*, New York: Scribner.

Lapoujade, D. (1999) 'William James: De La Psychologie à l'Empirisme Radical', *Philosophie*, 64: 15–30.

Lash, S. and Urry, J. (1994) *Economies of Signs and Space*, Theory, Culture & Society Book 26, Thousand Oaks, CA, London and New Delhi: Sage Publications.

Latour, B. (1986) 'Visualization and cognition: Thinking with eyes and hands', *Knowledge and Society: Studies in the Sociology of Culture Past and Present*, 6: 1–40.

Latour, B. (1987) *Science in Action*, Cambridge, MA: Harvard University Press.

Latour, B. (1988) *The Pasteurization of France*, Cambridge, MA: Harvard University Press.

Latour, B. (2005a) 'From Realpolitik to Dingpolitik', in B. Latour and P. Weibel (eds), *Making Things Public: Atmospheres of Democracy*, Cambridge, MA and London: MIT Press, pp 14–41.

Latour, B. (2005b) *Reassembling the Social: An Introduction to Actor-Network-Theory*, Oxford: Clarendon.

Latour, B. (2007) 'Turning around politics: A note on Gerard de Vries' paper', *Social Studies of Science*, 37(5): 811–20.

Latour, B. (2011) 'Reflections on Etienne Souriau's Les différents modes d'existence', in L. Bryant and N. Srnicek (eds), *The Speculative Turn: Continental Materialism and Realism*, Melbourne: re.press, pp 304–33.

Latour, B. (2016) On sensitivity arts, science and politics in the new climatic regime, Lecture at Performance Studies International Conference, Melbourne.

Latour, B. and Woolgar, S. (1979) *Laboratory Life: The Construction of Scientific Facts*, Princeton, NJ: Princeton University Press.

Law, J. (1994) *Organizing Modernity*, Oxford: Blackwell.

Liboiron, M., Tironi, M. and Calvillo, N. (2018) 'Toxic politics: Acting in a permanently polluted world', *Social Studies of Science*, 48(3): 331–49.

Lynch, M. and Edgerton Jr., S.Y. (1987) 'Aesthetics and digital image processing: Representational craft in contemporary astronomy', *The Sociological Review*, 35(1): 184–220.

Marres, N., Guggenheim, M. and Wilkie, A. (2018) *Inventing the Social*, Manchester: Mattering Press.

McAllister, J.W. (1996) *Beauty and Revolution in Science*, Ithaca, NY and London: Cornell University Press.

Moten, F. (2018) *Stolen Life*, 2, (Vol 2. of consent not to be a single being), Durham, NC and London: Duke University Press.

Nold, C. (2018) 'Turning controversies into questions of design: Prototyping alternative metrics for Heathrow Airport', in N. Marres, M. Guggenheim and A. Wilkie (eds), *Inventing the Social*, Manchester: Mattering Press, pp 65–93.

Osborne, T. (1997) 'The aesthetic problematic', *Economy and Society*, 26: 126–46.

Pignarre, P. and Stengers, I. (2011) *Capitalist Sorcery: Breaking the Spell*, Basingstoke and New York: Palgrave Macmillan.

Rancière, J. (2004) *The Politics of Aesthetics: The Distribution of the Sensible*, London and New York: Continuum International Publishing Group.

Richardson, J. (2006) *A Natural History of Pragmatism: The Fact of Feeling from Jonathan Edwards to Gertrude Stein*, Cambridge: Cambridge University Press.

Savransky, M. (2021) 'Problems all the way down', *Theory, Culture & Society*, 38(2): 3–23.

Sehgal, M. (2016) *Eine Situierte Metaphysik. Empirismus Und Spekulation Bei William James Und Alfred North Whitehead*, Konstanz: Konstanz University Press.

Sehgal, M. (2018) 'Aesthetic concerns, philosophical fabulations: The importance of a "new aesthetic paradigm"', *SubStance,* 47(1): 112–29.

Serres, M. (1982) *The Parasite,* Baltimore, MD: The Johns Hopkins University Press.

Shaviro, S. (2009) *Without Criteria: Kant, Whitehead, Deleuze, and Aesthetics,* Cambridge, MA: MIT Press.

Sherburne, D.W. (1963) *A Whiteheadian Aesthetic.*

Souriau, É. (2015) *The Different Modes of Existence,* Minneapolis, MN: Univocal.

Star, S.L. (1991) 'Power, technology and the phenomenology of conventions: On being allergic to onions', in J. Law (ed), *Sociology of Monsters: Essays on Power, Technology and Domination,* London and New York: Routledge, p 273.

Stengers, I. (2000) *The Invention of Modern Science,* Minneapolis, MN: University of Minnesota Press.

Stengers, I. (2005) 'The cosmopolitical proposal', in B. Latour and P. Weibel (eds), *Making Things Public,* Cambridge, MA: MIT Press, pp 994–1003.

Stengers, I. (2011) *Thinking with Whitehead: A Free and Wild Creation of Concepts,* Cambridge, MA and London: Harvard University Press.

Stengers, I., Massumi, B. and Manning, E. (2008) History through the Middle: Between Macro and Mesopolitics – Interview with Isabelle Stengers, http://www.inflexions.org/n3_stengershtml.html. (Accessed 7 November 2023).

Townsend, D. (1998) 'Baumgarten, Alexander Gottlieb', *Routledge Encyclopedia of Philosophy, Vol 1*, London and New York: Routledge.

Tresch, J. (2005) 'Cosmogram', in M. Ohanian and J.-C. Royoux (eds), *Cosmograms,* Lukas and Sternberg.

Van Dooren, T. (2014) *Flight Ways: Life and Loss at the Edge of Extinction,* New York: Columbia University Press.

Viveiros de Castro, E. (2014) *Cannibal Metaphysics,* Minneapolis, MN: Univocal.

Welsch, W. (1995), 'Aesthetics beyond aesthetics', *Proceedings of the XIIIth International Congress of Aesthetics, Lahti*, pp 18–37.

Welsch, W. (1996) 'Aestheticization processes: Phenomena, distinctions and prospects', *Theory, Culture & Society,* 13(1): 1–24.

Whitehead, A.N. (1967a) *Adventures of Ideas,* New York: The Free Press.

Whitehead, A.N. (1967b) *Science and the Modern World,* New York: The Free Press.

Whitehead, A.N. (1978) *Process and Reality: An Essay in Cosmology,* (corrected edn), D.R. Griffin and D.W. Sherburne (eds), New York: The Free Press.

Whitehead, A.N. (2004) *The Concept of Nature,* Amherst, NY: Prometheus Books.

Wilkie, A. (2010), *User Assemblages in Design: An Ethnographic Study,* Doctoral thesis, Department of Sociology, London: Goldsmiths, University of London, p 236.

Wilkie, A. (2016), 'Introduction: Aesthetics, cosmopolitics and design', in P. Lloyd and E. Bohemia (eds), *Proceedings of DRS2016,* Brighton, pp 873–79.

Wilkie, A. and Michael, M. (2018) 'Designing and doing: Enacting energy- and-community', in N. Marres, M. Guggenheim and A. Wilkie (eds), *Inventing the Social,* Manchester: Mattering Press, pp 125–47.

Wilkie, A. and Michael, M. (2023) 'Before the idiot, the poet? Aesthetic figures and design', in M. Tironi, M. Chilet, P. Hermansen and C. Marín (eds), *Design for More-Than-Human Futures: Towards Post-anthropocentric Worlding,* London; New York: Routledge.

Woolgar, S. (1981) 'Interests and explanation in the social study of science', *Social Studies of Science,* 11(3): 365–94.

PART I

Feeling and Experiencing

2

Whitehead, Dewey, Metaphysics, Aesthetics, Experience and Our World(s)

Michael Halewood

Introduction

This chapter will trace elements of the work of A.N. Whitehead and John Dewey in their attempts to give the aesthetic its due place and weight in both thinking and the world. The term 'aesthetic' has followed a convoluted path from its origins in Ancient Greek, where it evoked not beauty but the broad notion of sense perception. The narrower, more 'modern', conception of aesthetics as concerned with matters of 'the beautiful' or 'art' only developed through the ideas of Alexander Gottlieb Baumgarten (1714–62). Notably, Kant uses the term 'aesthetic' in both of these senses, in his first (Kant, 1986) and third (Kant, 1982) critiques respectively, reflecting the shift in its meaning during the 18th century, as will be discussed in more detail.

Why does this matter? Two points seem immediately important. First, when writing about aesthetics, or any concept, it is important to have a sense of what is meant by the term, even if that is only to point up its ambiguity. It is crucial *not* to take for granted that which falls under such a concept. The second point involves the notion of bifurcation, as discussed by Sehgal and Wilkie in Chapter 1 of this volume. If one concern of this collection, and this chapter, is to trace what might be involved in, or required by, attempts to integrate the aesthetic into thinking and the world while avoiding any unhelpful or unwarranted bifurcations, then a sense of where such bifurcations come from could be helpful. With regard to the two senses of the aesthetic mentioned already – sense perception and the study of beauty – there are a host of competing bifurcations rather than one simple gulf. For example, within the traditional philosophical version, there is the possibility of bifurcating the perceiver from the world that is perceived, or the knower from the known. Treating aesthetics as concerned with matters of beauty risks producing other bifurcations; for example, between beauty considered solely as a matter of human perception which is divorced from the object that is perceived and whose molecules would not normally be considered to be beautiful in themselves. The identification of such bifurcations does not entail that the task at hand is to reintegrate a separate realm (of art, perception, beauty or representation) back onto or into a placid realm of inert matter. This would be to accept, tacitly, the very bifurcation which enables beauty and reality to be conceived as separate. The more demanding task is to avoid that which leads our thought and lives into such bifurcations. The manner in which Whitehead and Dewey took up this task will be the mainstay of this chapter. As will be seen, both writers, though with different shades of meaning, insist that experience and feeling are primary. Feeling constitutes the process and outcomes of reality. Such feeling is not inert; it always happens in a certain way. There is a qualitative aspect which is constitutive of all existence; it is not an addition. One key role of the 'aesthetic' for both Whitehead and Dewey is to give a place to these qualities of feelings, ones which are not reliant upon or solely produced by humans.

The first sections of the chapter will focus on Whitehead's placement of the aesthetic within his metaphysical treatise *Process and Reality* (1978 [1929]). To avoid the perils of the bifurcation of nature, Whitehead develops a metaphysical scheme in which feelings, and ways of feeling, occur within all existence and can do so without reference either to humans or to human consciousness. The later sections will focus on Dewey's ideas on the aesthetic and capitalism, as set out in *Art as Experience* (2005 [1934]). There is a key difference or a contrast between these two writers. One (Whitehead) imbibes the metaphysical, while the other (Dewey) feels that metaphysics, by definition, is unable to talk of specifics and to address the messiness of our industrialized and polluted world, and this means that talking solely of aesthetics in terms of metaphysics inhibits its reach and political import. Nevertheless, my feeling, my argument, is that Whitehead and Dewey are, at one level, trying to create similar perspectives, to make us view the world in a new way, but each of them does so in a different manner. As a result, I will present their texts as inhabiting the same plane of argument. This might produce a form of tension, but my position is that the difference in manner of argument and presentation is itself an example of the operation of the aesthetic as a contrast. Quite what this means will, hopefully, become clearer as the chapter unfolds.

Whitehead and the (metaphysical) need for aesthetics

At one point in *Process and Reality* (1978 [1929]), Whitehead describes his philosophical approach, which he calls 'philosophy of organism', as follows: 'The philosophy of organism aspires to construct a critique of pure feeling, in the philosophical position in which Kant put his Critique of Pure Reason. ... Thus in the organic philosophy; Kant's "Transcendental Aesthetic" becomes a distorted fragment of what should have been his main topic' (Whitehead, 1978: 113). To achieve this, Whitehead follows this adventure into transcendental aesthetics but insists that Kant has not gone far enough. Kant unnecessarily limits his own argument, according to Whitehead, as he only allows for humans to be involved in, or generate, perceptions. Kant's 'transcendental aesthetic' follows the original meaning of 'aesthetics' (in its pre-Baumgarten role) in that it is concerned with the very possibility of perception. It involves an a priori intuition of space and time which, he argues, is necessary to ground the very possibility of sense perception and experience of events in the world.[1] Questions of beauty or art are not involved at this stage. Only in his later critique (around 1790), the *Critique of Judgement*, does Kant use the term aesthetic in its more current sense, as concerned with matters of taste and beauty.

Whitehead argues (1978: 151–2) that in unnecessarily reducing the process of perception to the process of thought, Kant has constrained such activity to the operations of human minds – and here lie the roots of several bifurcations which plague modern thought. Kant's *Critique of Pure Reason* and his *Critique of Judgement* stand as two poles of such bifurcations. The aesthetic, be it in terms of the possibility of perception or the possibility of beauty, always refers to or is derived from either human cognition or human judgements. The objects of perception or of art always lie on the other side of a gulf unknowable or unfeelable as they are in themselves, as they feel themselves to be. Kant's first and third critiques deal with different aspects of *human* experience, both labelled as aesthetic, but divorced from that which is seen or felt. Moreover, post-Baumgarten aesthetics, including that of Kant's third critique, is always situated within *human* feeling. Whitehead argues that there is no need to make such an assumption, but this stance has major implications. Two of these are:

- Everything that exists is a subject which experiences or feels.[2]
- Whatever the aesthetic is, it cannot rely upon, or only be generated by, the feelings, perceptions or thoughts of humans.

This version of the aesthetic needs to be given its place within (the process of) reality. And this is what Whitehead sets out to do. One first move is to broaden the remit of perception: 'perception is a feeling' (Whitehead, 1978: 179) and is not predicated upon, or limited to, human sense perception. Whitehead goes further and extends the reach of 'feeling'.

> In feeling, what is felt is not necessarily analysed; in understanding, what is understood is analysed, in so far as it is understood. Understanding is a special form of feeling. ... Kant, in his Transcendental Aesthetic, emphasizes the doctrine that in intuition a complex datum is intuited as one. (Whitehead, 1978: 153–4).

Whitehead takes the first sense of the aesthetic, as concerned with perception, but expands its reach so that perception is no longer assumed to be solely a human affair. And yet, Whitehead is not simply engaged in advocating a return to pre-Baumgarten conceptions of aesthetics. He chose this term knowing that it would also evoke notions of beauty and art. The balancing act that he is trying to perform involves holding together, or entertaining,[3] that which is evoked by both senses of aesthetic.

What does this involve? How is it related to feeling? And what is 'aesthetic' about it?

One short, limited but important answer to such questions is to assert that whatever constitutes the aesthetic, it is certainly not beauty. In *Process and Reality*, Whitehead only uses the word 'beauty' twice (Whitehead, 1978: 213, 346) and 'beautiful' once (Whitehead, 1978: 48). Likewise, he uses 'aesthetic', in his particular metaphysical sense, on only a few pages of *Process and Reality* (pp 213, 279–80, 317), though he does use the word in its more current sense at other points. In total he uses the word 'aesthetic' about 25 times.

The composition of *Process and Reality* was not linear.[4] Whitehead revisited his text on various occasions but disliked and avoided wholesale rewriting, revising or even editing. Instead, he preferred to add a paragraph or a section to change the slant or implications of all that went before, or came after. This would certainly seem to be the case with his discussion of the aesthetic. Whitehead only uses 'aesthetic' in the metaphysical sense on a few pages (Whitehead, 1978: 213, 279–80, 317). The first two of the three passages which, in total, make up about four pages of the whole of *Process and Reality* are to be found not just at the end of a chapter, but in the final chapter of one of the five 'parts' of the text. The third discussion (Whitehead, 1978: 317) which comes towards the end of Part IV, is not situated in the final chapter, but Ford (1984: 233–5) lists the chapter in which it does occur (that of 'Strains', Whitehead, 1978: 310–21) as comprising one of the very final revisions of *Process and Reality*.

Such positional and temporal positioning within text matters. Parts II and III make up the main body of *Process and Reality* and are its core. And yet, at the end of each part, Whitehead feels that something is lacking, something needs restating, or a different emphasis needs to be given. And to address this lack, this need for restatement, Whitehead draws on the aesthetic. For some, this might suggest that Whitehead's concept of the 'aesthetic' is simply an add-on, something which can be taken out or ignored. I want to argue that the opposite is the case. The fact that Whitehead felt the need, not once but three times, to restate his metaphysics through the concept of the aesthetic tells us that it is the strongest way of understanding all that has gone before in each part of the book. As will hopefully become clear as this chapter unfolds, the positioning of these arguments within the text itself bears witness to the operation of the aesthetic within all elements of existence. To justify such a claim, some more detailed analysis is required.

Some details: Whitehead's use of 'aesthetic' within *Process and Reality*

As has been seen, for Whitehead, perception, intuition or feeling is not limited to human subjects. All things feel, and it is feelings that are fundamental to the composition of all entities. One name that Whitehead gives to this generalized (or metaphysical) form of being and becoming is that of 'actual entity' or 'actual occasion'. The becoming of an actual entity or an actual occasion incorporates feeling. This is not the feeling of the world (or of objects) by an already existing subject. Instead, the process of feeling generates the subject. This is still too simple an account. There are stages to this feeling.

> An actual occasion is nothing but the unity to be ascribed to a particular instance of concrescence. ... The analysis of the formal constitution of an actual entity has given three stages in the process of feeling: (i) the responsive phase, (ii) the supplemental stage, and (iii) the satisfaction. (Whitehead, 1978: 212)

Whitehead sets up actual occasions (or actual entities) as involving three stages of feeling but has not mentioned the aesthetic yet. It is, perhaps, hard to think about stages which are non-temporal, but that is what Whitehead is asking us to do. These stages are in neither space nor time. This is, perhaps, one first indication of the role of the aesthetic, in terms of the original sense of the possibility of perception (as evidenced in Kant's Transcendental Aesthetic, which attempts to posit an a priori intuition of space and time).

Yet there is another sense of the aesthetic which inhabits this more general account of the possibility of perception, and this develops in the second, supplemental, stage: 'The second phase, that of supplementation, divides itself into two subordinate phases. ... Of these two sub-phases, the former so far as there is an order is that of aesthetic supplement, and the latter is that of intellectual supplement' (Whitehead, 1978: 213).

The aesthetic element 'precedes' or has priority over the 'later' intellectual stage, and Whitehead soon provides some more detail: 'In the aesthetic supplement there is an emotional appreciation of the contrasts and rhythms inherent in the unification of the objective content in the concrescence of one actual occasion. In this phase perception is heightened by its assumption of *pain and pleasure, beauty and distaste*' (Whitehead, 1978: 213, emphasis added)

It is important to note the linkage between aesthetics and perception, as mentioned previously. This again situates the argument within the pre-Baumgarten realm, within the original Greek sense of aesthetics and within the Transcendental Aesthetic of Kant's first critique, which is now broadened so that it does not rely upon or emanate from human consciousness. Perception is a mode of feeling the world which does not have to involve sight or any other of the senses. All things feel, and all things perceive. This is one of the tenets of Whitehead's metaphysics. The aesthetic, therefore, inhabits all elements of existence, to a greater or lesser extent.

This is a surprising, if not bewildering, proposition – any 'thing' that exists both feels and perceives and partakes of the aesthetic. In recognition of the peculiarity, Whitehead, in the quotation given previously, attempts to explain his point in the second sentence, where he talks of 'pain and pleasure, beauty and distaste'. With this mention of 'beauty', surely Whitehead is drawing on some kind of notion of aesthetics? Perhaps, but it is important not to go too far too quickly.

Whitehead's metaphysical account of existence in terms of 'actual occasions' or 'actual entities' does not map onto human experience of the world. To assume that Whitehead's discussions of 'actual entities', 'actual occasions', feelings and so on can be immediately taken up and used to describe *our* world, *our* experiences is to misunderstand the metaphysical aspect of Whitehead's philosophy.[5] This philosophy is speculative precisely in so far as it is *not* merely a description of *our* existence. And yet, such metaphysical analyses need to be balanced with the requirement to *explain*.

Bearing this in mind, it is possible to return to Whitehead's mention of 'pain and pleasure, beauty and distaste'. Two points can be made. The first, rather tepid one, is that this phrase is simply an example of Whitehead trying to clarify his surprising proposition that all things feel and perceive by using terms with which we are more familiar. The second, more interesting point can build on this first one and ask us to extend our surprise. The mention of beauty and pain is offered to elicit an initial understanding of this point but then asks us to take the next step, to allow for the possibility that that which humans refer to as beauty, pleasure, pain or distaste is an element of all existence. No thing is inert. More than that, all things, in the metaphysically potential sense, could experience what humans call pleasure, pain, distaste and beauty. Our world, our planet, is constituted by its ongoing feelings of pleasure, pain, distaste, beauty and more.

A missing shade of blue

Another way of reading Whitehead's passages on the aesthetic is as a response to a major philosophical problem which is sometimes referred to as Hume's missing shade of blue. Indeed, Whitehead makes it clear that this is one of his goals (Whitehead, 1978: 260–1). David Hume, the arch empiricist, allowed for an exception to his empiricism which Whitehead wants to avoid. Hume maintains that a person confronted with a spectrum of shades of blue going from light to dark with one shade missed out will be able to conjure up this missing shade in their mind. Whitehead disagrees. The details of Whitehead's argument are dense, but I will give a flavour in the following quotation, which provides more detail on the supplemental phase (the one where the aesthetic 'occurs'):

> It is the phase in which blue becomes more intense by reason of its *contrasts*, and shape acquires dominance by reason of its loveliness. What was received as alien, has been recreated as private. This is the phase of perceptivity, including emotional reactions to *perceptivity*. In this phase, private immediacy has welded the data into a new fact of blind feeling. Pure aesthetic supplement has solved its problem. This phase requires an influx of conceptual feelings and their integration with the pure physical feelings. (Whitehead, 1978: 213–4, emphasis added)

Again, we are in the realm of 'perceptivity', of perception (or 'sensible intuition', as Kant might put it). There is also mention of 'conceptual feelings', and these invoke Whitehead's notion of eternal objects in their role of providing both potentiality and novelty (though there is not space to go into detail here). There is also mention of 'loveliness'. Is this a reference to aesthetics? Perhaps. But if so, it is not crucial to the argument being made and could perhaps be filed as another example of Whitehead's attempt to explain. What matters is the mention of contrast, of the 'emotional reaction' and the move from blind feeling into the conceptual. Contrast and contrasts are the porters of conceptuality and novelty. It is not a matter of conjuring up an absent shade of blue but of focussing on the intensity of this blue in contrast to other possible blues, or even reds or greens. The completion of this feeling ('that is a blue coat' or 'there is a shade of blue missing') turns that private event into a public fact. It also renders this fact as 'aesthetic', in that the contrast, the conceptual novelty, is integral to that fact, indeed to all facts in so far as they manage to populate the world and endure.

It is important to remember that Whitehead is partially in dialogue with Kant's Critique of Pure Reason, in that he is trying to establish a critique of pure feeling. The first stage of feeling is a blind feeling, where the public, the outside, the 'alien' begins to be felt privately. The second, supplemental phase of feeling, the one where the aesthetic occurs, involves those feelings which do not have the physical as their datum but have potentiality, alternatives or possibilities as their data – this is the realm of eternal objects and conceptual feelings. Feeling becomes more 'complex', and although it does not emanate from a subject, through the different stages of feeling, a subject emerges which is the conveyor and conveyance of such novel reactions to the world.

Whitehead makes this point clear when he returns to the notion of the aesthetic at the end of Part III of *Process and Reality*: 'an actual fact is a fact of aesthetic experience. All aesthetic experience is feeling arising out of the realization of contrast under identity' (Whitehead, 1978: 280). Contrast is crucial. The awareness, the inclusion, of the possibility of things being otherwise, of the world not being a procession of blind repetition bears witness to the integral character of novelty which is the hallmark of the aesthetic. So much so that all facts are an aesthetic fact.

One consequence of this is that the 'aesthetic' is widespread, one might say even 'commonplace' or 'banal'. If every fact has an aesthetic element, in that it comprises a contrast, then the aesthetic could be 'reduced' to boring contrasts between, for example, something being warm or cold. We are a long way from questions of beauty or 'art'. Perhaps this is not surprising, in that we are at the heart of Whitehead's metaphysics. Nevertheless, such considerations need to be given their place. And some indication of this is to be found in Whitehead's third and final discussion of the aesthetic in *Process and Reality*, where he states that '[t]he canons of art are merely the expression, in specialized forms, of the requisites for depth of experience' (Whitehead, 1978: 317). Art and beauty, whatever they may turn out to be, are no more or less than an example of the deeper form of (aesthetic) fact and feeling which suffuses existence and constitutes both objects and subjects.

Examples, metaphysics and John Dewey

One aim of this chapter is to outline the role of the aesthetic within Whitehead's metaphysics, as set out in *Process and Reality*. It transpires that any such outline might be felt to be lacking, in that the very instantiation of the aesthetic as a metaphysical element entails that any examples, or particular instances, need to be written out of the scheme or introduced only as secondary, 'explanatory' elements. As a result, those mentions of 'beauty, pain, pleasure etc' had to be removed from the scaffolding of the argument. Whitehead declares metaphysics to be 'a dispassionate consideration of the nature of things, antecedently to any special investigation into their details' (Whitehead, 1932: 195). Yet the demand for examples, for further explanation, is a strong one. Rather than turn to one of Whitehead's later, supposedly less metaphysical, texts, such as *Adventures of Ideas*, I will take a detour through a philosophical contemporary of Whitehead, namely John Dewey.

Where Whitehead, in *Process and Reality*, focusses on developing an abstract scheme which by definition cannot rely on example, Dewey eschews metaphysics and maintains that only through specific arguments and examples can any metaphysical point be made.

> In order to *understand* the esthetic[6] in its ultimate and approved forms, one must begin with it in the raw; in the events and scenes that hold the attentive eye and ear of man, arousing his interest and affording him enjoyment as he looks and listens: the sights that hold the crowd – the fire-engine rushing by; the machines excavating enormous holes in the earth; the human-fly climbing the steeple-side; the men perched high on girders, throwing red-hot bolts. The sources of art in human experience will be learned by him who sees how the tense grace of the ball-player infects the onlooking crowd; who notes the delight of the housewife in tending her plants. (Dewey, 2005 [1934]: 3)

When confronted with a piece of text which seems to assume that the word 'man' can stand in for all humans but that only men look and listen, that men perch high on girders while housewives tend their plants, the usual convention is to place [sic] after the offending text, and perhaps add a footnote mentioning that such attitudes represent no more than the academic convention of the time. I think it is important not to do this. Rather, let us take the text at its word. Reading this quotation is an experience among many other experiences. In trying to understand the passage, the reader will be confronted or affected by the skewed language and phraseology. To assume that it is possible to bracket and ignore the gendered language and the assumptions which lurk behind such language is to produce another bifurcation. It is to split the supposed fact, the meaning of the text, from the words and lexicon which are used to produce that text and its argument. It is to suggest that behind the words used there is a pure meaning which it is possible to identify and render differently, perhaps in a more palatable form. However, we need to remember Whitehead's argument as set out in the preceding discussion. The manner of presentation of all existence is where the aesthetic resides, and this applies to texts as well. This is not to deny facticity (of argument or meaning) but to insist that the manner in which fact and meaning are elicited and framed cannot be shorn from each other. 'There is no parting from your shadow' (Whitehead, 1932 [1925]: 23). And it is important not to smooth over or ignore incongruities or feelings of unease while trying to latch on to the 'fact' of the argument that the raw components of the aesthetic are to be found in machines, fire engines, building sites, sport and gardening. Unease can be an example of the aesthetic.

We need to *entertain*, in the original sense of the word – of holding together – rather than *enjoy* Dewey's text, at this stage at least. Our reaction is an example of the aesthetic at work throughout existence (though Dewey might not put it in so general a manner). For Dewey, as with Whitehead, what matters is experience. 'Even a crude experience, if authentically an experience, is more fit to give a clue to the intrinsic nature of esthetic experience than is an object already set apart from any other mode of experience' (Dewey, 2005 [1934]). It is a mistake, when thinking about the aesthetic, to start with supposed art objects and consider how they fit in with some notion of the aesthetic. Aesthetics, for Dewey, is a theory of specific feelings and experiences but, like Whitehead, he does not predicate such experience upon human individuality or subjectivity. Dewey gets rid of any notion of a fixed self which endures behind its experiences. He talks of the 'failure [which] is found when the self is regarded as the bearer or carrier of an experience instead of a factor absorbed in what is produced, as in the case of the gases that produce water' (Dewey, 2005 [1934]: 260–1). The self, insofar as one can talk of such a 'thing', comes and goes, is an element of a wider event. 'Because experience is the fulfilment of an organism in its struggles and achievements in a world of things, it is art in germ. Even in its rudimentary forms, it contains the promise of that delightful perception which is esthetic experience' (Dewey, 2005 (1934): 18–19). The hallmark of an aesthetic experience is that the organism and environment work together to constitute an experience within which it makes no sense to talk of the self and the world as separate. This hallmark is actually borne by all experiences; it is simply that the aesthetic experience brings it most fully to light:

> the uniquely distinguishing feature of esthetic experience is exactly the fact that no such distinction of self and objects exist in it, since it is esthetic in the degree in which organism and environment cooperate to institute an experience in which the two are so fully integrated each disappears. (Dewey, 2005 [1934]: 259)

Albeit via a different route, Dewey has brought us to a conclusion which was made towards the end of the discussion of Whitehead's placement of the aesthetic within his metaphysics. Aesthetics is not a creation of the human mind or of human feeling. It is wider than that and incorporates the external world – the environment – in a cooperation with a range of organisms (including humans). The aesthetic has a wider remit than first thought; indeed, it has such an extraordinarily broad reach that it might even be felt to be commonplace or banal. This might constitute a problem, in that the aesthetic has been so diluted as to have lost the purchase upon feelings (of beauty, distaste, or otherwise) that both Whitehead and Dewey want to retain, or at least be able to encompass within their theories, without predicating their arguments upon the specificity of human feelings.

Dewey renders this troublesome consequence as follows: 'The problem of conferring esthetic quality upon all modes of production is a serious problem. But it is a human problem for human solution; not a problem incapable of solution because it is set by some unpassable gulf in human nature or in the nature of things' (Dewey, 2005 [1934]: 84). To address the problem, it is necessary to address that which generates the problem. There is no actual gulf, no bifurcation, within human nature, within nature or between human nature and nature. That is not the source of the problem. It is not that there is aesthetic on one side and reality on the other. The problem, as signalled by Dewey's use of the more familiarly Marxist phrase 'modes of production' is one situated within the very *character* of the economic, political, psychological and industrial environs of that which we call, don't call or want to call 'aesthetic'.

Capitalism has reduced 'art' and the aesthetic so that the emphasis is placed on the objects of art and the ownership of them, whether in private collections or museums (see Dewey, 2005 [1934]: 7). One important consequence of the argument made throughout this chapter is that the extent and remit of the aesthetic has often been underestimated. It has been restricted to the human realm, predicated on consciousness and lifted off from nature or reality. Whitehead and Dewey aim to give the aesthetic its rightful place within existence, as occupying a much broader plane. In doing so, although without always making this clear, they make a distinction between the aesthetic and what might be termed 'art'. For Dewey, whatever art involves, it will involve work. 'The product of artistic activity is significantly called the *work* of art' (Dewey, 2005 [1934]: 290). Art is a form of work. Can it be said that work is a form of art? Not exactly, but there will always be an element of the latter within work. This turns attention from Whitehead's metaphysical description to Dewey's focus on the metaphysical within the everyday, through the inherence of the aesthetic within the processes of production. Recalling that the self and environment cohere within specific experiences, it is not possible to generalize, to posit laws which govern the processes of production. 'The psychological conditions resulting from private control of the labor of other men for the sake of private gain, rather than any fixed psychological or economic law, are the forces that suppress and limit esthetic quality in the experience that accompanies processes of production' (Dewey, 2005 [1934]: 357).

Capitalism is slippery. It evades our grasp, mentally and physically. Capitalism is not a thing, a substantive, a noun, which can be isolated and named. Capitalism is a way of doing things, hence the term *mode* of production: there are *market-like* relations rather than markets in which such relations occur (see Halewood, 2020: 71–88 for a fuller discussion of this). Capitalism, like art, 'is a quality of doing and of what is done. Only outwardly, then, can it be designated by a noun substantive ... it is adjectival in nature' (Dewey, 2005 [1934]: 222). Where Dewey uses the adjectival to express the qualitative character of the aesthetic, I would like to add the adverbial to emphasize the modes of activity and experience. The environment within which work occurs is not governed by immutable economic or psychological laws; the conditions of work do, however, 'suppress and limit [the] esthetic quality' which necessarily inheres in all experiences that accompany work. This mention of the environment is instructive, for both Whitehead and Dewey would insist that there is no such thing as the 'environment in general'; there is only ever *this* environment or *that* environment. Our world, our worlds, incorporate an environment, or environments, in which capitalism and its ecological implications are deeply imbued. The project of broadening the remit and import of aesthetics is important not just for modern society and culture but for the planet, for example in relation to its experience and expression of radical novelty in terms of a changing climate. The world does not simply undergo or suffer such changes; it conveys both us and itself through the pain, pleasure, beauty and distaste which populate our worlds.

Notes

1. Kant's 'transcendental aesthetic', which comprises one of the earliest sections of his monumental *Critique of Pure Reason* (1986), 'discovers' that space and time are not, as Newton held, receptacles which contain the things of the world but are a priori intuitions (not concepts) which make *perception* of the world possible.
2. '[A]part from the experiences of subjects there is nothing, nothing, nothing, bare nothingness' (Whitehead, 1978: 167).
3. In *Process and Reality*, Whitehead makes extensive use of the word 'entertain' (see, for example, Whitehead, 1978: 43, 147, 188, 193, 195, 197, 258, 259) with a slightly unusual usage of the term which refers to its root meaning, that is, to 'hold together' or to 'hold among'.
4. See Ford (1984) for a fuller discussion of some of the complexities involved in the composition and publication of this text.
5. The kind of experiences that we (humans) have of the world involve Whitehead's specific understanding of what he terms 'societies' (Whitehead, 1978: 89–109). Such societies are collections which endure and are far removed from apparently ultimate metaphysical entities such as 'actual entities'. Many Whitehead scholars missed the crucial distinction between actual entities and societies, and it took some real effort to bring the importance of societies in his philosophy to the forefront (see Debaise, 2006: 133–72; Halewood, 2011: 79–104; Stengers, 2011).
6. Dewey chose to use this spelling. I could have changed it to 'aesthetic' to fit in with the other uses within this chapter. However, I have kept it in its original version as I have the feeling that this slight alteration or disturbance in some way fulfils an aesthetic role, in the sense being set out in this chapter.

References

Debaise, D. (2006) Un empirisme spéculative, Lecture de Procès et réalité de Whitehead, Paris: Vrin.

Dewey, J. (2005 [1934]) *Art as Experience*, New York: Perigree.

Ford, Lewis. S. (1984) *The Emergence of Whitehead's Metaphysics 1925–1929*, Albany, NY: University of New York Press.

Halewood, M. (2011) *A.N. Whitehead and Social Theory: Tracing a Culture of Thought*, London: Anthem Press.

Halewood, M. (2020) *Language and Process: Words, Whitehead and the World*, Edinburgh: Edinburgh University Press.

Kant, I. (1982) *Critique of Judgement*, trans J. Meredith, Oxford: Oxford University Press.

Kant, I. (1986) *Critique of Pure Reason*, trans N. Kemp Smith, London: Macmillan.

Shaviro, S. (2009) *Without Criteria: Kant, Whitehead, Deleuze, and Aesthetics*, Cambridge, MA: MIT Press.

Stengers, I. (2011) *Thinking with Whitehead: A Free and Wild Creation of Concepts*, Cambridge, MA and London: Harvard University Press.

Whitehead, A.N. (1932 [1925]) *Science and the Modern World*, Cambridge: Cambridge University Press.

Whitehead, A.N. (1978 [1929]) *Process and Reality: An Essay in Cosmology* (Gifford Lectures of 1927–8), corrected edn, ed D. Griffin and D. Sherburne, New York: The Free Press.

3

Eternal Objects of Nuclear Waste Futures

Thomas P. Keating

I was walking along the road with two friends – the sun was setting – suddenly the sky turned blood red – I paused, feeling exhausted, and leaned on the fence – there was blood and tongues of fire above the blue-black fjord and the city – my friends walked on, and I stood there trembling with anxiety – and I sensed an infinite scream passing through nature.

Edvard Munch, painted onto the
frame of The Scream (1985)

Introduction

What is an eternal object? On one level, one might begin with how in *Process and Reality* Whitehead (1978) seeks to define eternal objects directly in terms of potentiality: different to actual occasions, eternal objects are 'the pure potentials of the universe' (149). As pure potentials, eternal objects are not reducible to actualized things, occasions or predicates of matter since they exist in themselves: they exhibit an *inherent value* that needs no qualification through recourse to other abstractions of experience. Against a purely transcendental metaphysics of experience, Whitehead's eternal objects are 'eternal' in the precise sense that they always exceed actual occasions localized in a given time and space. In this way, eternal objects inhere a fundamental, if not a transcendental, orienting possibility of the universe – one that both *informs* and *exceeds* the production of an actualized event. By participating in the actualization of events, or what he terms actual occasions, eternal objects share something in common with Simondon's (2020) notion of the 'pre-individual', consisting of singular, orientating potentialities informing individuating events. They also connect to Deleuze's (1990; 2004) expansive concept of the 'virtual' (Halewood, 2005) – particularly in the sense that the virtual might be understood in terms of non-individuated intensities directing events of difference. This collective effort to theorise eternal objects of pure potentiality is to account for how actualized occasions are always structured by intangible relations in excess of the event.[1] In this reading, eternal objects are pure indefinite potentialities that always retain an unactualized remainder from actuality – a 'complete world of abstract potentiality' (Whitehead, 1948: 152) characterized by 'its unchanging relationless unity' (Allan, 2008a: 332) that can never be fully expressed in any given event.

On another level, eternal objects can be understood in an explicitly aesthetic mode concerning the function of pure potentials to instil capacities for feeling. In this aesthetic mode, eternal objects 'such as colours, sounds, scents, geometrical characters' can be understood as the 'ingredient' (Whitehead, 1948: 105) of actual occasions. These ingredients are absolutely not captured by the concrete space and time of actual occasions, nor the solipsistic materialism implied by Aristotle's substantialism. They evade this capture because, for Whitehead, there is an abstract character of eternal objects that is not explained by substantialist claims about a fundamental base-reality of matter. When Whitehead (1948: 158; 1978: 256) refers to 'red' as an eternal object, in doing so he is not necessarily arguing for a new theory of aesthetics but pinpointing the way eternal objects can be understood in terms of 'colour' that always retains a *wider, fuller* capacity for feeling that has hitherto never been experienced. Colour is an eternal object because a subject apprehends the possibility that alternative experiences of the colour red can be actualized in the future: the potential for experiencing red differently is never exhausted. Eternal objects, therefore, concern a speculative empirical question concerning the capacity of abstractions to 'thicken' experience by providing a sense of the alternative (Debaise and Stengers, 2022): how to account for events of sense not merely through dominant abstractions of experience but rather in terms of a wider universe of possible experience?

This chapter considers some of the implications of eternal objects for thinking about a particular environmental problem: namely, current plans for the underground storage of 20th- and 21st-century nuclear waste into the distant future within so-called 'final repositories'. This is the name given to a recent plan to store the most radioactive substances produced by nuclear energy production – spent nuclear fuel – within underground burial chambers for the entire 100,000 years that these materials pose a danger to organic life. The construction of final repositories for nuclear waste is currently under way in Sweden and Finland, with similar schemes being considered elsewhere in Europe and North America. One of the implications of constructing final nuclear waste repositories is that problems arise regarding how to communicate the existence of these burial sites into the future.

Addressing this problem is difficult not least because present-day human language systems and representational structures are entirely unsuitable for communicating over 100,000-year post-human timeframes. Indeed, the very premise of burying nuclear waste underground for 100,000 years clearly involves a certain form of hubristic thinking – including an assumption that it is possible to engineer the communication of a message about nuclear waste sites through millennia (Wikander, 2015). Such hubris might be also understood as symptomatic of a wider tendency within the Anthropocene for the human subject to understand itself as having a wider agency and capacity for managing earth process over geological time scales (Bjornerud, 2018).

The relevance of Whitehead's eternal objects to the problem of communicating the existence of nuclear waste repositories into the distant future can be understood as follows: for around 40 years, the social and physical sciences have been variously involved in debates and planning for final repositories for nuclear waste by imagining their own 'eternal objects' – understood, in this context, as the literal production of material things (signs, obelisks, markers, landscape art, time capsules, archives etc) designed to communicate into eternity (Madsen, 2010). This formal planning of final repositories for nuclear waste (see Ast et al, 1992) has involved wider engagements with nuclear art (Decamous, 2019) and semiotics (Sebeok, 1984) that aim, in part, to understand the capacity of aesthetic forms to communicate in a manner that *exceeds* any given time and place, and in doing so *inform* the actualization of the future. The aim of this chapter is to consider to what extent Whitehead's notion of eternal objects might speak to research concerning the communication of memory of final repositories for nuclear waste (Keating and Storm, 2023) and the kinds of aesthetic forms of thinking it demands. Here, the intention is not to seek some kind of synthesis of thinking between these contexts. Rather, and beginning with the idea that aesthetics directly concerns a capacity to feel and be affected (Stengers, 2000; Sehgal, 2018), this chapter engages the aesthetic through Whitehead's articulation of forms of aesthetic value entirely freed from the localized placings of the phenomenological human subject. Doing so helps consider how eternal objects, like that of colour, speak to the environmental problem of communicating the existence of final repositories through the production of *different* nuclear waste futures (Joyce, 2020). Focussing on Whitehead's articulation of the eternal qualities of colour is potentially fruitful in this context, not least due to his focus on indefinite aesthetic expressions that remain open to different futures – expressions concerning a force of feeling that are not overdetermined by imaginations of the future derived from the actualized present.

While bringing Whitehead's thought into conversation with nuclear waste management practices clearly involves a degree of risk, the effort in doing so is to consider how the recent practice of imagining and theorizing nuclear signs and messages designed to last at least 100,000 years might reveal something about this unlikely genealogy of eternal objects. The key argument is to say that Whitehead's eternal objects chiefly involve the production of values – an argument first made by Raymond Ruyer (1948) – and that these values are revealed by eternal objects in the actualization of actual occasions that open the possibility for collective forms of transvaluation. The remainder of this chapter proceeds over three parts. The first considers the relationship between eternal objects and the production of values; the second suggests how this relationship speaks to recent research in nuclear semiotics – focussing especially on the legacy of Edvard Munch's painting *The Scream*; the third concludes by reflecting on some of the problems and opportunities offered by this commingling of thought. As this chapter shows, *The Scream* has proved a source of inspiration for discussions around the eternal objects of final repositories for nuclear waste, while Munch (1895) himself was moved to create his artwork after an experience with a striking red sky expressing, in his words, 'an infinite scream passing through nature' – an experience that invokes an element of compatibility with Whitehead's own conceptualization of eternal objects.

Eternal objects: definiteness in experience and the indefinite production of values

Whitehead is not necessarily an obvious starting point for a theory of aesthetics. Thanks to the respective contributions of Stengers (2011) and Debaise (2017), among others, he is more obviously associated with process philosophy and in defining the function of philosophy in speculative terms as the 'critic of abstractions' (Whitehead, 1948: 59) – or what he will also refer to as the 'critic of cosmologies' (1948: viii). Thought about in this context, he is perhaps more immediately recognized for his metaphysical contributions, as well as his writings on the philosophy of science that consider how the production of abstractions produces thinking in ways that are often difficult to discern.

And yet, some have observed the way Whitehead considers aesthetics a fundamental component of existence (Sehgal and Wilkie, Chapter 1, this volume; Allan, 2008b; Shaviro, 2014; Sehgal, 2018). If, for Whitehead, aesthetics refers not to a phenomenological experience of beauty and the sublime but to 'a production of existence that concerns one's capacity to feel' (Stengers 2000: 147), then this notion of aesthetics at once defines the evaluative frames that structure feeling prior to a subject's sense of conscious experience and wilful decision making. The critical importance of aesthetics for addressing this modern dualism of thought, as Sehgal (2018: 127) argues, lies in the Whiteheadian gambit that 'changing habits of thought requires and presupposes changes in habits of feeling'. This is to understand the aesthetic as something that directs thought towards Deleuze's (2004: 176) oft-cited 'something' that 'forces us to think': as a mode of existence, aesthetics as capacity for feeling would be capable of accounting for forms of experience that slip past the human subject with its tendency to qualify feeling through subjective and objective categories. Aesthetics, therefore, becomes something directly concerning those lures of feeling, existential territories, and pre-individual potentials that constitute a much wider 'ecology of experience' (Manning and Massumi, 2014).

As 'forms which determine the specific character of any actual entity, or which determine the 'kind' of feeling the subject of any occasion experiences' (Hooper, 1942: 47), eternal objects clearly offer something specific to this understanding of Whiteheadian aesthetics. If eternal objects can be understood in terms of certain aesthetic forms, as Hooper argues, this is because these pure potentials are subject to what Whitehead terms 'creativity'.[2] When Whitehead (1967) coined the term creativity, in doing so he aimed not at a new notion of invention implying an active subject of formation (such as an inventor) but at conceptualizing the way occasions arise as something that 'has gathered the creativity of the Universe into its own completeness' (p 212). Creativity, in this enigmatic complete and universal mode, is not simply a term of invention or novelty (Meyer, 2005), but an inherent power of actualization that defines the initial phase of an occasion of experience:

> The initial situation includes a factor of activity which is the reason for the origin of that occasion of experience. This factor of activity is what I have called 'Creativity'. The initial situation with its creativity can be termed the initial phase of the new occasion. It can equally well be termed the 'actual world' relative to that occasion. It has a certain unity of its own, expressive of its capacity for providing the objects requisite for a new occasion, and also expressive of its conjoint activity whereby it is essentially the primary phase of a new occasion. It can thus be termed a 'real potentiality'. (Whitehead, 1967: 179)

Reminiscent of eternal objects, and thus different to an ultimate transcendental condition, 'real potentiality' in this passage refers to how the creativity of the universe comes to provide the necessary conditions – or 'objects' – for the becoming of occasions of experience. As Duvernoy (2019) explains, what Whitehead and Deleuze both develop is a metaphysics of 'authentic creativity' – one amounting not to a theory of difference and individuation, but rather the actual enactment of difference and individuation in thought itself. Creativity, in this authentic sense, can therefore be understood in connection to eternal objects: if creativity concerns 'real' potentials rather than 'pure' potentials, this might be because for Whitehead creativity is about the unfolding of an actual occasion in the world, whereas eternal objects are resolutely indeterminate and distinct from actual occasions.

Yet Whitehead (1978: 257) is quite clear that eternal objects are not 'mere undifferentiated nonentities' entirely abstracted from actuality but are potentials that relate to one another and participate, often subtly, in the actualization of events. As Duvernoy (2019: 175) notes, eternal objects 'are not static universals or forms that instantiate in a top-down relationship of one-to-one resemblance, but are rather potentials of relation that "ingress" into actual occasions in differing degrees and intensities'. The term ingress is used here because Whitehead theorizes the relationship between eternal objects and the unfolding of actual occasions through what he terms 'modes of ingression': 'each eternal object has its own proper connection with each other such occasion, which I term its mode of ingression into that occasion' (Whitehead, 1948: 159). Mode of ingression refers to the way eternal objects are differently realized in actual occasions due to the existence of alternative possibilities oriented by eternal objects with which it has a proper connection. To understand the proper connections of eternal objects, one can think of the way red might be actualized as another possible sense perception of colour but not as a geometric form that itself is another eternal object involving its own mode of ingression.

Through this formulation, Whitehead's eternal objects account for the way feelings emerge in experience through modes of ingression that prefigure, to some degree, how actual occasions of experience take shape. Two key implications can be discerned from this reading of eternal objects. The first is that eternal objects have a specific power to provide definiteness to actual occasions. Definiteness, in this context, refers to the way that an actual occasion takes on a quality that makes it entirely distinct from any other occasion that will precede or follow it. Eternal objects provide definiteness in a variety of ways – returning to the example of red, Whitehead writes:

> an eternal object refers only to the purely general any among undetermined actual entities. In itself an eternal object evades any selection among actualities or epochs. You cannot know what is red by merely thinking of redness. You can only find red things by adventuring amid physical experiences in this actual world. This doctrine is the ultimate ground of empiricism; namely, that eternal objects tell no tales as to their ingressions. (Whitehead, 1978: 256)

It is because red is an eternal object that the quality of an actualized experience of redness is able to take on a definiteness that is a distinct and singular occasion of experience. Eternal objects reveal nothing of their ingressions because this realm of indefinite potential cannot be reduced to actualized experience. Yet, what can be known is a sense that the eternal object of red inheres a 'conceptual feeling' (Whitehead 1967: 194) that is never quite captured in its categorization into the subjective or objective. The definiteness of an actual experience of red, meanwhile, is not an eternal object but something that can *only* be experienced and whose singular experience offers an inexhaustible source of empiricism.

The second, and related, implication is the way that eternal objects are crucial to how actual occasions provide a sense of *alternative possibilities* by being defined as an indefinite quality of nature. What at first seems like a contradiction between the definite and indefinite is a crucial part of Whitehead's whole notion of eternal objects insofar as it explains their participation in the production of alternatives within actual occasions of experience: 'Potentiality becomes reality; and yet retains its message of alternatives which the actual entity has avoided. In the constitution of an actual entity: whatever component is red, might have been green; and whatever component is loved, might have been coldly esteemed' (Whitehead, 1978: 149). Which is to say that an experience of red, however strong and affecting this may be, brings with it the premise that this experience of colour could have been different. Part of the importance of this notion of eternal objects to Whitehead's metaphysics, as Shaviro (2012: 40) notes, is that they 'always imply alternatives, contingencies, situations that could have been otherwise'. When Whitehead (1948: 89) exemplifies eternal objects of sense by referring to William Wordsworth's evocation of 'The light that never was, on sea or land', in doing so he is pointing towards an inherent, yet inexpressible, aesthetic value of nature that can never be realized by any actualized occasion.

Thinking with this same eternal object of colour, in *Le Monde des Valeurs* (1948) Raymond Ruyer develops four theses on the relation between values and colour by referring to the following passage from Whitehead's *Science and the Modern World*: 'Colour is eternal. It haunts time, like a spirit. It comes and it goes. But where it comes, it is the same colour. It neither survives nor does it live. It appears when it is wanted' (Whitehead, 1948: 88).

Unpacking something of this passage, Ruyer (1948: 11–14) makes four specific arguments concerning the relationship between values and colour: (1) colours and values have the same status of subsistence (as existence); (2) the experience of colour is non-transferrable due to its value being situated in the self-enjoyment of the perceiver; (3) 'Values and colors are both subjective and transsubjective, relative and cross-relative' (p 12) since colour is part of the eternal constituent of things; (4) and that there are systems of colours – defined by systems of evaluation of qualities of shade and luminosity – which are analogous to a culture's system of values. What is remarkable about Ruyer's reading, and particularly the fourth stage of his argument, is that eternal objects bring with them a specific evaluative function: the actualization of the future is not purely an outcome of indeterminate relations between pure potentials, but also of the mode of ingression of pure potentials that prefigure actualized systems of valuation coming into being.

The pursuit of eternal objects in nuclear semiotic markers

By connecting an indefinite and unactualized capacity of nature to the production of definiteness in experience, there is much to distinguish between Whitehead's reading of eternal objects and the pursuit of what might be termed 'eternal objects' in practices of planning final nuclear waste repositories into the future. Not least is how the eternal objects of nuclear waste management practices are mostly imagined as actualized things that are concerned – for the most part – with the way matter might be construed to produce messages and forms of signification suitable for communicating over thousands of years. The most concentrated effort to develop eternal objects to communicate memory of final nuclear waste repositories began in the 1980s with the formation of the Human Interference Task Force by the United States government's Department of Energy. This task force, which led to an associated Expert Judgement on Markers to Deter Inadvertent Human Intrusion into the Waste Isolation Pilot Plant panel in the 1990s, brought together experts from anthropology, nuclear engineering, behavioural science, linguistics, psychology and semiotics – to name a few – to develop ways of communicating memory of nuclear waste sites over 10,000–100,000 years. Their solution, invariably, was to create universal 'markers' and 'signs' to communicate into the future to indicate the existence of highly radioactive nuclear waste buried underground. As with Sagan's (1978) *Murmurs of Earth* archive, these eternal signs were strongly influenced by the notion of the time capsule as something capable of communicating a universal message through time to any subject whatsoever. One proposal to emerge from these discussions includes the *Landscape of Thorns* (1993) concept by Michael Brill and Safdar Abidi, which utilizes environmental things as a universal mode of communication by using the physical presence of jagged aesthetic forms that emanate affects of inhospitality and deterrence (Keating, 2022).

One of the enduring difficulties encountered by the Human Interference Task Force and the Expert Judgement on Markers panel in the 1980s and 1990s included how to communicate into the future without falling back onto current anthropocentric frames – that is, how to create an eternal warning sign for final repositories of nuclear waste that does not rely on contemporary aesthetic genres of, for example, fear, danger or deterrence? Perhaps the most notable attempt at responding to this problem includes the enrolment of Munch's *The Scream* (Ast et al, 1992) in creating specific nuclear waste repository markers (Figure 3.1). As Van Wyck (2004: 53) explains, the

Figure 3.1: Universal facial icons in Waste Isolation Pilot Project subsurface markers.

Source: United States Department of Energy. *Permanent Markers Implementation Plan* (2004: 23).

aim in incorporating *The Scream* into these formalized proposals was to attain the 'structure of universal meaning – faces expressing horror, revulsion, fear, pain, anguish providing support for an essential, phenomenological or haptic mode of perception'. To supplement the use of *The Scream* in creating an eternal warning sign, the 1990s Expert Judgement on Markers panel also drew upon a taxonomy of supposedly 'universal' facial expressions taken from Eibl-Eibesfeldt's (1989) *Human Ethology* – opting, for the final nuclear repository, to use something between the 'nauseated' and the 'physically hurt, tormented' facial icons (see Eibl-Eibesfeldt, 1989: 454). As the panel concluded, faces are understood to offer 'universal expressions' because 'human facial expressions of emotion and feeling, such as pain, anger, disgust and fear communicate in the same way universally, regardless of cultural differences' (Ast et al, 1992: F-43).

If, for Munch, the faciality of *The Scream* concerns the qualities of a red sky to evoke a sense of anxiety and an infinite expression of nature itself, then in the context of nuclear semiotic markers it could be said to take on a quite different sense involving the presumed universality of a 'human' facial expression. In considering the implications of these universal markers for nuclear waste sites, perhaps what is of most critical importance here is not how they variously fail to achieve a sense of universal expression, but a question of how and why certain abstractions of thought – such as a male, American-European sense of the human face – can become so dominant that they are falsely associated with a sense of the eternal, the universal or timelessness itself.

Inhibited by the overdetermining force of present-day abstractions, the proposals for universal nuclear warning signs created by those in Human Interference Task Force and the Expert Judgement on Markers panel produce a number of critical problems that undermine their effectiveness as universal signs to last across millennia. One problem includes the way that these experts themselves recognize the limits of actualized entities to act as eternal warning signs. Indeed, the panel report describes an initial proposal to use a skull and crossbones as an eternal warning sign, which was rejected when members concluded that in places like Mexico the appearance of bones might differently invoke a sense of human vitality and health rather than death, fear and deterrence (Ast et al, 1992: F-43). As Joyce (2020: 182) reflects, in their search for signs that would last for eternity, the expert discussions in the 1980s and 1990s were marked by a certain 'obsession with signification', as well as a failure to recognize how 'meanings are produced in specific, contingent, and unpredictable, or better, open and productive ways' (p 181). The enduring problem here is the way that the commitment to time capsules and markers invoking an aesthetics of fear is itself a product of a contemporary sense that future generations cannot be trusted. This mistrust concerns both a future subject's capacity to remember the existence of nuclear waste repository sites, but also whether they would act 'safely' if they were to accidentally discover the existence of a repository. It perhaps comes as no surprise, therefore, that the expert groups would go on to conclude that the best management strategy for 100,000 years would be if societies were to forget about the existence of final nuclear waste repositories altogether.

What, therefore, can be said about the way the eternal object of red has acted as a lure for thinking and feeling in the legacies of both Whitehead's and Munch's respective endeavours? Most obvious, perhaps, is that applying Whitehead's eternal objects to the problem of nuclear waste involves a degree of conceptual violence – particularly given that Whitehead never conceived of his eternal objects in terms of the actuality of physical things like semiotic markers and warning signs. It is worth being clear that I am hesitant to overstate the connections between these different approaches to thinking eternal objects. One irreconcilable point of departure includes the way these contexts address quite different problems. Indeed, the pursuit of universal signs for final nuclear waste repositories by expert groups in the United States is arguably closer to a Bergsonian false problem whose terms of solution are, at least in part, pre-defined. If there remains something fruitful about this comparison, it is precisely because there exists a surprising genealogy of thought traversing Munch and Whitehead that considers the way certain forces of expression, such as the colour red or the impressionistic power of a face, can come to operate abstractly as an affect freed from any localized placing in time and space. Both Munch and Whitehead detected in red not a colour that is actualized in the experience of an individuated subject, but something that exhibits an indefinite quality of nature. If *The Scream* offers something distinct to formalized practices of nuclear waste management, this might be because it suggests certain parallels to Whitehead's conceptualization of eternal objects, which also concerns a question of the communication of expressive forms no longer subsumed by actual occasions.

To develop these parallels a little further, and by way of conclusion, I want to highlight two connected points. The first concerns the way Whitehead recognizes in the ingression of actual occasions the potential for beauty. For Whitehead (1967: 255), beauty is not an eternal object but something that can be actualized in an occasion of experience. This notion of beauty would not be subjective in a phenomenological sense but concerns the capacity for the ingression of eternal objects of pure potential into a *self-enjoyment of an actual occasion* – such as a red sky that invokes an alternative sense of nature that is no longer split between primary and secondary qualities (Sehgal and Wilkie, Chapter 1, this volume). Crucially for Whitehead, 'beauty, in itself, has no aim other than its own realisation' (Duvernoy, 2019: 176): it concerns the *fullest* actualization, or what Whitehead refers to as the *absolute* self-enjoyment, of an actual occasion of experience. In having no external aim, beauty defines something inherent to, and localized within, actual occasions: it is the actualization of occasions of experience that define beauty, and thus absolutely not a human subject with a privileged capacity to judge beauty according to preconceived criteria.

Freed from the judgement of preconceived criteria, the relationship between eternal objects and beauty instead offers the prospect of thinking the emergence of actual occasions of experience no longer localized in a given individual experience *here and now*. Something of this reading of eternal objects in excess of the here and now is countenanced by Simondon, who writes:

> The experience of eternity must be left at the level of what it veritably is: the basis of an affectivo-emotive regime. If there is a certain sort of reality that is eternal, it is the individual as a transductive being and not as a subject-substance, body-substance, consciousness, or active matter. Already during its objective existence, the individual, insofar as it experiences, is a being-in-relation. It is possible that something of the individual is eternal and is somehow reincorporated into the world with respect to which it was individual. (Simondon, 2020: 275)

For Simondon, there is no veritable experience of eternity at the level of an individual subject, but rather the existence of an 'eternal' that exists resolutely as an affective-emotive regime. In this case, the eternal serves as something that orientates the arrival of actualized events. According to Simondon (2020: 261), it is possible to understand the eternal through the way that young children exhibit an innate understanding of the posture of an animal as expressing a 'hostile or trusting attitude' – where this innateness is not properly of a subject but of an individuation of experience itself. Understanding the eternal element of individuated experience becomes a key task in nuclear memory communication practices, I contend, because it demonstrates all too clearly the need to aspire to forms of beauty defined in terms of the self-enjoyment of events themselves. This conceptual manoeuvre would be to counteract the tendency to create nuclear markers founded on the most territorialized tendencies of human life and aesthetic judgement as it is composed today. However, for nuclear semiotics and markers to be made sensitive to expressions of beauty – understood as the full self-enjoyment of actual occasions – is no easy feat, and it promises no easy solutions or methodological guarantees. Directing nuclear memory communicating practices to this notion of beauty may require, for example, drawing on 'rhetorical method/ologies' that are themselves able to enact alternative aesthetic modes of enquiry (Kalin and Gruber, 2022). It also invites cognate speculative research into how the differing production of abstractions through time can pluralize a subject's sense of the emergent properties of material things (Wakefield-Rann and Lee, 2022). The pluralization of experience, in this manner, thus demands minor disruptive modes of nuclear aesthetic intervention reminiscent of what Decamous (2019: 297) terms the capacity of art and aesthetics to reveal the 'dark side of radiance' that may otherwise remain opaque and difficult to discern.

The second point concerns the role of eternal objects in theorizing the production of contingency and a sense of alternative possibility within actual occasions. Such a focus on the alternative connects closely to recent approaches to speculative philosophy (Debaise and Stengers, 2017). It also intersects with recent discussions around nuclear memory communication emphasizing the need to create techniques that account more *openly* for the different kinds of contingency and possibilities involved in imagining and thinking possible nuclear waste futures (Joyce, 2020; Keating and Storm, 2023) – futures that become poorly conceived by predictive calculation based on a model of imagining the future as an extension of the present. For Whitehead, actual occasions invoke other contingent possibilities because 'every actual occasion is set within a realm of alternative interconnected entities. ... It is the realm of alternative suggestions, whose foothold in actuality transcends each actual occasion' (Whitehead, 1948: 158). Whitehead's insistence that a realm of alternative suggestions is expressed by, and transcends, actual occasions is because they are connected to the functioning of eternal objects. When Ruyer (1948) extracts from Whitehead a theory of the emergence of systems of value, in doing so he is also interested in the way eternal objects may offer alternative ways to understand the production and transvaluation of collective values. As Massumi (2017: 364) develops, this is because Ruyer and Whitehead see in eternal objects the emergence of alternative possibilities or values – such as the way red can appear green under certain conditions of light – but since this 'alternate realization is not treated as a value in itself', this expression of contingency offers opportunities to recuperate other ways of both evaluating and experiencing events of sense. It would be worthwhile, therefore, if nuclear semiotics, and nuclear memory communication practices more widely, might think with the evaluative and experiential implications of Whitehead's eternal objects, which can already be said to be communicating through time in a manner that exceeds the contemporary human condition. To do so requires one to follow Whitehead's (1978: 256) call to think with eternal objects 'by adventuring amid physical experiences in this actual world'.

Notes

[1] Indeed, when Deleuze (1990: 21) develops through the Stoics the ability to 'distinguish between green as a sensible color or quality and "to green" as a noematic color or attribute', he is able to discuss green as an eternal object whose function is not exhausted in an actualized event but is something that is expressed in terms of singularity-events that disturb any phenomenological distinction between the noumena and phenomena.

[2] While not pertaining to a transcendental metaphysics, Whitehead conceptualizes the creativity of eternal objects in relation to 'God'. In doing so, God is positioned not as a transcendental creator but as a necessary figure for the logic of a whole cosmology explaining the becoming of actual occasions of experience. As Stengers (2006) explains, for Whitehead the entire point of conceptualizing eternal objects is not to reify an ultimate creative origin but, quite differently, to 'deprive any cause of the power to define how it will cause, and more generally to protect any becoming against its reduction to a function of something else'. It is in the effort to avoid reproducing any ultimate transcendental cause of becoming that the notion of God in eternal objects is, for Whitehead, better understood as a primordial 'infinite variety of forms' (Emmet, 1966: 119).

References

Allan, G. (2008a) 'A functionalist reinterpretation of Whitehead's metaphysics', *The Review of Metaphysics*, 62(2): 327–54.

Allan, G. (2008b) 'Aesthetic', in M. Weber and W. Desmond (eds), *Handbook of Whiteheadian Process Thought*, Frankfurt: Ontos Verlag, pp 41–54.

Ast, D.G., Brill, M., Goodenough, W., Kaplan, M., Newmeyer, F. and Sullivan, W. (1992) Appendix F: Team A Report: Marking the Waste Isolation Pilot Plant for 10,000 Years. *Expert Judgment on Markers to Deter Inadvertent Intrusion into the Waste Isolation Pilot Plant*. Sandia Report SAND92-1382. Albuquerque, NM: Sandia National Laboratories.

Bjornerud, M. (2018) *Timefulness*, Princeton, NJ: Princeton University Press.

Brill, M. and Abidi, S. (1993) *Landscape of Thorns*. https://m.ammoth.us/blog/wp-content/uploads/2009/11/landscape-of-thorns.jpg (Accessed on 28 November 2023).

Debaise, D. (2017) *Speculative Empiricism: Revisiting Whitehead*, Edinburgh: Edinburgh University Press.

Debaise, D. and Stengers, I. (2017) 'The insistence of possibles towards and speculative pragmatism', *Parse*, 7: 12–19.

Debaise, D., and Stengers, I. (2022). 'An ecology of trust? Consenting to a pluralist universe', The *Sociological Review*, 70(2): 402–15.

Decamous, G. (2019) *Invisible Colors: The Arts of the Atomic Age*, Cambridge, MA: MIT Press.

Deleuze, G. (1990) *The Logic of Sense*, London: Continuum.

Deleuze, G. (2004) *Difference and Repetition*, London: Continuum.

Duvernoy, R.J. (2019) Deleuze, Whitehead, and the 'Beautiful Soul', *Deleuze and Guattari Studies*, 13(2): 163–85.

Eibl-Eibesfeldt, I. (1989) *Human Ethology*, New York: Aldine de Gruyter.

Emmet, D. (1966) *Whitehead's Philosophy of Organism*. London: Palgrave Macmillan.

Halewood, M. (2005) 'On Whitehead and Deleuze: The process of materiality', *Configurations*, 13(1): 57–76.

Holtorf, C. and Högberg, A. (2020) 'What lies ahead? Nuclear waste as cultural heritage of the future', in C. Holtorf and A. Högberg (eds), *Cultural Heritage and the Future*, London: Routledge, pp 144–58.

Hooper, S.E. (1942) 'Whitehead's philosophy: Eternal objects and God. *Philosophy*, 17(65): 47–68.

Joyce, R. (2020) *The Future of Nuclear Waste: What Art and Archaeology Can Tell Us about Securing the World's Most Hazardous Material*, Oxford: Oxford University Press.

Kalin, J. and Gruber, D.R. (2022) 'Rhetoric, methodology, and a question of onto-epistemological access', *Philosophy & Rhetoric*, 55(2): 127–51.

Keating, T. (2022) 'Nuclear remains', in N. Williams and T. Keating (eds), *Speculative Geographies: Ethics, Technologies, Aesthetics*, Singapore: Palgrave Macmillan, pp 173–86.

Keating, T. and Storm, A. (2023) 'Nuclear memory: Archival, aesthetic, speculative', *Progress in Environmental Geography*, 2(1–2): 97–117. https://doi.org/10.1177/27539687231174242

Madsen, M. (director) (2010) *Into Eternity: A Film for the Future*, London: Dogwoof.

Manning, E. and Massumi, B. (2014) *Thought in the Act: Passages in the Ecology of Experience,* Minneapolis, MN: University of Minnesota Press.

Massumi, B. (2017) 'Virtual ecology and the question of value', in E. Hörl and J. Burton (eds), *General Ecology: The New Ecological Paradigm*, London: Bloomsbury, pp 345–73.

Meyer, S. (2005) 'Introduction', *Configurations*, 13(1): 1–33.
Munch, E. (1895) *The Scream*, Pastel on cardboard.
Ruyer, R. (1948) Le *monde des valeurs: études systématiques*, Paris: Aubier.
Sagan, C. (1978) *Murmurs of Earth: The Voyager Interstellar Record*, New York: Ballantine Books.
Sebeok, T. (1984) *Communication Measures to Bridge Ten Millennia*, Columbus, OH: Battelle Memorial Institute, Office of Nuclear Waste Isolation.
Sehgal, M. (2018) 'Aesthetic concerns, philosophical fabulations: The importance of a 'new aesthetic paradigm', *SubStance*, 47(1): 112–29.
Shaviro, S. (2012) *Without Criteria: Kant, Whitehead, Deleuze, and Aesthetics*, Cambridge, MA: MIT Press.
Shaviro, S. (2014) *The Universe of Things: On Speculative Realism*, Minneapolis, MN: University of Minnesota Press
Simondon, G. (2020) *Individuation in Light of Notions of Form and Information*, Vol 1, Minneapolis, MN: University of Minnesota Press.
Stengers, I. (2000) *The Invention of Modern Science*, Minneapolis, MN: University of Minnesota Press.
Stengers I. (2006) Whitehead and science: From philosophy of nature to speculative cosmology, https://www.mcgill.ca/hpsc/files/hpsc/Whitmontreal.pdf (Accessed 1 March 2023).
Stengers, I. (2011) *Thinking with Whitehead: A Free and Wild Creation of Concepts*, Cambridge, MA: Harvard University Press.
U.S. Department of Energy (2004) Permanent Markers Implementation Plan. United States Department of Energy. doi:10.2172/990726, p 23.
Van Wyck, P. (2004) *Signs of Danger: Waste, Trauma, and Nuclear Threat*, Minneapolis, MN: University of Minnesota Press.
Wakefield-Rann, R. and Lee, T. (2022). 'Dust and soil: Speculative approaches to microecological sensing', in N. Williams and, T. Keating (eds), *Speculative Geographies: Ethics, Technologies, Aesthetics*, Singapore: Palgrave Macmillan, pp 269–83.
Whitehead, A.N. (1948) *Science and the Modern World,* New York: Pelican Mentor.
Whitehead, A.N. (1967) *Adventures of Ideas,* New York: Free Press.
Whitehead, A.N. (1978) *Process and Reality: An Essay in Cosmology* (corrected edn), New York: Free Press.
Wikander, O. (2015) Don't push this button: Phoenician sarcophagi, 'atomic priesthoods' and nuclear waste. Vetenskapssocieteten i Lund Årsbok 2015.

4

Geo-Narrativity: Anthropocene, Aesthetics, Forensics

Alexander Damianos

Deep-time aesthetics

It was May 2018, the end of a three-day meeting of the Anthropocene Working Group (AWG), held at the Max Planck Institute for Atmospheric Chemistry, in Mainz, Germany. The generosity of AWG members is such that I was permitted to attend in my capacity as 'participant observer' as part of my doctoral research concerning the AWG's ongoing effort to formalize an Anthropocene geological unit. I was supposed to stay with a friend in Frankfurt for a few days, but the proceedings of the meeting were such that I decided I needed to get home and write up my thoughts and observations as soon as I could. When a senior geologist, who carries a formidable reputation within the community of chronostratigraphers who are dedicated to the construction and maintenance of the Geological Time Scale – a chart that lists the categories of planetary time and space for the entirety of Earth's 4.5 billion years – offered to drive me all the way back to London together with his colleague, I figured this would be a unique opportunity to access a slightly different narrative about the Anthropocene hypothesis. This geologist has voiced some of the most well-articulated reservations concerning the case for an Anthropocene unit; not because they do not sympathize with the premise that human activity has altered the material constitution of the planet, but on the methodological grounds that such a unit would simply be too recent in time to merit formalization. Besides, a geological unit premised on the advent of human activity already exists: the Holocene has as one of its markers the first appearance of homo sapiens remains in the fossil record.

During a rest stop at a petrol station on the outskirts of Frankfurt, the geologists called me over to a balcony that overlooked an impressive vista of the Rhine valley. Both geologists had spent some time in that region conducting geological surveys. I told them that the view was beautiful. They agreed and proceeded to describe the material transitions that the landscape had undergone over the course of several million years. I didn't understand what they were talking about. Where I saw a mountain, they saw a text-book specimen of late Eocene rift flank uplift. They described the formation of glaciers many thousands of years ago, cracking open the mountain, forming deep ridges, eventually subsiding into rivers and strips of abundant vegetation. They recounted the events with enthusiasm, albeit with a certain casualness, as if it was a story that was familiar to us all, as if we had heard it all before. My ignorance persisted. What struck me instead was the gap between what was immediately before us and what they could see. Using their hands, they orchestrated the trajectory of the landscapes unfolding over *deep time*, indicating the rhythm of inter-glacial and tectonic events. I took more from their ability to recount geological episodes and narrate material landscapes than from the content of their description. At my request, we took a selfie with the vibrant landscape behind us before continuing our drive.

Geologists tend to perceive Earth as a dynamic entity. Not so much in the sense of Lovelock's Gaia, which has often been misinterpreted to assign mystical sentience to Earth as a single, conscious entity (Clarke, 2020). Rather, Earth is understood as geologically dynamic to the extent that, as Charles Lyell put it in the subtitle of his *Principles of Geology* (Lyell, 1883), former changes of Earth's surface are often explainable by reference to causes now in operation. A geologists ability to 'see' ongoing processes where a layperson like myself sees mountains is then more properly a demonstration of what Latour (1999: 24–79) called *circulating reference*. In his own participant observation, Latour recounts the gradual process of conversion enacted by a group of soil scientists working in the Amazon rainforest, which saw the translation of a patch of soil into a universal, scientific *fact* about the encroachment of the savannah into the forest. What interested Latour, by his own admission, was how 'the transformation undergone by the soil [becomes] bound up in words' (1999: 68). Latour refers to 'chains of reference' that iteratively link 'world' to 'words'. The soil scientists use string to delineate an area of soil; they divide samples into discrete boxes; they assign a code to each sample using a coloured swatch sample; that code then stands in for the material sample, allowing them to communicate specific details to a lab on the other side of the world in France. Through successive stages of material practices, the local, particular material is 'amplified' into the compatible, standard, calculable and universal.

The point here is not simply the *agency* of the cardboard boxes, swatch panels and other artefacts that facilitate this process of conversion. Rather, what interests me in the case of the geologists is the way in which those material practices present a counter-intuitive account: the geologists solicit the narrative competencies of objects such as fossils, rocks and sediment samples in such a way as to remove themselves from the equation. The geologists' art lies in their ability to speak *on behalf* of landscapes *as if* they were *not* fabricating a particular narrative but instead simply recounting testimony solicited from the material artefacts comprising the mountain-range. So compelling was the narration of shifting landscapes just beneath that Frankfurt balcony that, more than 'just' a demonstration of geo-narrative technique, the occasion suggested a distributed sensibility of geologist and landscape. Rivers meander; glaciers expand and retreat; flora and fauna migrate; and geologists measure, observe, interpret and narrate. Keeping Lyell's aphorism in mind, in which planetary materiality demonstrates procedures still in operation, the geological dynamics narrated are constituted equally by a practice of narration as much as by a sensitivity towards experience particular to the landscape itself: an appreciation of what *it* has endured irrespective of the temporal and historiographic frames familiar to, or imposed by, any human.

Attendants of the Mainz conference witnessed the contingency of narrative practices and what might popularly be called 'more-than-human' sense perception in geology. In presentation after presentation, AWG members shared meticulously crafted graphs, charts and infographics supported by a range of complex analyses of sediment samples collected from around the world, at great expense of time, money and expertise (the AWG had, at that time, failed to secure funding for its research endeavours from any of the traditional sources). Since its founding in 2009, the AWG has worked to assemble this material into a compelling narrative. Its success hinges on the willingness of the group's peers to adopt the story in their own accounts of ongoing planetary dynamics. The geologists who narrated the trajectory of the Rhine valley to me during our drive, however, remain vocal sceptics of accounts provided by AWG members. They simply do not believe them, yet they do not dispute the materiality of the sediment samples and rock cores that the AWG's charts, graphs and analyses are based on. Rather, they perceive methodological and conceptual problems in understanding how raw material is folded into the narration of 4.5 billion years of planetary history. The hypothesis of an Anthropocene geological unit, in other words, is only as successful as the willingness of a community of geologists, in particular those affiliated with the Geological Time Scale, to accept the story told to them by the AWG and to implement it into their own narrative practices.

Fossils: planetary forensics

At this point, it is useful to speak directly to the AWG's narratives of Earth history and how an Anthropocene unit fits therein. Formalization of an Anthropocene unit would be an unprecedented event for geology. Geology is a discipline that occupies itself with vast spans of time, stretching up to four and a half billion years. Geological research, and the decision-making procedures involved in the formalization of a new unit (Damianos, 2022), often feels similarly expansive in its tempo. The AWG was commissioned in 2009 to examine the suitability of the Anthropocene hypothesis, as articulated by Paul Crutzen and Eugene Stoermer in a series of articles (Crutzen and Stoermer, 2000; Crutzen, 2002; Zalasiewicz, 2019), as a unit of the Geological Time Scale. Since then, there has been a remarkable effort to designate the material characteristics such a unit would possess. With the possible exception of the Jurassic, no other unit of the Geological Time Scale has achieved the reputation of the as-yet unformalized Anthropocene. Almost all other units of the Time Scale, even those that are currently under consideration by a Working Group and not yet formalized, have been proposed this side of the 20th century. While several units have been formalised since 2000, those units were invariably first discussed long ago. The Anthropocene is the only geological unit to be *hypothesised* since the beginning of the 21st century. That is to say that the Anthropocene unit was assembled remarkably quickly, by geological standards, and that its reception beyond the geological community has taken all those involved in the formalization process, whether for or against an Anthropocene unit, by surprise. For that reason, the AWG's formalization effort provides a unique insight into the process of constructing geo-historical narratives.

To the extent that the unit was first proposed 'outside' of geology, the AWG has had to work somewhat counter-intuitively.[1] As Pottage has observed, the AWG's efforts have entailed 'a reversal of the forensic approach of modern geology'. Rather than 'beginning with the fossil and eliciting context from it, one begins with the context and finds the *Leitfossil* for that context' (Pottage, 2019: 154). In the AWG's own words, the object is to identify 'the environmental trends picked out as of major significance to contemporary global change by the Earth system science community', and consider 'whether or not they will leave a recognizable signal within strata' (Zalasiewicz et al, 2017: 88). As such, the AWG attempts a speculative geology. Rather than piecing together material evidence to (re)construct a narrative of what happened in the deep past, the AWG seeks to apply methodology and knowledge in order to advance a speculative account of the near and deep future. Geological techniques of narrating the *deep time* of Earth's 4.5-billion-year historical accumulation, in other words, are applied *speculatively* to consider what sediments *will* amass, as well as how their legibility might be determined in advance.

What kinds of techniques facilitate the speculative geologies of the Anthropocene? How do they cultivate a sensitivity to geological deep time unfolding in the present? A key strategy that I wish to focus on in this chapter involves the appropriation of palaeontological techniques – according to which fossil remains in sediments are used to correlate and thereby chronologize the planet's material archives – to the present and future accumulation of geological deposits. Such practices are characteristic of the AWG's *speculative forensics*, drawing on established practices of geological dating and correlation but taking them out of their familiar habitat of the deep past and instead applying them to the future.

Geological observation has always been characterized by a practice of associating material deposits to temporal markers. To that extent, geology could be thought of as the original forensic science. In the late 17th century, 'natural historians' made initial attempts to narrate planetary history by reference to artefacts. Sharks' teeth encased within rocks, the large bones of unfamiliar creatures or the acknowledgement that *kinds of rocks* (chalk, limestone, marble) tended to appear in a predictable order led observers to characterize 'natural antiquities' as a distinct class of artefact from the vases, coins and tablets used to piece together accounts of pre-historic human civilizations. Using 'natural antiquities' as a category of artefact facilitated access not only to former times and places but also to novel modes of verification. Take, as an example, the efforts of the 17th-century priest Athanasius Kircher, who was so impressed by the size of some fossils that he sought to apply his findings to verify the facticity of scripture. If *The Book of Genesis* recounts the episode wherein Noah's Ark carries two of every creature, then given the size of fossil remnants, how large would the vessel have been? How was it constructed? How would animals have entered; and where would they have slept and eaten? In total earnestness, Kircher drafted blueprints of the vessel as suggested by the size of these newly discovered fossils, along with illustrations of the Ark's construction (Kircher, 1675; Rudwick, 2017). Kircher's story is just one among several that demonstrate a profound shift in the perception of spatio-temporality evinced by the advent of *fossils* as a novel category of epistemic artefact. In short, it was no longer the case that scripture provided the authoritative account of planetary genesis. With the advent of 'natural antiquities', it became possible to verify the account provided by scripture with reference to the experience and observation of a material environment. It is in this sense that geology can be understood as the original forensic science.

Most ways of reading the 'signals', or material indicators, of an Anthropocene unit are derived from insights afforded by early natural historians who took an interest in 'natural antiquities', developing these insights to devise techniques of geological narratology. For example, *superposition*, first posited by Nicolas Steno in the 17th century, holds that rocks are composed of regularly deposited layers of sediment, which may subsequently be disrupted by volcanic eruptions, plate tectonics or bioturbation (the movement of plants and animals) (Rudwick, 1985; Gould, 1987). The signals can be referenced, or *correlated*, to rock bodies across the world to weave together an account of truly *geological* – that is *planetary* (rather than local) and *synchronous* (rather than diachronous) – events that are then used to break the vastness of 4.5 billion years of Earth history into smaller, more manageable chunks of time and space known as 'units'.

Chicken bones, cement foundations of buildings, an explosion in synthetic fertilizers and the proliferation of infrastructures such as dams, ports and roads are just some of ways in which the novel sediments that would characterize the Anthropocene act as a decisive break from all previous bodies of rock, thereby justifying the Anthropocene as a novel *unit* (Waters et al, 2016; Head, 2023). Yet the primary signal that the AWG is pursuing for its formalization effort is the global spread of artificial radionuclides resulting from nuclear weapons testing beginning in the mid-twentieth century. Traces of this material are evident globally and can be dated with remarkably high precision using radiometric dating of isotopic half-lives that nuclear fallout leaves wherever it is deposited. In this way, the onset of nuclear weapons testing leaves a *global* and *synchronous* geological signal that will be evident for vast spans of time to come (Waters et al, 2015).

What to make of the insight that fossils constitute a material practice of experiencing and narrating relations of space and time? One option is to focus on the shared epistemological terrain between geology and law. 'Forensics' provides an appropriate frame with which to do so. The term is derived from the Latin word *forensic*, which refers to the *forum* and thus to the practice and skill of making an argument before a professional, political or legal gathering. Forensics indicates a common method of science and law. It entails a nurturing of the capacity to elicit accounts from artefacts, *wherein the object is apprehended as a witness*. In law, the practice of acknowledging the agential capacities of artefacts dates back at least to Ancient Greece, where a special branch of the judiciary, known as the *prutaneion*, concerned themselves with adjudicating the culpability of objects. Miguel Tamen recounts an episode wherein a statue was tried for killing a man when it fell on top of him: 'The statue was tried, convicted, and sentenced to be cast into the sea' (Tamen, 2004: 79–80). 'In the prutaneion, the revenge for the dead person who was killed by an animal or by an inanimate object was taken at a symbolic level, by the punishment of the animal or object, as a form of retribution' (Arnaoutoglou, 1993: 129–30).

In a somewhat related register, Eyal Weizman and Thomas Keenan (2012) recount the conditions under which the skull of the Nazi phrenologist Josef Mengele was brought to trial (a trial of a specific kind, as we shall see) to attain a form of retribution for victims of the atrocities he had been complicit in. Mossad agents were able to capture Adolf Eichmann in the Spring of 1960 at his refuge in Argentina. They knew that Mengele was in the country too, but fearing any activity that could jeopardize the success of the Eichmann operation, Mossad agents opted to return with Eichmann to Jerusalem and return at a later date to capture Mengele. In the interim, Mengele 'went underground'. In February 1979 he suffered from a stroke and drowned while swimming near Bertioga, Brazil, where he was buried under the false name Wolfgang Gerhard. Nevertheless, a skull that was believed to be that of Mengele was found when a body was exhumed in June of that same year, and Weizman and Keenan describe how a kind of retribution, or justice, was attained through the forensic process of identifying the skull as Mengele's in place of a trial of the man himself.

Weizman and Keenan proceed to recount the forensic investigations that took place to establish that the skull was *almost certainly* (absolute certainty being an impossibility) that of Mengele. As a result of this process, they argue, forensic anthropologists contributed a host of techniques to the armoury of human rights law as well as to international and criminal law, to say nothing of the various genres of television entertainment that precipitated therefrom. In doing so, the media of law and, as a consequence, the practice and understanding of law, changed as well. 'The difference between a witness and a piece of evidence might seem to be that evidence is merely presented while a witness is interrogated', explain Weizman and Keenan. 'However, the experience of forensic anthropology in the context of war crimes investigations seems to undo this distinction' (2012: 65). In the case of Mengele, scientific evidence comes to stand in for a kind of justice. A kind of closure is presumed, allegedly facilitated by law, through the mobilization of scientific, forensic methodologies. What forensics contributes in this instance is the truth of the skull as that of Mengele. And that truth is presumed by law to be the truth of his culpability, the truth of his conviction, in the absence of a sentence. For in this instance, the question forensic techniques were invoked to answer was not 'how did this person die?' but rather 'to whom do these bones belong?'

Extending the parallel between science and law, Weizman and Keenan assert that the recovery of Mengele's bones, and the investigation into the determination of the identity of those bones, 'opened up what can now be seen as a second narrative, not the story of the witness but that of the *thing* in the context of war crimes investigation and human rights. If the trial of Eichmann marks the beginning of the era of the witness, we would suggest that the exhumation of a body thought to be that of Mengele in June 1985 signals the inauguration of an era of forensics in human rights and international criminal justice' (Keenan and Weizman, 2011). Using a turn of phrase that seems to designate simultaneously what is common and distinct between science and law, by way of the example of Eichmann's and Mengele's respective fates, Weizman and Keenan remark that 'one faced a legal forum; the other a scientific one' (Keenan & Weizman, 2012: 11).

Technofossils: the Anthropocene's speculative forensics

In their effort to give form to a proposed Anthropocene thesis, members of the AWG seek to define a new class of artefact: not the fossil, but the technofossil. In doing so, AWG members perceive Earth's future material record in the present. The technofossil is perhaps the clearest example of the speculative geology designated by the Anthropocene hypothesis, even if its normative dimensions have not been fully thematized. Technofossils are the material remnants of the technosphere. AWG members define the technosphere as 'the interlinked set of communication, transportation, bureaucratic and other systems that act to metabolize fossil fuels and other energy resources ... considered to be an emerging global paradigm, with similarities to the lithosphere, atmosphere, hydrosphere, and biosphere' (Haff, 2014: 301). Admittedly vague in definition, the technofossil nevertheless suits the purposes of the AWG in articulating a way of perceiving a geological future within the requirements of geological unit definition. 'Recent anthropogenic deposits contain new minerals and rock types', explains an AWG-authored paper, 'with rapid global dissemination of novel materials including elemental aluminium, concrete and plastics, shaped into abundant rapidly-evolving "technofossils"' (Waters et al, 2016). With the technofossil concept, geologists interested in formalizing an Anthropocene unit have sought to fashion a forensic medium that renders contemporary artefacts such as microplastics (Ivar do Sul and Labrenz, 2022), cement ('the most abundant novel rock type of the Anthropocene'; Waters and Zalasiewicz, 2017) and the remains of popular eating habits in the form of discarded chicken bones (Bennett et al,. 2018) as objects of geologically significant experience – and indicators of time and process endured by the planet itself – which designate a stratigraphy particular to the Anthropocene: a technostratigraphy (Zalasiewicz et al, 2014).

The technofossil is generative of a novel aesthetic remarkably successful at facilitating a sensitivity to geological deep time (Zalasiewicz et al, 2021). As a narrative technique, the technofossil is an attempt to render planetary dynamics sensible in such a way as to emphasize material and strata set apart as 'novel', both temporally and categorically. The technosphere hypothesis amounts to a strategy by which the AWG expands the category of rock and fossil to include 'contemporary strata' (even though there is nothing 'contemporary' about technology), encapsulating both what is thought to be novel about the Anthropocene hypothesis and the ways in which it is asserted as entirely consistent with the requirements of formal unit definition within the discipline of stratigraphy. The technofossil concept, in other words, does something peculiar and slightly paradoxical. On the one hand, the technofossil suggests a distinction between deposits particular to the past century or so, and older deposits (which would still be *fossils* but *just* fossils, rather than *techno*fossils). On the other hand, and at the same time, the technofossil idea suggests a folding of the contemporary into the vastness of 4.5 billion years of geological *deep time*. Extending the meaning of 'fossil', technostratigraphy incorporates the wider themes surrounding Anthropocene discourse into geological practices of classification. Specifically, the 'technofossil' allows the AWG to speak of a very recent temporality *as geological* through the familiar and procedurally acceptable idiom of the fossil. Simultaneity of conflicting temporalities, recalling Koselleck's particular development of the 'simultaneity of the non-simultaneous' (Koselleck, 2018), is characteristic of the aforementioned 'novel aesthetic' of geo-narrativity: time is not just the time of human history; it is what former AWG Chair Jan Zalasiewicz calls 'simply time' (Chakrabarty, 2018; Zalasiewicz, 2019). The human/non-human distinction is redundant in the context of the experience of duration. To that extent, although the Anthropocene theme is problematic insofar as it conflates conflicting histories and subjectivities into the singular theme of 'anthropos' (Haraway 2015; Yusoff, 2018), the material practices of geologists are nevertheless remarkably effective in displacing anthropocentric notions of time, or to put it differently, *re*-placing historical experience within a wider context of planetary durational experience, whether that be the meandering of rivers or the retreat of glaciers over billion-year time frames.

The crucial point is that forensic practices, such as those entailed in any reference to fossils, are normative. Forensics is, after all, a strategy of persuasion. It is a technique of speaking on behalf of entities, artefacts and their experiences, and of rendering sensible the experience of planetary dynamics otherwise imperceptible within traditional historical timeframes. It extends the domain of the witness, whereby testimony becomes a competency that is no longer exclusive to the witness but can be extended to objects, either directly or via the subject that speaks on its behalf. And as a consequence of the technofossil, not only the object itself but also the manner of its comprehension is altered. 'The making of facts depends on a delicate aesthetic balance, on new images made possible by new technologies, not only changing in front of our very eyes, but changing our very eyes – affecting the way we can see and comprehend things' (Keenan and Weizman, 2012: 27). It is in this sense that the technofossil constitutes a novel forensic aesthetics, to the extent that it alters the manner of judgement and sensation.

The normative dimension of forensic practices arises from novel configurations of objects and observers. The advent of fossils inaugurated a distinct method for verifying knowledge. In the examples of Kircher and Steno, *verification* of knowledge proceeds as *construction* of knowledge. Reference to skeletal remains not only confirmed belief in scripture (perhaps uncomfortably so insofar as Steno then devoted himself exclusively to the clergy) but also inaugurated geological study, insofar as their techniques remain as cornerstones of geological practice. New technologies entail novel observations arising from associations of, for example, skeletal remains with scriptural passages or chicken bones with the Geological Time Scale. A normative dimension arises from the choices observers make concerning the interpretation and communication of those associations. 'When we speak of an "Anthropocene", we only seem to be sitting in a geoscientific seminar', remarks Peter Sloterdijk. 'In reality, we are taking part in a court case – in a preliminary hearing before the main trial, to be more precise – in which, as a first step, the accused's culpability is supposed to be settled' (Sloterdijk, 2018: 2). In the era of a pending Anthropocene unit, geology's speculative capacity is perhaps more properly an extension (or appropriation) of forensic capacities in the service of designating culpability. The technofossil, in other words, facilitates not only the designation of recent time and sediments within the vernacular of stratigraphic practice; it also engenders a proxy *juridical* certainty, invoking *measurement*, for example of the frequency of certain skeletal remains in a rock section, as an instance of *normative assertion*.

The normative dimension of Anthropocene geology is, in part, a demonstration of the precision of geological practices of correlation and dating. In addition to traditional dating techniques facilitated by fossils, whereby geologists arrive at a *relative* classification of strata by observing similarities in the accumulation of skeletal remains in rocks from across the world, the advent of radiometric dating in the 20th century allows *absolute* dating and correlation by measuring the decay of radioactive isotopes found in rocks and fossils. Consequently, geologists involved in the Anthropocene formalization effort assert that they can *already* acknowledge the material consequences of mid-twentieth century nuclear weapons detonation on sediments across Earth with remarkable precision, sufficient to qualify a novel geological unit despite the brevity of those changes (so far), by comparison with existing, and far older, units of the Geological Time Scale. Such precision in measurement underlies the normative assertion of an Anthropocene as an index of human-led modification to Earth's material constitution. That assertion is justified, it is argued, by reference to the material analysis of cores of rock extracted from eight sites across the planet.

The advent of nuclear weapons testing in the mid-twentieth century resulted in 'geologically speaking, a virtually instantaneous global release' of radiometrically datable plutonium deposits (Cundy et al, 2022). As evidence of the remarkable precision that radiometric dating of deposits provides, consider that AWG members claim that they can identify 'distinct, globally recognizable phases, such as the 1959 weapons testing moratorium, a fallout "pulse" in 1963 (resulting from an acceleration of testing in 1962), and a rapid decline following the Partial Nuclear Test Ban Treaty of 1963)' (Cundy et al, 2022) . This overlapping of *historical account* and *geological dating* is characteristic of the narrative that the AWG is developing in its efforts to realize a formal Anthropocene geological unit. The significance of the technofossil concept, and the geological modes of observation particular to the AWG, lies in the justifiability of such conflated narratives, providing a node wherein 'modern' history translates into geological 'fact'. The AWG is careful, however, to negotiate the way in which such acts of translation are read. 'The use of the signature of weapons of mass destruction to mark the beginning of the Anthropocene may be considered by some to be morally controversial or undesirable', note the authors of an article on the use of radiometric dating of radioactive fallout as a marker of an Anthropocene unit, 'but such a designation would be valid in stratigraphic terms and should not be regarded as commemorating or celebrating the use of atomic weapons' (Cundy et al, 2022). History becomes geological fact, but only on the condition of a reassurance of disinterest and impartiality. An Anthropocene unit marked by the onset of nuclear weapons testing would be, they argue, simply 'an appropriate marker, given that it marks the point at which humans not only began to steer the functioning of the Earth system itself, but also realized the capability to destroy our own civilization on a global scale' (Cundy et al, 2022). The effort to cast a historical account of the twentieth century, replete with questionable assertions of 'humanity' and a 'civilization' that is 'our own', is less convincingly cast as geological fact. AWG-authored articles that reflect explicitly on the consequences of such translation practices are rare precisely for that reason. Nevertheless, the very fact that opportunities for such comparison have arisen in the first place demonstrates the peculiar consequences of a technofossil aesthetics, wherein geologists, who have otherwise restricted themselves to the deepest archives of planetary pre-history, find themselves in a position of having to navigate the socio-technical and military legacies of the Second World War and Cold War.

Of course, neither the Anthropocene nor any of the assertions made by the AWG are, as of yet, *geological fact*. By this is meant that the Anthropocene is not yet a unit of the Geologic Time Scale and as such remains an informal designation (Gibbard et al, 2021; Koster et al, 2023; Merritts et al, 2023; Swindles et al, 2023). Their status as such is pending the deliberation of three tiers of committees that will review the AWG's proposal once submitted (Damianos, 2022). Their deliberation entails an assessment of whether an Anthropocene unit, as defined by the AWG, would be consistent with the existing assembly of unit types that currently constitute the Geologic Time Scale, as well as what kind of *precedent* an Anthropocene unit would set for further amendments to the Scale. Each level of the three committees must agree on the amendment by way of a supermajority vote of at least 60 per cent. The significance of that deliberative process cannot be understated, insofar as an Anthropocene unit would mark a radical shift in the temporalities and types of signals that can be acceptably folded into Earth's geo-historical and stratigraphic narration.

In other words, and to conclude, what the AWG's formalization efforts demonstrate most forcefully is the extent to which the material constitution of the planet is not so much *read* from the rocks as it is *written*. And to that extent, the process reveals how *rock* and *strata* are not simply media to be *decoded* but are rather a medium with which to *encode* or *write* that history. Technofossils, technostratigraphy and radiometric dating of nuclear fallout, may (or may not) be convincing techniques for narrating an Anthropocene unit, yet their success is ultimately contingent on the willingness of the voting panels to incorporate that narrative into their own accounts of Earth's material and historical composition. At the time of writing, the AWG has relayed its intention to submit a formal proposal to the voting committees by December 2023. Submission would conclude a process that has taken almost 15 years, having begun in 2009. What the fossils say, or rather, the capacity of geologists to solicit testimony from fossils, is only as successful as the willingness of colleagues to adopt those accounts themselves.

Note

1   The term 'Anthropocene' was first proposed by Paul Crutzen, an atmospheric chemist who received the Nobel Prize for demonstrating the effects of aerosols on the atmosphere. See Crutzen and Stoermer, 2000; Crutzen, 2002.

References

Arnaoutoglou, I. (1993) 'Pollution in Athenian Homicide Law', *Revue Internationale des Droits de l'Antiquite*, 40: 109–37.

Bennett, C.E., Thomas, R. Williams, M., Zalasiewicz, J., Edgeworth, M., Miller, H. et al (2018) 'The broiler chicken as a signal of a human reconfigured biosphere', *Royal Society Open Science*, 5(12): 180325.

Chakrabarty, D. (2018) 'Anthropocene Time', *New Literary History*, 57(1): 5–32.

Clarke, B. (2020) *Gaian Systems: Lynn Margulis, Neocybernetics, and the End of the Anthropocene*, Minneapolis, MN: University of Minnesota Press.

Crutzen, P. (2002) 'The Geology of Mankind' *Nature*, 415(23).

Crutzen, P. and Stoermer, E. (2000) 'The "Anthropocene"', *Global Change Newsletter*, 41: 17–18.

Cundy, A., Hajdas, I., Saito, Y. and Waters, C. (2022) 'Radioactive fallout as a marker for the Anthropocene', in C. Rosol and G. Rispoli (eds), *Anthropogenic Markers: Stratigraphy and Context, Anthropocene Curriculum*, Berlin: Max Planck Institute for the History of Science. https://doi.org/10.58049/hwgt-9a13.

Damianos, A. (2022) 'Law and Geology for the Anthropocene: Toward an Ethics of Encounter', *Law & Critique*, 34: 165–83. https://doi.org/10.1007/s10978-022-09320-7.

Gould, S.J. (1987) *Time's Arrow, Time's Cycle: Myth and Metaphor in the Discovery of Geological Time*, Cambridge, MA: Harvard University Press.

Gibbard, P.L., Bauer, A.M., Edgeworth, M., Ruddiman, W.F., Gill, J.L., Merritts, D.J. et al (2021) 'A practical solution: The Anthropocene is a geological event, not a formal epoch', *Episodes* 45(4): 349–57.

Haff, P. (2014) 'Humans and technology in the Anthropocene: Six rules', *The Anthropocene Review*, 1(2): 126–36.

Haraway, D. (2015) 'Anthropocene, Capitalocene, Plantationocene, Chthulucene: Making kin', *Environmental Humanities*, 6(1): 159–65.

Head, M., Zalasiewicz, J., Waters, C.N., Turner, S.D., Williams, M., Barnosky, A.D. et al (2023) 'The Anthropocene is a prospective epoch/series, not a geological event', *Episodes*, 46(2): 229–38.

Ivar do Sul, J.A. and Labrenz, M. (2022) 'Microplastics into the Anthropocene' in T. Rocha-Santos, M.F. Costa and C. Mouneyrac (eds), *Handbook of Microplastics in the Environment*, Cham: Springer International Publishing. https://doi.org/10.1007/978-3-030-39041-9_25

Keenan, T. and Weizman, E. (2011) 'Mengele's skull: From witness to object', *Cabinet* 43. https://www.cabinetmagazine.org/issues/43/keenan_weizman.php (Accessed 9 November 2023).

Keenan, T. and Weizman, E. (2012) *Mengele's Skull: The Advent of a Forensic Aesthetics*, Berlin: Sternberg Press.

Kircher, A. (1675) *Arca Noë*.

Koselleck, R. (2018) *Sediments of Time: On Possible Histories*, Stanford, CA: Stanford University Press.

Koster, E., Gibbard, P.L. and Maslin, M. (2023) 'Optimising the Anthropocene definition: An epistemological view with briefings on four 2022–23 conferences', *Episodes*, 46(2): 325–36.

Latour, B. (1999) *Pandora's Hope: Essays on The Reality of Science Studies*, Cambridge, MA: Harvard University Press.

Lyell, C. (1997) *Principles of Geology*, London: Penguin.

Merritts, D., Edwards, L.E., Ellis, E.C., Walker, M., Finney, S., Gibbard, P. et al (2023) 'Response to Waters et al (2022) The Anthropocene is complex. Defining it is not', *Earth-Science Reviews*, 238: 104340.

Pottage, A. (2019) 'Holocene jurisprudence', *Journal of Human Rights and the Environment*, 10(2): 153–75.

Rudwick, M.J.S. (1985) *The Meaning of Fossils: Episodes in the History of Palaeontology*, Chicago, IL: University of Chicago Press.

Rudwick, M.J.S. (2017) *Earth's Deep History: How It Was Discovered and Why It Matters*, Chicago, IL: University of Chicago Press.

Sloterdijk, P. (2018) *What Happened in the 20th Century?*, Cambridge: Polity Press.

Swindles, G.T., Roland, T.P. and Ruffell, A. (2023) 'The 'Anthropocene' is most useful as an informal concept', *Journal of Quaternary Science*, 38(4): 453–54.

Tamen, M. (2004) *Friends of Interpretable Objects*, Cambridge, MA: Harvard University Press.

Waters, C.N. and Zalasiewicz, J. (2017) 'Concrete: The most abundant novel rock type of the Anthropocene', in *Reference Module in Earth Systems and Environmental Sciences*. https://www.researchgate.net/publication/313825741_Concrete_The_Most_Abundant_Novel_Rock_Type_of_the_Anthropocene#:~:text=Concrete%20is%20the%20most%20abundant,greater%20than%20natural%20geological%20processes

Waters, C.N., Syvitski, J.P.M., Gałuszka, A., Hancock, G.J., Zalasiewicz, J., Cearreta, A. et al (2015) 'Can nuclear weapons fallout mark the beginning of the Anthropocene epoch?', *Bulletin of the Atomic Scientists*, 71(3): 46–57.

Waters, C.N., Syvitski, J.P.M., Gałuszka, A., Hancock, G.J., Zalasiewicz, J., Cearreta, A. et al (2016) 'The Anthropocene is functionally and stratigraphically distinct from the Holocene', *Science*, 351: 6269.

Yusoff, K. (2018) *A Billion Black Anthropocenes or None*, Minneapolis, MN: University of Minnesota Press.

Zalasiewicz, J. (2019) 'The extraordinary strata of the Anthropocene', in A. Bilgrami (ed), *Nature and Value*, New York: Columbia University Press, pp 29–45.

Zalasiewicz, J., Waters, C.N., Ellis, E.C., Head, M.J., Vidas, D., Steffen, W. et al (2021) 'The Anthropocene: Comparing its meaning in geology (chronostratigraphy) with conceptual approaches arising in other disciplines', *Earth's Future*, 9(3): e2020EF001896. https://doi.org/10.1029/2020EF001896

Zalasiewicz, J., Steffen, W., Leinfelder, R., et al (2017) 'Petrifying Earth Process: The Stratigraphic Imprint of Key Earth System Parameters in the Anthropocene', *Theory, Culture & Society*, 34(2–3): 83–104.

Zalasiewicz, J., Williams, M., Waters, C.N., Turner, S.D., Barnosky, A.D., Head, M.J. et al (2014) 'The technofossil record of humans', *The Anthropocene Review*, 1(1): 34–43.

5

Race and Reality: Towards a Social Aesthetics of Race

Michael L. Thomas

A civilization that proves incapable of solving the problems it creates is a decadent civilization.
A civilization that chooses to close its eyes to its most crucial problems is a stricken civilization.
A civilization that uses its principles for trickery and deceit is a dying civilization.
      Aimé Césaire, *Discourse on Colonialism* (31)

Introduction

Whitehead's speculative philosophy is a generative method which aims for the enhancement of experience through adventures of thought. My thinking with Whitehead initiated a journey led by the concept of the aesthetic as a field of feeling which permeates social life but is limited in an epistemically oriented society which aims at forms of truth abstracted from experience. It is from this perspective that I have attempted to develop a 'social aesthetics' from the work of Alfred North Whitehead, a critical analysis of the role of abstractions and forms of feeling in the production, maintenance and transformation of societies.[1]

In this chapter, I draw upon the social aesthetics of Whitehead to argue for a social aesthetics of race. The social aesthetics of race draws on the aesthetic dimensions of social life in response to the function of race as a predatory abstraction which bifurcates human societies between worlds of colour. These worlds realize themselves through the maintenance of hierarchical, segregated material conditions alongside an ideology of liberal universalist progressivism. This contradiction, I argue, generates forms of sensibility that ontologize the fundamental distinction between worlds and people as a necessary feature of our experience. Thus, our engagement with social aesthetics should work on cultivating forms of sensibility grounded in collective practices that draw upon these forms to identify their origins in lived experience, critique their ideological underpinnings and develop novel sociological ideals for the advancement of societies out of their colonial forms.

The social aesthetics of A.N. Whitehead

The aesthetic holds a central place in the cosmology of Alfred North Whitehead. Actual entities, 'the final real things of which the world is made up', are composed of prehensions, relations of feeling that establish what is included and excluded from experience, providing it with a value-laden emotional tone (Whitehead, 1978: 18). Speculative philosophy is an attempt to prevent these relations of feeling from being bifurcated in the search for knowledge, presenting us a world of dead facts rather than an experience of reality as life 'among a democracy of fellow creatures' (Whitehead, 1978, 50). It aims to produce novel concepts that lure us towards a wider sense of the relations involved in our experience. In this sense, Whiteheadian philosophy opens a path to considering 'aesthetics as first philosophy' (Segall, 2011) as aesthetic feeling provides the core of its epistemic and metaphysical basis, leaving open the question of the ethical and sociological implications that we draw from speculative flights.[2]

When we turn from cosmology to sociology, Whiteheadian philosophy presents reality as a collection of societies of feeling.[3] Whitehead's aesthetic cosmology proposes that what we experience as individual entities are relational creatures who owe their form of experience to their internal and external relations of feeling. They are societies, each with its own enduring form and defining characteristic that enables its persistence over time. Reality is fundamentally societal and, as societal relations are relations of feeling, life in a democracy of fellow creatures is primarily aesthetic life. The emphasis on creativity and novelty in Whitehead's work may lure us to treating him as a philosopher of sociological progress; however, this is far from the case. In *Adventures of Ideas* (1938) and *Symbolism* (1927), Whitehead warns us that the life and death of societies depends on their capacity to develop conditions for their endurance and enhancement. Societies that fail to produce such conditions become decadent. Thus, societal endurance and transformation require adventure and risk. As he writes in *Symbolism:*

> It is the first step in sociological wisdom, to recognize that the major advances in civilization are processes which all but wreck the societies in which they occur:– like unto an arrow in the hand of a child. The art of free society consists first in the maintenance of the symbolic code;

and secondly in fearlessness of revision, to secure that the code serves those purposes which satisfy an enlightened reason. Those societies which cannot combine reverence to their symbols with freedom of revision, must ultimately decay either from anarchy, or from the slow atrophy of a life stifled by useless shadows. (Whitehead, 1927: 104)

Whitehead's philosophy offers the speculative proposition that human societies, organized through modes of symbolism found in laws, principles and values, must enliven themselves through aesthetic transformation (the revision of symbolic codes) or face their own destruction. This claim is descriptive rather than prescriptive. Whitehead is alerting us to the forms of destabilization and stabilization at work in the maintenance of societal order over time. We are taught 'the age of revolutions' of the 18th century or the technological revolutions of the 19th as moments of rapid transformation of societies and their ideals. These periods are characterized by massive forms of social upheaval, which were resolved by establishing new modes of politics and economic relations that fundamentally altered the societies of North America and Europe.[4] The use of 'civilization' in the quotation also brings to mind the civilizing projects of the 17th and 18th centuries, which deployed 'civilized' values as a means of justifying the extraction of wealth and resources from Asia, Africa and the Americas through the enslavement of their peoples and overdevelopment of their lands. The tension between these two notions of civilization is manifest in values of freedom, rationality, humanity and beauty that become a fulcrum for deciding who is able to participate in 'civilized' society and who must be excluded and seasoned into participation through servitude. Within 'civilized' societies, this distinction plays itself out in forms of class and gender oppression which exclude women and people of a lower economic means from full participation in civil life despite the prevalence of universalist ideals. The speculative flight generated by Whitehead's concept of 'sociological wisdom' highlights the utility of his concept of civilization as a starting point for a multidimensional investigation of societies through their self-conception, values, material structure and the forms of sensibility that emerge within them.

This feature of Whitehead's social aesthetics makes it a useful starting point for work on a social aesthetics of race. In national contexts of Euro-Anglo-American societies in which race talk is not prohibited, it is generally accepted that 'race' is a social construction, an identity category historically used to differentiate between superior and inferior groups of human beings, presuming that inferiority and humanity can be thought simultaneously in their particular racial discourse. Typically, the appeal to social construction is a move towards racial eliminativism, the idea that we should abandon racial categories and, in doing so, be done with the problems associated with racism.[5] However, the empirical persistence of racial disparities and forms of violence in societies in which race is a discursive taboo in public life (for example, France) falsify this ideology. The existence of races is realized in the historical forms of classification, violence and exploitation that begin in the 'civilizing project' of colonization and continue in various forms into the present. The persistence of racist exploitation and violence rests on a bifurcation between the category of race and its manifestations in experience, which generates an experience of tension between the democratic ideals of Euro-Anglo-American societies and the reality of racist violence that persists within them. This tension generates forms of sensibility such as the anaesthetic responses to violence, Black self-alienation or forms of radical consciousness that aim to bridge the gap between ideals and reality.

Whitehead's social aesthetics provides a vocabulary for synthesizing work in Black Studies and the Philosophy of Race in order to trace the historical formation of race categories, examine their material effects and identify the forms of sensibility they produce. In the next section, I will provide an account of the aesthetic problem(s) of race, emphasizing the impact of Whitehead's aesthetics as a vehicle for synthesizing work in existing discourses of racial aesthetics in these fields.

The aesthetic problem(s) of race

Work in the critical philosophy of race analyses the operations of race through several frames. There is work on the ontology of race, which attempts to define what race is or what races are; theories of racialization that trace its socio-political effects on the organization of societies; and racial phenomenologies, which trace the effects of racialization on human perspectives. My version of a social aesthetics of race aims to synthesize work in these areas using foundations in Whitehead's social aesthetics that link these frames together into a unified account.[6] In this section, I trace three key features of the aesthetic dimensions of race, each of which points to the value of Whitehead's social aesthetics as an impetus for work in these areas.

The fiction(s) of race

The social aesthetics of race begins with the proposition that the concept of race emerges as part of a project that aims to abstract peoples from a shared world of nations and territories and place them into divided worlds differentiated by culture and biology. In his analysis of the concept, Paul Taylor (2013) frames the adventure of this concept in two periods – classical and modern – which mark its move from a biological marker to a social or cultural category. In its early modern form – the monogenic account – races are distinct groups of people that emerge from a common human origin, who diverge due to their geographical locations and environments. Their features solidify themselves over time as these disparate populations develop as separate breeding communities. As the dominant paradigm moves from monogenesis to polygenesis, races lose their anchor in a common human origin and become groups distinguished by heritable intellectual and physical differences. The shift from the first to the second phase is accompanied by a shift in arguments for the colonization of African and American lands and the enslavement of their peoples. In the former case, there is a natural difference between peoples that explains the superiority of the colonizer alongside a principle of abstract human value that can justify abolitionist positions. In the latter, colonization and enslavement become means of civilizing inferior peoples. This is the thought motivating positions like J.S. Mill's notion of 'tolerant imperialism' (Tunic, 2006) towards societies 'in their nonage'. This paternalistic approach to civilization is simultaneously present in abolitionist movements, symbolized in material objects such as the Wedgewood medallion, which couples the phrase 'Am I not a man and a brother?' with an image of a Black man as a pleading supplicant, bent low and in need of rescue. This image persists in the memorialization of Black progress, appearing in the Tuskegee statue of Booker T. Washington 'lifting the veil' of ignorance from a formerly enslaved person and the Emancipation Memorial in Washington DC's Lincoln Park, which replaces Washington with Lincoln, who stands above a now freed Black man, still kneeling in supplication, both dedicated in 1922.

These statues demonstrate the persistence of the past biological race concept in its 'late modern' and 'post-modern' deployment, where race shifts from its biological foundations to a category of sociological and cultural difference. In its sociological form, racial differences are manifested in mores and problems generated by a history of cultural degeneracy due to socio-political inequality. The political project of civilization continues through forms of integration that maintain relations of hierarchical difference. The shift is that those differences are no longer inherent, but politically caused. Although it shifts from the biological to the socio-political, the narrative of Black inferiority persists, embodied in documents such as the Moynihan Report, which blames the problems of the Black community on the lack of Black males and the failures of the Black family (Geary, 2015). In the subsequent 'post-modern' moment, races become cultural groups whose differences are not essentially social or political. Contemporary racial discourse follows this lineage, inheriting anti-racism as a principle of social transformation required to change the hearts and minds of racists while organizing people of good will in the cause of transforming society. However, a hierarchical principle remains. The progressive ideal, that the social principle is ideal but simply imperfectly realized, fixes our current societies in a moment where racial hierarchy is maintained as a flaw in the system or reality rather than a fundamental feature of its organization, necessary for its success. This tension is manifested in the conception of Black people enshrined in the National Museum for African American History and Culture in Washington D.C. The largest room of the historical exhibition features a history of constitutional amendments and post-reconstruction social conditions, overseen by the thematic statement 'Making a Way out of No Way'. This statement enshrines a concept of Black Americans as always succeeding in the face of oppression but never achieving liberation in the United States. From the perspective of the social aesthetics of race, this establishes the role of Black Americans in the national narrative as characters given over to perpetual suffering, existing as a marker of the nation's contradictions.

This story of the development of the concept of race illustrates its fictional quality. Beginning as a principle of social organization, it shifts form in line with evolving scientific, socio-cultural and political thought, distancing itself from its character as a principle of hierarchy while maintaining conditions of domination. As a result, it generates a bifurcation between the ideals of progressive liberal societies and the reality of the experiential difference between racialized worlds that these societies contain. From the Whiteheadian perspective, I argue that race is a predatory abstraction (Debaise, 2021: 314) which thins the political imagination. Du Bois' unanswered question, 'How does it feel to be a problem?' (1997: 3) alerts us to the fact that this division is felt in experience, maintained by sensual relations that necessitate forms of racial hierarchy as they simultaneously disavow them.[7] Racial projects are aesthetic projects insofar as the naturalization of racist forms of difference is embedded in values and ways of viewing that justify forms of domination. In contrast, work in the social aesthetics of race aims to generate new racial fictions to revise the concept for deployment in emancipatory projects. Du Bois' early essays, for example, are a first attempt to tell new stories about race through his own experience, sociological research and political activity, redeploying the concept into a set of new fictions that invert common-sense racism into a false paradigm for apprehending the reality of societies. In response to racial eliminativists, who argue that the end of racism requires the end of race talk, we can respond that their project is already active in the process of recasting race as a cultural or categorical concept rather than an evolving term for capturing the forms of hierarchy inscribed through the history of anti-Blackness. In addition, we can point to the ways that racial identity has been used by Black people as a starting point for solidarity and cultural formation that aims to construct new worlds of experience. It is not the concept of race itself but the fictions it facilitates which serve as the ground for illuminating and contesting the history of racist division into worlds of Black and White. Work in Black Studies and Decolonial Thought forms part of a larger theoretical tradition that responds to these felt conditions with alternative fictions and novel abstractions that thicken our experience in line with historical reality. Their works link the epistemic and the aesthetic to situate contemporary struggles in their historical foundations, attuning our senses to the reality of race.

Racial projects as aesthetic projects

The second feature of the social aesthetics of race is an approach to racial projects as aesthetic projects (Wynter, 1992; Roelofs, 2014: 29–56). This follows work in Black studies that traces the production of forms of experience that necessitate racist division through epistemic, material and political means. The aesthetic foundations of these projects also motivate the intertwining of the aesthetic and epistemic in Black liberation, which appears clearly in the contemporaneous emergence of the Black Studies movements, the Black Arts Movement and the Black power movement in the post-civil rights culture of the United States. As Sylvia Wynter (2006: 108) argues, these movements emerge and take their force from the uprisings after the murder of Dr Martin Luther King Jr., which mobilized Black communities and generated a form of national trauma that pressured institutions of higher education to act. The institutionalization of these movements aligned their interests with forms of liberal universalism, shifting their aims to integration into institutions.[8] As the uprisings subsided, founders shifted to more radical political formations to avoid the trap of liberalism, and a post-structuralist critique of Blackness emerged which aimed to replace an 'essentialist' notion of Blackness that these movements assumed (109–11). We should immediately feel parallels to the upswell of support for 'anti-racism' following the uprisings of 2020 that led universities to recommit themselves to 'diversity, inclusion and equity' as institutional structures that should stabilize university cultures and ensure their continued financial viability.

These conditions mark the emergence of the Black Arts, Black Studies and Black power movements as a struggle over conditions of experience through a recasting of aesthetics, epistemology and politics. They mark a psychic rupture against a hegemonic sociogenic code (Wynter, 2006: 118) that establishes Black self-alienation as a condition for sociological reality. The encoding of these movements back into larger frameworks occurs because the forms of liberation experienced failed to move from the 'map' establishing the 'systemic de-valorization of Blackness and correlated over-valorization of whiteness', to the 'territory' of the 'overall devalorization of the human species' at work in the organization of our societies. For Wynter, 'the systematic revalorization of Black peoples can be fundamentally effected only by means of the no less systemic revalorization of the human being itself, *outside* the necessarily devalorizing terms of the biocentric descriptive statement of *Man,* over represented as it were by that of the human' (119). This problem is an aesthetic problem insofar as it involves the encoding of values of beauty and worth on skin, with the effect that these value codes generate relationships of kinship, satisfaction, and dissatisfaction that establish divisions between worlds (Wynter, 1992). The fictions of race become real insofar as they encode human relationships through the political, epistemic and aesthetic structures that form the sociogenic code which characterizes societies in the wake of slavery and colonialism.[9] The human itself is an abstraction used to differentiate peoples between 'civilized' and 'uncivilized', distancing 'human' from 'nature' and devalorizing the concept of human by human beings from their relations to the environment and others.

Wynter and Du Bois show us that Blackness in its political, epistemic and aesthetic forms is allowed to maintain its particularity only in terms of a liberal universalist ideal of human being that was constructed with the exclusion of Blackness as a condition of its appearance. For example, the current model of liberal anti-racism treats racial identities as one perspective among others which should be included in interpersonal and political life to enrich democratic discourse and economic development. The solutions to the problem of exclusion are inclusion, bringing in more bodies, and belonging, creating a sense that these bodies deserve to participate in economic and political relations. These strategies fail due to the disconnect between racialized identity and political ideals. England's Conservative Party, for example, have a prime minister and home secretary who are both people of colour yet respond to the country's influx of immigrants with a policy of increased police enforcement and deportation rather than providing mechanisms for safe immigration or relocation to countries who will accept them (Braverman, 2023). In the United States, there has been an increase in the election of Black politicians since the uprisings of 2020. However, these politicians are notable for their extreme political disconnect from the demands of Black protestors. Most recently, Eric Adams, the Democrat mayor of New York City, is a former police officer who has responded to calls to abolish or defund the police with an increase in their budget (David et al, 2022). These phenomena reinforce the sense that calls for justice will be met with sympathy but that the resulting actions will always reinforce status-quo racial violence and exploitation. The code must be respected. Situations such as these have generated new forms of cynicism and pessimism that see modes of racial progress as one more narrative to continue racist forms of domination through the neo-colonial deployment of Black people.

If we turn back to Whitehead's proposition on sociological wisdom, we see the risks involved in conceptual revision. Beyond the epistemic shifts required for sociological transformation, we require a shift in forms of feeling tied to material conditions that come to characterize the lived experience of the members of a society. The opening quotation from Césaire presents us with an anti-colonial sensibility that orients us to feel the extent to which our current forms of civilization still fail their own test of legitimacy. We can sense the 'infinite distance' between colonization and civilization in the ongoing extraction of raw materials for technology in Africa and Latin America, the slow privatization and elimination of institutions of care, and the so-called 'migrant crisis', which has populated Euro-Anglo-American capitals with people from Latin America, Africa, the Middle East and Eastern Europe who are provided little to no access to resources for legal immigration. These phenomena are naturalized as features of our societies through the material benefits secured by 'developed' nations from their persistence and a sense of their necessity as features of our common world. The problem of social transformation is not fundamentally epistemic. There are knowledgeable debates about sociological problems which leave the underlying structures that perpetuate them intact. Nor is the problem a matter of understanding or recognizing the humanity of others. This response relies on us forgetting, as per Wynter, that the evolution of societies from their colonial roots continues a long process of the devaluation of humanity, or 'man', along with the destruction of the non-human environment. The social aesthetics of race aims to focus on an interrogation of the forms of sensibility that naturalize these uncivilized conditions and the production of new forms of feeling that can provide an experiential and ontological relation of societal codes.

Forms of racial sensibility

The third element of the social aesthetics of race is an analysis of the forms of racial sensibility that naturalize or contest racist structures and violence. 'White Ignorance' for example, is theorized by Charles Mills as 'a moral cognitive distortion' that legitimizes concepts of equality and justice in contexts organized around exploitation and domination (1997, 95). It captures moments in which one 'takes for granted the appropriateness of concepts legitimizing the racial order, privileging them as the master race and relegating nonwhites to subpersonhood' by 'derace[ing] the polity, denying its actual racial structuring' (1997: 95, 2017). For Mills, this distortion emerges by virtue of the 'racial contract' underlying the social contract, which necessitates a disavowal of the horrors and inequalities of liberal societies to preserve their progressive ideals. Mills' White Ignorance is a manifestation of what James Baldwin terms 'white innocence', the complex by which his fellow citizens 'have destroyed and are destroying hundreds of thousands of lives and do not know it and do not want to know it' (1998: 292). I contrast these views to mark how the epistemic focus of Mill's understanding of ignorance elides with Baldwin's moral valence, marking the role of feeling as a bridge between epistemology and ethics. In Baldwin's theorization, societies are structured systems of reality ('codes') which produce a 'sense of reality' relative to one's position in the society's structure (1998: 714). Following Baldwin, I offer the hypothesis that this sense of reality manifests in forms of sensibility described in racial phenomenologies, which illustrate that the societal problems generated by race are not simply a problem of bad beliefs, as contemporary anti-racists hold. They are forms of experience, ways of feeling, which organize perspectives in line with a society's code for its maintenance and valorization.

On the psychological level, following Baldwin (1962), we know that a response to facing the horrors of the past often leads to panic.[10] It is this panic, which is captured in the concept of 'white ambush' (Yancy 2008: 217–42), in which one is interpellated as a racialized (as White) racist in an encounter with someone racialized as a minority. On the material level, we should remember that 'Whiteness' is a desirable social identity insofar as it comes with social benefits for many, though not all. The concept of the 'N***r', as Baldwin also argues, is needed to secure a sense of superiority in an anti-Black world. Even the poorest White person in the US can lean on the proposition that they are, at least, not Black. On these grounds, Linda Alcoff has proposed the cultivation of a 'white double consciousness' that uses an awareness of one's racialization as 'a potential source for a new and more accurate understanding of social conditions' (2015: 169–70). As she notes, this form of split consciousness differs from Du Bois' experience insofar as seeing oneself through the gaze of Black people is not a form of oppression. It is 'living out the necessary effects of white vanguardist ideologies' (Alcoff 2015: 170). It is a form of adjusting one's sense of reality to view the system of reality more clearly, developing the possibility of viewing material changes beyond epistemic shifts.

Shifting worlds from White to Black, Afro-pessimism presents itself as another form of sensibility, a response to the long history of failed attempts at the liberation of Black people in Euro-Anglo-American societies. The Afro-pessimist argues that Black people are ontologically slaves, given over to the experience of gratuitous violence, natal alienation and social death (Wilderson, 2010, 2020; Sexton, 2016). Coalitional politics and liberation are impossible since, in an anti-Black world, any efforts will always return to the ontological abjection of Black people from societies. Thus, Wilderson (2014) argues, citing Fanon, that the liberation requires 'the end of the world'. While Wilderson and Sexton treat their analysis as ontological, from the perspective of a social aesthetics of race the ontology of social death is a historically contingent result of a philosophy of liberal universalism built on denying the humanity of those exploited to build new cosmopolitan societies. There is a sense, when living in the United States and Europe, that survival as a Black person or person of colour requires something beyond assimilation or integration. In France, for example, an appeal to Blackness is met with the charge of *communautarisme*, a term which expresses 'a general distrust of allowing ethnic, cultural, or religious communities of origin to express their identities over and above republican universalism' (Lizotte, 2020: 2; see also Fleming, 2017: 74–6). Its use against Black activists and visible Muslims marks a paranoia about the failure of the French nation to maintain its social ideas in the face of ongoing neo-colonial relations with its formerly colonized peoples. Although the country, thanks to Christine Taubira, has acknowledged its enslavement of colonized peoples as a crime against humanity, Haiti remains underdeveloped due to the huge reparation payments demanded by France at the end of the slave trade and a century of financial control by the United States (Rosalsky, 2021; Toure, 2021; Méheut and Porter, 2023).

Thus, Afro-pessimism follows on a history of racial realist positions, such as Critical Race Theory, which argue that a struggle against racist societies must assume the permanence of their racist forms (Bell, 1992). Along with 'white innocence' and 'white double consciousness', it represents another form of racialized sensibility that engages with the effects of racialization on our experience of reality to link our subjective experience to the societal structures that generate it. This connection demonstrates the importance of aesthetic feeling as a site to link our epistemic, political and ethical concerns into a realistic view of life in uncivilized societies despite their claim of civilized ideals. These forms of sensibility reflect a felt sense of permanent conflict that inhibits the ability to act on the contradictions faced in our societies. The energy contained in radical movements, once denied, remains in a psycho-social feeling of unease which is soothed by innocence, ignorance and pessimism, anaesthetic positions that thin experience, numbing our sense of reality. In response, the social aesthetics of race aims to provide forms of feeling that thicken our experience, balancing pain with possibility to direct our energies to sociological transformation.

Towards a social aesthetics of race

In the social aesthetics of Alfred North Whitehead, civilization is the art of forging relations of a massiveness and intensity of experience that stimulates a zest for adventure and sense of peace. This form of experience depends on a relationship between truth and beauty that exposes us to a wider encounter of reality than our epistemic categories allow. This conception echoes Du Bois' (1926, Sec 11) early characterization of himself as 'one who tells the truth and exposes evil and seeks with Beauty and for Beauty to set the world right'. For him, the 'apostle of beauty' is compelled by a sense of truth and goodness to speak the truths which are thrust upon them by experience to motivate the goodness of peoples for the transformation of their worlds (Secs 27–9). In both philosophies, truth and beauty are linked such that propositions about the world carry the force of experience, which contains the values that make them important, the values that motivate them and the circumstances they mean to address. Joy and suffering, youth and tragedy are contained within the process as beauty, like civilization, is never an absolute achievement. These processes require activity and attention to the fact that we are engaged in practices that refresh them or allow their slide into decadence.

As Michael Halewood reminds us, Whitehead turns to sociology to examine 'the changing modes of mentality' that characterize epochs of civilization (2014: 142). In the Black aesthetic tradition I am attempting to carve out, Black theorists are interested in the aesthetic as a vehicle for the articulation of values and analysis of experience that retains the connection between propositional understanding and the urgency of life. On this basis, I argue for a reading of their works as 'models of Black thought' which should be treated as situated perspectives combining propositional and aesthetic form for the transformation of experience. Rather than sources for political debate, they are perspectives aimed at concrete transformations in their times, associated with the authors' own political projects. Propositionally, these models analyse the role of feeling in the production and maintenance of oppressive structures, offering counter-narratives and conceptual critiques against the codes of our systems of reality. Aesthetically, they are constructed to intervene in forms of sensibility that maintain these structures, working at the sites of contestation they identify and setting lures for alternative forms of sensibility that thicken our experience of the roles race plays in the structure of our societies. These connections form relations of aesthetic feeling that link our worlds and perspectives through articulations of experience, allowing us to identify the material conditions of our experience and sense possibilities inhibited by societal anaesthesia (and amnesia). Following the work of Audre Lorde (1984), I argue that forms of oppression operate materially on the possibilities for agency afforded in society and our sense of the world of others in connection with our own. Rather than a rejection of past forms of thought or a romanticization of their ideals, we require forms of thought that evolve perspectives with a view to how our positions are informed through struggle and short-circuited by systems of domination. Individuality is not lost in this collective pursuit. For Lorde (1984), our guiding force is the erotic, which animates our relations between one another and gives the individual a sense of what is valuable for themselves. It generates relations of feeling that connect communities to the needs of their members in shared political projects. I believe that this strategy, along with those outlined by Baldwin and Du Bois, provide initial steps towards interventions into our social code which can animate a process that moves our societies from decadence to advance.

Notes

[1] Social aesthetics has different meanings depending on the disciplines in which its conducted. In sociology, it is concerned with the aesthetic dimensions in sociological

phenomena (Carnevali, 2017). In philosophy, it addresses the societal sources of aesthetic norms and values and the activities of aesthetic communities.
2. Recent works have highlighted the role of feeling in Whitehead's philosophy, producing a view of the aesthetic as an essential feature of his philosophy. Along with Shaviro's *Without Criteria* (2009) is *Process and Aesthetics* (Dadejík et al, 2021).
3. In Whitehead's philosophy, 'society' and 'societies' are deployed as metaphysical terms, while 'sociology' and sociological' are reserved for discussions of human societies (Halewood, 2014: 140–1). The former refers to 'the manner in which things come to endure' (140) and the latter 'the changing "modes of mentality" which suffuse different epochs' (142). The latter sense opens a space for an examination of modes of sensibility, termed as such to highlight the role of feeling in the development of mentality.
4. In *Adventures of Ideas* Whitehead refers to 'barbarians and steam' (1938: 5) as 'senseless agencies' that generate shifts in the forms of societies with contemporary shifts in ideas. The contrast between the two points to the 'uncivilized' effects of industrialization and mechanization of human societies, emphasizing their violence against human and non-human life.
5. The eliminativist position in the philosophy of race is associated with the early work of Kwame Anthony Appiah (1985, 1996) and Naomi Zack (2002), along with Ron Mallon (2006). For an overview of the contemporary philosophy of racial ontology see, *What is Race?: Four Philosophical Views* (Glasgow et al, 2019).
6. This is not to say that Whitehead's work is a precondition for synthetic work in these areas. The tradition of social aesthetics I propose is already present in the work of several authors in Africana Philosophy and Black Studies (for example, Sylvia Wynter) who have analysed the role of aesthetics or aesthetic feeling in the production and maintenance of racist or colonial societies. The aim of this project is to use Whitehead's framework as an extension of these examinations for contemporary projects.
7. See Chapter 1 of this volume for a further discussion of felt abstractions.
8. This analysis follows work in Critical Race Theory on 'interest convergence' (Bell, 1980), the idea that moments of racial progress do not mark moments of moral clarity in societies and their political institutions. Instead, they are moments where the maintenance of these societies requires ceding ground to Black political movements to maintain their own interests.
9. I interpret the use of 'codes' in both Wynter and Whitehead as a term for the organization of propositions about race and the structures of society into an interpretive framework that ties together articulated social ideals and their material relations. These codes maintain the contradictions between ideals and lived conditions of experience in societies and are the object of counter-narratives produced in the work of Black thinkers, such as Du Bois' 'Study of Negro Problems', which deploys a sociological concept of racial division to redefine 'social problems' as a societal failure rather than a pathology of Black people (Gordon, 2000). Work in Critical Race Theory and Saidya Hartman's (2008) 'critical fabulations' are a contemporary, speculative form.
10. Baldwin writes:

> The entire purpose of society is to create a bulwark against the inner and the outer chaos, in order to make life bearable and to keep the human race alive. And it is absolutely inevitable that when a tradition has been evolved, whatever the tradition is, the people, in general, will suppose it to have existed from before the beginning of time and will be most unwilling and indeed unable to conceive of any changes in it. They do not know how they will live without those traditions that have given them their identity. Their reaction, when it is suggested that they can or that they must, is panic.

He presents echoes of the tension surrounding the revision of social codes which emerges psychologically at the thought of overturning implicit assumptions about the structure of societies that mask the horrors that ground them.

References

Alcoff, L.M. (2015) *The Future of Whiteness,* Cambridge: Polity.

Appiah, K.A. (1985) 'The uncompleted argument: DuBois and the illusion of race', *Critical Inquiry,* 12(1): 21–37.

Appiah, K.A. (1996) 'Race, culture, identity: Misunderstood connections', in A. Appiah and A. Gutmann (eds), *Color Conscious*, Princeton, NJ: Princeton University Press, pp 30–105.

Baldwin, J. (1998) *Collected Essays,* New York: Library of America.

Baldwin, J. (1962) 'The creative process', in *Creative America*, New York: Ridge Press.

Braverman, Suella. 'Home Secretary statement on the Illegal Immigration Bill', 7 March 2023. https://www.gov.uk/government/speeches/home-secretary-statement-on-the-illegal-immigration-bill (Accessed 3 May 2023).

Bell, D. (1980) 'Brown v. Board of Education and the interest–convergence dilemma', *Harvard Law Review,* 93(3): 518–33.

Bell, D. (1992) 'Racial Realism', *Connecticut Law Review*, 24(2): 363–80.

Carnevali, B. (2017) 'Social sensibility. Simmel, the senses, and the aesthetics of recognition', *Simmel Studies*, 21(2): 9–39.

Dadejík, O., Kaplický, M., Ševčík, M. and Zuska, V. (2021) *Process and Aesthetics: An Outline of Whiteheadian Aesthetics and Beyond,* Chicago, IL: University of Chicago Press.

David, G., Gonen, Y. and Honan, K. (2022) 'Mayor Eric Adams proposes boost to police and jail spending in nearly $100B budget', *The City,* 27 April. https://www.thecity.nyc/2022/4/26/23043827/eric-adams-budget-police-jail (Accessed 29 May 2023).

Debaise, D. and Keating, T. (2021) 'Speculative empiricism, nature and the question of predatory abstractions: A conversation with Didier Debaise', *Theory, Culture & Society,* 38(7–8): 309–23.

Du Bois, W.E.B. (1926) 'The criteria of Negro art', *The Crisis*, 32: 290–7, http://www.webdubois.org/dbCriteriaNArt.html (Accessed 9 November 2023).

Du Bois, W.E.B. (1997) *The Souls of Black Folk,* Amherst, MA: University of Massachusetts Press.

Fleming, C.M. (2017) *Resurrecting Slavery: Racial Legacies and White Supremacy in France.* Philadelphia, PA: Temple University Press.

Geary, D. (2015) 'The Moynihan Report: An annotated edition', *The Atlantic,* 14 September. https://www.theatlantic.com/politics/archive/2015/09/the-moynihan-report-an-annotated-edition/404632/ (Accessed 8 June 2023).

Glasgow, J., Hasslanger, S., Jeffers, C. and Spencer, Q. (2019) *What is Race?: Four Philosophical Views*, Oxford: Oxford University Press.

Gordon, L. (2000) *Existentia Africana: Understanding Africana Existential Thought*, New York: Routledge.

Halewood, M. (2014) *Rethinking the Social through Durkheim, Weber, Marx, and Whitehead*, London: Anthem.

Hartman, S. (2008) 'Venus in two acts', *Small Axe* 12(2): 1–14.

Lizotte, C. (2020) 'Laïcité as assimilation, laïcité as negotiation: Political geographies of secularism in the French public school', *Political Geography*, 77. https://doi.org/10.1016/j.polgeo.2019.102121 (Accessed 9 November 2023).

Lorde, A. (1984) *Sister Outsider: Essays and Speeches*, Berkeley, CA: Freedom Crossing Press.

Mallon, R. (2006) 'Race: Normative, not metaphysical or semantic', *Ethics*, 116(3): 525–51.

Méheut, C. and Porter, C. (2023) 'Macron honors Haitian revolutionary, but leaves much unsaid', *The New York Times*, 27 April. https://www.nytimes.com/2023/04/27/world/europe/macron-toussaint-louverture-speech.html (Accessed 9 November 2023).

Mills, C. (1997) *The Racial Contract*. Ithaca, NY: Cornell University Press.

Mills, C. (2017) *Black Rights/White Wrongs*, Oxford: Oxford University Press.

Rosalsky, G. (2021) ' "The greatest heist in history": How Haiti was forced to pay reparations for freedom', *NPR.org*, 5 October. https://www.npr.org/sections/money/2021/10/05/1042518732/-the-greatest-heist-in-history-how-haiti-was-forced-to-pay-reparations-for-freed (Accessed 9 November 2023).

Roelofs, M. (2014) *The Cultural Promise of the Aesthetic*, New York: Bloomsbury.

Segall, M. (2011) 'Whitehead: Aesthetics as first philosophy', *Footnotes to Plato*, 11 March. https://footnotes2plato.com/2011/03/11/whitehead-aesthetics-as-first-philosophy/ (Accessed 8 June 2023).

Sexton, J. (2016) 'Afro-pessimism: The unclear word', *Rhizomes*, 29. Available at: http://www.rhizomes.net/issue29/sexton.html (Accessed 9 June 2023).

Shaviro, S. (2009) *Without Criteria: Kant, Whitehead, Deleuze and Aesthetics*, Cambridge, MA: MIT Press.

Taylor, P. (2013) *Race: A Philosophical Introduction*, London: Polity.

Toure, F. (2021) 'The day France recognized slavery as a crime against humanity', *Le Journal de l'Afrique*, 10 May. https://lejournaldelafrique.com/en/the-day-France-recognized-slavery-as-a-crime-against-humanity/ (Accessed 6 June 2023).

Tunic, M. (2006) 'Tolerant imperialism: John Stuart Mill's defense of British rule in India', *The Review of Politics*, 68: 1–26.

Whitehead, A.N. (1927) *Symbolism: Its Meaning and Effect*, New York: Macmillan.

Whitehead, A.N. (1938) *Adventures of Ideas*, New York: Free Press.

Whitehead, A.N. (1978) *Process and Reality: An Essay in Cosmology*, (corrected edn), ed D.R. Griffin and D.W. Sherburne, New York: The Free Press.

Wilderson, F. (2010) *Red, White, & Black: Cinema and Structures of U.S. Antagonisms*, Durham, NC: Duke University Press.

Wilderson, F. (2014) '*We're Trying to Destroy the World*': *Anti-Blackness and Police Violence after Ferguson*, Ill Will Editions.

Wilderson, F. (2020) *Afropessimism*, New York: Liveright.

Wynter, S. (1992) 'Rethinking aesthetics: Notes towards a deciphering practice', in M.B. Chaim (ed), *Ex-iles: Essays on Caribbean Cinema*. Trenton, NJ: Africa World Press.

Wynter, S. (2006) 'On how we mistook the map for the territory, and re-imprisoned ourselves in our unbearable wrongness of being, of Désêtre: Black Studies towards the human project', in J. Gordon and L. Gordon (eds), *Not Only the Master's Tools: African American Studies in Theory and Practice*, London: Paradigm, pp 107–69.

Yancy, G. (2008) *Black Bodies/White Gazes: The Continuing Significance of Race*, Lanham, MD: Rowman and Littlefield.

Zack, N. (2002) *Philosophy of Science and Race*, New York: Routledge.

PART II

Problematizing and (Re)Valuing

6

A New Taste for Life? Value Ecologies and the Aesthetics of the Outside

Martin Savransky

> Inasmuch as the disaster is thought, it is nondisastrous thought, thought of the outside. We have no access to the outside, but the outside has always already touched us in the head, for it is the precipitous.
>
> Maurice Blanchot, *The Writing of the Disaster* (1995)

Swan songs

Like the high-pitched ringing sound in one's ears in the wake of acoustic trauma, the swan song of a frequency resonating with our bodies perhaps for the last time, there is something eerie in the gesture of seeking to reclaim the notion of aesthetics today, of looking for new ways of thinking and feeling, new knowledges and practices that might open 'aesthetics' up to the possibility of an adventure it never quite had. For amid ongoing catastrophic processes of ocean acidification, mass extinction, wildfires, deforestation and desertification, and the depletion of biodiversity – only some of the latest dimensions of the ongoing socio-ecological disaster that the conjoined histories of capitalism, colonialism and extractivism constitute – one can hardly shake off the sense that the contemporary planetary condition is in certain respects the latest ripple of a radically (an)aesthetic event: precipitating the devastation of myriad forms of value, of sense and sensation, of modes feeling and manners of being that once populated the earth. The sense of an ending which seems to coincide with a certain ending of sense. What, at the enduring end of this world (already in the process of recomposing itself in the name of technocratic climate change governance), is there of 'aesthetics' that could be reclaimed from such a deeply anaesthetized present? Is there anything in what we have associated with aesthetics that could render it other than the last sensible sediment, the very swan song of the many modes of sensation, perception and sensibility, of the multiple modes of feeling lost to the earth?

It is all too tempting to succumb to the ominous tone of the swan song, presaging the imminent coming about of a fading future, sublime in its destruction, diminished just in the sense in which it intimates itself today. And yet, the fact is that swan songs are also aesthetic events. The fading ring in our ears, those parting gestures, moments or experiences of intensity right at the bitter end, are themselves so many testaments to fugitive forms of experience no amount of extermination and fossilization can ever hope to repress, to regions of existence no abstract *Anthropos* can ever manage to subsume, to a riotous outside no Golden Spike can ever wipe out. And the very name of the 'swan song' makes perceptible that our many lives and deaths are in spite of all shaped by traditions of legend, myth and storytelling that insist and persist amid the rubble of all that the modern world has disqualified and disavowed. Indeed, the figure of the swan song binds us to a timeless legend which told that swans, who remain atonal during much of their lives, sing beautifully only before they die. But the omen-like quality of the legend of the swan song is only one of its multiple threads. For like all legends, its survival is intimately tied to its ongoing metamorphosis, to the manner in which its sense is rewoven by new threads laced through its various incarnations and relays. In this way, whereas in Aesop's (1998) classical fable 'The Swan and the Goose' the swan song is the clarion call that, from the still of the dark, 'saves' the swan from the knife of the cook who was about to take its life so as to eat it – thereby exchanging its fate with that of the goose – in Leonardo Da Vinci's (2006) rendering the swan sings sweetly *as* it dies, the song actively *ending* its life.

If the swan song might generatively resonate as a musical tone for this epoch – rather better, perhaps, than the name 'Anthropocene' – as well as for the possibility of reclaiming aesthetics today, it is not because it would only too late remind us of our finitude or reconcile us melodically with our fate. Rather, it is precisely because, in the course of its various transformations and permutations, the swan song has acquired a truly ambiguous and unsettling value, at once tangling and upending otherwise melancholy images of salvation or damnation in whose hold much contemporary thinking and feeling, knowing and doing on climate change dwells. At once the sense of an ending and something *intensely sensed*, the paradoxical figure of the swan song simultaneously reminds us that salvation is never innocent and that endings are never absolute, that there is value even in and amid loss, an after to every ending. It reminds us that if it is not a matter of saving swan, goose or civilization from their ends, that if the end of this world is, in the end, something we might strive not to avert but to begin – to recall Aimé Césaire (2013: 39; see also Savransky, 2021a) – it matters what openings the end might engender in the echoes and breaks its song makes reverberate. It is for this reason that, while it may in some sense be *too late* to save aesthetics from the anaesthetic disaster that the modern-colonial world system constitutes, perhaps this swan song of socio-ecoaesthetic devastation that pulsates through it might itself be a vector of intensity, of a fugitive sensation that might make of the idea and possibility of an aesthetics of the outside something worth thinking and living for after all. The 'too late' is a time of finitude, not finality. And we continue to inhabit the problem of composing interstitial forms of life, improvised socialites, a feel for the outside in spite of the inhospitable conditions of habitation (Savransky, 2021b).

As we grope for the possible in the dark, for lives worth living and deaths worth living for while we still can, it might be then, now, that giving 'aesthetics' over to the insistence of another sense, of an outside, might be worth an always risky and incomplete chance. At the end of the day – perhaps even at the end of days – what is at stake is no less than the question of whether it might still be possible to wrest the meaning and force of *aesthesis* from the deleterious modern history that parsed it away from multifarious worlds of feeling and value, confined it within the all-too-human judgement of the beholding eye, reduced it to a set of *general* values – of beauty and the sublime – and delegated it to a limited set of artistic practices and objects held in and for judgement (Sehgal, 2018). Indeed, the rise of modern aesthetics in the 18th century made its own swan songs reverberate in its wake, alongside 'the general evolution' that, as Félix Guattari (1995: 99) rightly observed, tended 'towards an accentuation of the individuation of subjectivity, towards a loss of its polivocality', a general evolution which precipitated the 'autonomisation of Universes of value of the order of the divine, the good, the true, the beautiful, of power' and led to a 'sectorisation of modes of valorisation' which 'is now so deeply rooted in the cognitive apprehension of our era that it is difficult for us to trace its economy when we try to decode past societies'.

The correlate to the vectorization and autonomization of a universe of aesthetic value as a distinct form of experience was, of course, the 'aestheticization' of practices and rituals into tightly demarcated artistic forms, which became sterile except insofar as they elicited pleasure or judgement – which is to say except insofar as they became bound to commercial institutions which displayed and managed them for the pleasure and judgement of their clientele (see Demos, 2020). And it was such reduction of *value itself* to an act of judgement that precipitated the devaluation of immanent values incarnated in always singular forms of existence, rendering them liable to extraction, sites of revenue and capital, anonymous points on the imperial cartography of homogenous space. Hence the paradox that, to borrow Nicholas Mirzoeff's (2014: 220) words, 'the conquest of nature, having been aestheticized, leads to a loss of perception (*aesthesis*), which is to say, it becomes an anaesthetics'. In this sense, modern aesthetics perceives little beyond its own horrible pleasures, the pleasures of sublime horror engendered in ongoing processes of appropriation and devastation. What is more, regarding those who now publicly dream of bioengineering the resurrection of mammoths and other extinct forms of life, the fact is no engineered resurrection will bring back the modes of *aesthesis* through which devastated worlds made themselves felt. There are real losses, and no longing gesture of melancholy or nostalgia will enable us to reclaim the modes of sensing lost to value extraction, colonial destruction and environmental collapse. Not, that is, without in so doing confusing the sensing of bygone worlds with what Nietzsche (1996) came to call *ressentiment*, that sense of impotence that fuels contempt for this world, for the reasons that make this world, rather than another, exist. Encouraging us to judge this impoverished world in the name of some other world we would have lost, from which we would have fallen, such *ressentiment* would have no other consequence than that of reinforcing the very reactive operation by which values became general in the first place, mobilized as weapons through which worlds could be judged once again.

Resisting both the reactive temptation of salvation and the resentful lure of nostalgia, what I seek in what follows is to affirm the possibility of reclaiming 'aesthetics' – the concept, its meaning, the events it might perhaps still precipitate – while allowing the echoes of the swan song to continue ringing in our years. For after all, if the contemporary condition of generalized ravage deserves to be called 'ecological', it is because, more than animals, plants, soils, toxic particles, new diseases or extreme weather events, it is the collective 'ways of living on this planet that are in question' (Guattari, 2005: 28). To allow the swan song to continue ringing in our ears, therefore, is to insist that, amid ongoing processes of anaesthetization, the task is not to save a modern notion of aesthetics whose general values have never prevented worlds from enduring the slow violence that have depleted much of the earth's ability to make itself felt. It is rather to gamble on the chance of sensing the glimmers of what Guattari (1995) called 'a new aesthetic paradigm'. Which is to say, to step outside so as to affirm, in the outlaw edges of that which we have and might still continue to call aesthetics, the possibility of becoming sensitive to the immanent creation of values elaborated in divergent practices of thinking and feeling that insist and persist amid the disaster. Values that might, just perhaps, inspire in us the thoughts, feelings and beliefs that may be required to cultivate speculative methodologies of life and death – unruly ways of inhabiting the earth.

Immanent values and the ecology of the virtual

At the heart of the possibility of reclaiming 'aesthetics' while allowing the swan song to ring in our ears lies, it seems to me, the question of the nature of value. First, of course, because the rise of modern aesthetics in the 18th century was itself premised upon the very modern bifurcation between facts and values, objectivity and subjectivity: 'the nature apprehended in awareness and the nature which is the cause of awareness' (Whitehead, 2004: 31). As Alexander Baumgarten (2013) and Immanuel Kant (1987) turned 'aesthetics' into a theory of sensuous perception and the perceiving subject, they enabled the realm of the aesthetic to be carved out from the expansive field of experience while simultaneously allowing the realm of the sciences to reign supreme over the new world of matter.[1] Indeed, such a transformation in the conceptualization of the nature of self and knowledge – or at least a creative adaptation of Kant's conceptualization – 'spread like wildfire in the first half of the nineteenth century', affecting every domain of intellectual and collective life, 'from science to literature' (Daston and Galison, 2010: 205). But it also allowed something else. The withdrawal of values from the world precipitated their own *transcendentalization*, rendering the presence of values the function of a faculty of judgement which would evaluate concrete experience on the basis of pre-existing universal principles of taste. On this account, 'beauty is not a property of the flower itself. For a judgement of taste consists precisely in this, that it calls a thing beautiful only by virtue of that characteristic in which it adapts itself to the way we apprehend it' (Kant 1987: 145). Which is to say, by virtue of the way in which the flower conforms to a general value vouchsafed by a transcendent power (Massumi, 2017).

It is this modern transcendentalization of values and of the nature of value that haunts not only contemporary notions of aesthetics but our very relations – in and out of the modern confines of the aesthetic realm – to values themselves: in science, where the value of 'truth' is said to depend upon the conformation of facts to pre-established methods of verification; in ethics, where the value of 'the good' is actualized not in the concrete configuration of a situation but in the principle of moral judgement which assesses it; in politics, where appeals to 'democratic values' – whatever they're meant to imply in any given circumstance – are mobilized as a means of certifying the legitimacy of a whole array of political acts; in political economy, where values are subsumed either into functions ('use-value') or into a rule of generalized equivalence ('exchange-value') which endows the market with the transcendent power to determine the way in which practices, things and forms of life must adapt themselves to the way it apprehends them; or in ecology, where earthly values are either judged on the basis of their extraction-value or according to a logic of 'rights' and the would-be universal conservation principles of balance, harmony or sustainability. Indeed, everywhere value 'is recomposed, as reified individuation, from Universals laid out according to an arborescent hierarchy' (Guattari, 1995: 104). Which is why it is no surprise that Guattari (1995: 104) would suggest that such a 'sectorisation and bipolarisation of values can be defined as capitalistic due to the neutralization, the systematic dequalification, of the materials of expression from which they proceed'.

The overwhelming character some of these general values have acquired in the apprehension of our time – infecting the imagination to such a degree that the possibility of appraising not only the value of other values but also another mode of appraising values themselves becomes staggeringly difficult to envisage – is no doubt a testament to that Nietzschean (1996) proposition, that we always have the values that we *deserve* given to our way of being or our style of living (see also Deleuze, 2006; see also Savransky, 2019, 2021c). Yet it is precisely in this sense, which is to say in the attempt to induce a process of metamorphosis of our manner of being and our ways of living on earth, that we may approach Guattari's (1995) proposition for what he came to call 'a new aesthetic paradigm'. As a call, in other words, to reactivate a notion of aesthetics no longer confined to its modern sphere of relevance, no longer limited to a restricted number of practices and objects or to a special kind of experience, but rather spreading over and infecting a radically expanded landscape of practices of creation and plural modes of existence. And if it is thus that one may approach this new aesthetic paradigm, it is because key to its novelty and potential is the attempt to think *aesthesis* in the presence of a multiple and radically fragmentary outside, of that which escapes the confines of the actual and the sectorization of divergent forms of value, of that which is outside the sovereignty of the subject, of the One and of the Whole, of that which remains improper and unnamed, unformed and indeterminate, unknown and impossible, under way and yet to be made. Hence Guattari's (1995: 92) proposition that such an aesthetics of the outside requires not a subjection of all values to yet another transcendental mode of evaluation but an 'ecology of the virtual', the speculative lure of the unformed and indeterminate whose power is not just 'to preserve the endangered species of cultural life but equally to engender conditions for the creation and development of unprecedented forms of subjectivity that have never been seen and never felt'.

An aesthetics of the outside is therefore nothing if not a speculative mode of sensation attuned to virtual ecologies, which is to say, to the *creation* of values and modes of evaluation that, 'far from being fearful of finitude – the trials of life, suffering, desire and death – embraces them like a spice essential to the cuisine of life' (Guattari, 1995: 90). In its flight after the unformed and indeterminate, the unknown and the impossible, it exposes the present to the insistent presence of a multifarious and fragmentary outside, whose intensification may not just challenge dominant values but burst within and 'recast the *axes* of values' – infecting and regenerating our collective imaginations so as to precipitate a revaluation of values (1995: 91). Indeed, at stake is nothing less than the wager on the chance to 'create new systems of valorisation, a new taste for life' (Guattari, 1995: 91). It goes without saying that no new taste for life will be created from transcendent values already subordinated to general principles, subsumed under the aegis of the judging subject. No new modes of valuation can be brought into existence unless we also dare affirm that values presuppose that which is valuable: that the beauty of the flower is owed *to the flower* and not merely to the subject who judges it. No aesthetics of the outside would be imaginable, in other words, unless we dare affirm that values are not what we appraise but what *makes us* appraise – sensible intensities that are indissociable from the heterogeneous multiplicity of singular ways existing, of living and of feeling that compose the earth (Savransky, 2019).

Experimenting with what Guattari called an ecology of the virtual therefore requires, in the first instance, the refusal to prolong the transcendentalization of universes of value that the socio-ecoaesthetic disaster of modernity engendered, so as to give oneself over to an experimental affirmation of the most radical immanence. William James (2003: 75) made this daring point earlier than most when, in his *Essays in Radical Empiricism,* he proposed that we 'discover beauty just as we discover the physical properties of things'. For it is not as a function of our awareness and attention that things are endowed with value, but rather the very value-intensities subtended in things, 'those very appreciative attributes of things, their dangerousness, beauty, rarity, utility, etc, that primarily *appeal* to our attention'. He goes on:

> In our commerce with nature these attributes are what give *emphasis* to objects; and for an object to be emphatic, whatever spiritual fact it may mean, means also that it produces immediate bodily effects upon us, alterations of tone and tension, of heartbeat and breathing, of vascular and visceral action. The 'interesting' aspects of things are thus not wholly inert physically, though they be active only in these small corners of physical nature which our bodies occupy. That, however, is enough to save them from being classed as absolutely non-objective. (James, 2003: 79)

Values, in other words, do not descend upon the world from the heights of sovereign judgement. Beings, bodies, environments – human and more – the socialites they improvise and the configurations they become capable of immanently uphold their own value-intensities. It is their concrete value-intensities that make an emphatic appeal to the attention, that renders them *interesting,* which is to say capable of inhabiting and stealing away in the interstices of being, the milieux of the between, infecting lives with their emphases, engendering variations in more-than-human sensoria, precipitating visceral metamorphoses.

When values are immanent, indissociable from the concrete forms of existence that subtend and express them, aesthetics becomes groundless, anarchic, without foundations, and so-called 'principles' become little more than 'such axioms as that a note sounds good with its third and fifth, or that potatoes need salt' (James, 1950: 672). For *aesthesis* itself no longer names the subjective faculty or act of perception but the impersonal event of sensation activated in the scintillation of heterogeneous values. Stepping out of the sovereign imperium that is constituted in the operation of judgement, this groundless aesthetics of immanence precipitates an ongoing and unfinished experimentation with heterogeneous value-intensities, improvised aesthetic configurations involving not sovereign ruin but the insistence of that which is outside both the sovereign and its ruination, something that is not in opposition but in apposition to it, which festers in its interstices and eludes its grasp. For to say that each manner of existing upholds concrete value-intensities through which it appeals to the manner of being of others is also to say that no being is, on its own, a master of its own values. To make, by virtue of one's own manner of being, an appeal to others is to be given over to an irreducible sociality of immanent values, to enter into an always unstable and precarious *value ecology* that connects habits and habitats, forms and regions of existence in such a way that each manner of being is altered by the intensities which insist and persist in the interstices, in the milieu of the between engendered in the ongoing and always unstable experiment of a shared life.

It is thus that we might come to a renewed understanding of what it means to say that we have the values we deserve according to our manner of being or our way of living. For what the ongoing socio-ecological disaster has engendered is the orchestration of a deleterious value ecology wrought through earth-wide processes of homogenization, commensuration, transcendentalization and systematization, which renders value-intensities subject to the general law of equivalence instituted in and by the modern mode of evaluation. Making visible what this anaesthetic disaster has rendered so many of us unable to sense is at the heart of many – but not all – contemporary 'aesthetic' responses to climate change.[2] The now obvious case in point concerns, of course, the totemic images of polar bears, which have become 'the key figure through which the entanglement of the loss and the flourishing of the biophysical world, and the politics of life and energy turn' (Yusoff, 2010: 75). But one could also point to a host of more generative endeavours which, like the Centre of PostNatural History in Pittsburgh, seek less iconic and more insidious ways of visualizing how histories of selective breeding, domestication and genetic engineering have given shape to a whole host of living organisms and their habitats – from the transgenic chestnut tree to the Biosteel™ Goat – thereby proffering sensible genealogical testaments to some of the ways in which modern modes of habitation have transformed the origins, habitats and evolution of forms of living, feeling and sensing on earth.

Amid the general devaluation of all values, arts concerned with making our transgenic companions as well as some of its victims present are not to be discounted. And yet, while potentially effective in rendering witnesses cognisant of the poisonous value ecologies that capitalism and modern technoscience have woven together, presumably such efforts at telling the history 'of the origins, habitats, and evolution of organisms that have been *intentionally* and *heritably* altered by humans' (Centre for PostNatural History, n.d.) also have to contend with the fact that the human witnesses' own manner of being itself belongs to the same history they are seeking to relate, not just as agents of practices of engineering and fossil-burning but also as one of the very 'postnatural' organisms such practices have forged (for example, D'Abramo and Landecker, 2019). What value-intensities are upheld in such re-presentations? What sort of appeal do they make? Can one bear witness to such histories without in so doing giving in to the temptation to try the judge's gown on? Can one sense them without either admiring the creative powers of a modern technoscience seemingly capable of giving birth to the paradox of a transgenic chestnut tree designed 'to proliferate in the wild', or mourning the loss of a bygone 'natural' world, when polar bears roamed the Arctic freely and goats remained genetically unrelated to spiders?[3] I do not know – even when one might suspect that the mere act of *representing* loss and restoration will not, by itself, render us worthy of different values. The 'nonhuman aesthetic charisma' of some of these representations may occasionally be a 'vital motivating energy that compels many people to get involved in biodiversity conservation' (Lorimer, 2007: 921). But, as is the case with representation more generally, they can also be deeply *reactive,* intensified by an entrenchment of values of sameness, such that 'organisms that are most dramatically other to us humans are unlikely to encounter us – given the alterity of their ecology – and when these encounters do occur they are less likely to engender sympathetic affections' (Lorimer, 2007: 921).

In any case, it is not a matter of knowing, of being able to judge, at a distance and in general, what sort of appeal such artistic representations might be capable of making on the very manner of being of those to whom they are addressed. What matters is that the test can no longer be the judgement of recognition, which is bound to reproduce the prevailing axes of value, but a more unsettling form of existential apprehension which involves the bursting in of the outside and which Guattari (1995: 92–3) called 'affective contamination': the way in which, by making an emphatic appeal to your own manner of being, to your own way of living, other value-intensities 'start to exist in you, in spite of you'. Which is to say that if we do have the values we deserve according to our manners of being and our ways of living, it cannot be simply a matter of thinking or representing our way into another way of living, but rather one of becoming implicated in the much riskier and groundless task of groping, experimentally, with practices of affective contamination capable of bursting in our midst and transforming our lives into other modes of thinking, of sensing, of evaluating the value of values. At stake, in other words, is the 'thunderous refusal of the plausible: the outside in its becoming, which is that of bursting' (Blanchot, 1995: 124).

Aesthetic machines and the arts of existence

Hence the speculative aim of an aesthetics of the outside in its thunderous refusal of the plausible and the probable: to relinquish the judgement of taste so as to engender a new taste for life. To step outside so as to elaborate from the interstices and outlaw edges of the modern confines, conditions for the creation and improvisation of runaway value-intensities, of events of aesthesis that might upend the prevailing axes of value, affectively contaminating them so as to make exist, inside and in spite of the socio-ecological disaster we inhabit while we still can, values yet to be intensified, a sense of the unthought, a feel for the unformed, the glimmers of another ensemble of existences yet to be composed. Here, aesthetic judgement is done away with twice over: first, through the profusion of immanent values, always situated and never general enough to allow for the descent of judgement; and second, because no judgement can apprehend the new and runaway values that have begun to contaminate a concrete manner of being, the revaluations this contamination precipitates, or the ways of living and manners of being otherwise that such revaluations might be capable of engendering. 'What expert judgement, in art, could ever bear on the work to come?' (Deleuze, 1997: 135). Indeed, in seeking experimentally to intensify runaway values so as to recast the axes of value and engender a new taste for life, it is not only the nature of values, or the concept of 'aesthetics', that undergoes a profound metamorphosis lured by the insistent possibility of inhabiting the earth otherwise.

So too does whatever we may (come to) mean by 'art'. For when aesthetics no longer names a special kind of experience, a well-demarcated universe of value, but belongs to the process of rendering value-intensities sensible, what we call 'art' can no longer be contained within the established contours of the realm of the 'fine' arts, which in no way guarantees that such metamorphic processes might come about. Above all, it is most certainly not a matter of renewing the compulsions of what T.J. Demos (2020: 15) calls an 'ecocritical art history', which tirelessly turns this long anaesthetic event into an object of aesthetisization, 'into a thematic concern (often celebrating exclusively nonhuman realms), picturing and materialising ecology and thereby containing its radical relationality within the artistic frame'. Whatever the contemporary pontifications of critics, art 'does not', Guattari (1995: 106) suggested, 'have a monopoly on creation', yet it can take 'its capacity to invent mutant coordinates to extremes', thereby engendering 'unprecedented, unforeseen and unthinkable qualities of being'. It is not a matter of opposing art confined, art spectated, art exhibited. It is a matter once again of experimenting with the possibility of giving oneself over to another art of sense and sensation. In other words, it is a question of affirming that art need not be 'fine', for what it here comes to designate, what it begins to name, is the improvisational assembling of 'aesthetic machines' capable of 'extracting full meaning from all the empty signal systems that invest us from every side' (Guattari, 1995: 90). Outside the gallery and the biennale, in their interstices and margins, aesthetic machines are unleashed in what are multiple and divergent ensembles, ongoing and unfinished experiments. These appraise value-intensities otherwise so as to give way to the reassembling of forms and regions of existence in a new event of *aesthesis* that renews the experiments' own 'materials of expression and the ontological texture of the percepts and affects it promotes', and does so in order to bring about, 'if not a direct contamination of other domains then at least a highlighting and re-evaluation of the creative dimensions that traverse all of them' (Guattari, 1995: 106).

Aesthetic machines are assembled and unleashed in the outlaw edges, in that space out-on-the-outside of risky improvisations with sociality in spite of the ongoing collapse. They take and make place, just for example, in the forests of Notre-Dame-des-Landes, where local farmers and a host of activists have opposed the construction, planned since the 1960s, of an airport by the multinational corporation Vinci, an enormous development project that would have evicted the former from their homes and devastated the land that provided a habitat in which humans, ewes, cows, goats, sheep and myriad other creatures elaborated a shared life. And they opposed it by occupying and reinhabiting the space, fighting against capitalist and State forces while experimenting with autonomous forms of life, cultivating vegetable plots, setting up a brewery, a pirate radio station and a bakery to make bread from locally grown grains, as well as engaging in new herding and agricultural practices, learning the powers of medicinal plants and participating in spiritual rituals.[4] Indeed, this *zone à défendre* (ZAD), as it has become known, was not only a case of autonomist resistance, an experiment in reclaiming the commons against the extractive powers of capitalism. Resisting the airport *and its world,* the ZAD also involved the creation of new and unexpected collective valuations: of what it means to live well in an autonomous space, whether and how to negotiate with the State, as well as collective questions and negotiations concerning how to live, eat and die with others – humans and more, vegans and carnivores – amid the plurality of value-intensities that divergent manners of being and multifarious political sensibilities bring into play when making earth in common is at stake (Vidalou, 2017; Glowczewski, 2019).

Other (cosmo)aesthetic machines have been unleashed in the region of Tohoku, in northeastern Japan, when in the wake of the catastrophic tsunami that in 2011 devastated the area, killed tens of thousands of people and left hundreds of thousands without a home, a collective of priests of the Buddhist, Shinto and Protestant faiths found themselves eschewing theological principles in order to experiment pragmatically with ways of responding to the profusion of ghosts that began to populate the area. The priests set up a mobile café that they called *Café de Monk*, playing on different senses of the word: 'Monku' is the Japanese word for 'complaint'; 'monk' is also the English term for priest; and it was the improvisational jazz of Thelonious Monk that accompanied their practices. The *Café de Monk* would travel around the devastated area, providing a space for survivors to gather together around some tea and cakes, to remember the dead and to share their stories. What is more, the collective of priests would also proffer a number of spiritual practices, from massages to sutras and hymns, devoted to addressing especially tricky cases of spirit possession and suffering. By trusting the possibility of threading the story of the disaster otherwise, they learned not only how to inspire a new taste for life among those who survived but also how to take care of the dead who had lost their living to the wave and whose well-being in the afterlife depended entirely on the care that their living families took of them (Savransky, 2021b, 2022).

And yet other (agro)aesthetic machines are assembled in Battir, where the Palestine Heirloom Seed Library (PHSL) sets out to reactivate and heal, share and sow Palestinian seeds and the forms of life which they gather together and to which they give rise, against the backdrop of the sinister partnership between the eroding effects of climate change and the Israeli occupation, appropriation and interiorization of the land and soil. Assembled as an 'interactive art and agriculture project', the PHSL seeks to gather stories and forms of life 'that may have been buried away' and are 'waiting to sprout like a seed', thereby not only healing devastated lands and lives but enabling the value-intensities of seeds to begin to exist in us as 'subversive rebels' capable of 'travelling across borders and checkpoints to defy the violence of the landscape while reclaiming life and presence'.[5] It is the activation of speculative forms of more-than-human presence outside the horrors and aesthetic disasters of the occupation that this agroaesthetic machine precipitates what it makes burst within. For unlike the Svalbard Global Seed Vault, the Millennium Seed Bank or various other government-backed seed *banks* which store seeds as reserves for a probably future world that might vitally need them but which for the same reason might be unable to carry them, this seed *library* is subtended not in the promise of a world to come but in the new taste for life which is sown and grown in the sociality of heterogeneous practices, stories and foods, in a debt to ancestral biocultures and knowledges which is shared rather than paid, reactivated rather than reclaimed. Indeed, at stake in this experiment is nothing less than an attempt to revaluate the value of collective existence subtended in defiance and persistence – one no longer defined by the ongoing socio-ecoaesthetic disaster of settler colonialism, with which it must nevertheless contend, or overshadowed by the melancholic yearning for a severed past that may never return, but marked instead by the aesthetic gesture of appraising life otherwise inside and, in spite of the ongoing devastation, precipitating a mode of evaluation capable of contaminating and upending ecological assemblages built through colonial settlement, international development and extractive capital (see Meneley, 2021).

Contending with and bursting within the depleted environments, bodies, practices and values that the sociological disaster has left in its wake, these and other experiments found neither alternative societies, post-capitalist economies nor balanced and harmonious ecologies. Neither do they set the general foundations for an ecological aesthetics or an ecological civilization that might come to save, restore or replace the devastation that surrounds and permeates multiple worlds in this world (Savransky, 2022). Echoes of the swan song keep reverberating, resounding through the rustle of the forest, whispered in the voices of those who have been lost, sensed in the difficult liveliness of seeds, bodies and stories of occupied and eroded soils. And yet, springing from their specific histories and situations, they each make an emphatic appeal to certain manners of being, to certain forms of living, cultivating runaway value-intensities that begin to radiate inside and in spite of the ravage. These and other experiments therefore constitute a challenge to established values precisely insofar as they contaminate and recast the axes of value, giving way to divergent value ecologies where habits and habitats are assembled otherwise. In this sense, these experiments are nothing if not *artful*. For rather than celebrate 'life' or resent 'death', rather than issue a judgement on their lives, on their worlds, on the reasons that make their lives and worlds be what they are, these experiments confer upon their own divergent ways of living otherwise the power to posit their own values, to appraise themselves through the ecologies that their aesthetic machines precipitate and throw up. Which is to say that, when it is precisely our ways of living on this planet that are in question, it is the very cultivation of other manners of being, of ways living and dying otherwise, that become *an art*: the art of engendering unprecedented, unforeseen and unthinkable qualities of being while groping collectively, immanently, with the question of how to live and die well with others inside and despite the ongoing devastation. Such aesthetic machines and the experiments to which they give rise testify, in other words, to the activation of multiple and divergent *arts of existence* in direct connection with an immanent but inappropriable outside. The arts, in other words, of giving yourself over to that which starts to exist in you, in spite of you.

Notes

1. For an in-depth discussion of the invention of modern aesthetics from the perspective of Whitehead's protest against the bifurcation of nature, see Sehgal (2018).
2. This in no way means that this is all that aesthetic or artistic responses to the ecological catastrophe amount to. For some generative experiments and projects, see Cevernack (2021) and Demos (2020).
3. Biosteel™ Goats are genetically modified to produce the protein from Golden Orb Weaver Spider (*Nephila clavipes*) silk in their milk, thereby turning them into 'biofactories' for the production of pharmaceuticals.
4. For information on the ZAD, see their blog www.zadforever.blog.
5. For a description of this project by its founder and spokesperson, Vivien Sansour, see https://viviensansour.com/Palestine-Heirloom.

References

Aesop (1998) *The Complete Fables*, New York: Penguin.
Baumgarten, A. (2013) *Metaphysics: A Critical Translation with Kant's Elucidations, Selected Notes, and Related Materials*, trans C.D. Fugate and J. Hymers, London: Bloomsbury.
Blanchot, M. (1995) *The Writing of the Disaster*, trans A. Smock, Lincoln, NB: Nebraska University Press.
Centre for PostNatural History (n.d.) About, https://www.postnatural.org/About (Accessed 10 November 2023).
Césaire, A. (2013) *Return to My Native Land*, Brooklyn, NY: Archipelago Books.
Cevernak, S.J. (2021) *Black Gathering: Art, Ecology, Ungiven Life*, Durham, NC and London: Duke University Press.
Da Vinci, L. (2006) *The Complete Works*, trans C. Frost. Newton Abbot: David & Charles Ltd.
D'Abramo, F. and Landecker, H. (2019) 'Anthropocene in the Cell', *Technosphere Magazine*. https://technosphere-magazine.hkw.de/p/Anthropocene-in-the-Cell-fQjoLLgrE7jbXzLYr1TLNn (Accessed 10 November 2023).
Daston, L. and Galison, P. (2010) *Objectivity*, Brooklyn, NY: Zone Books.
Deleuze, G. (1997) *Essays Critical and Clinical*, trans D.W. Smith and M.A. Greco, Minneapolis, MN: University of Minnesota Press.
Demos, T.J. (2020) *Beyond the World's End: Arts of Living at the Crossing*, Durham, NC and London: Duke University Press.
Glowczewski, B. (2019) 'Se soigner en soignant la terre', *Multitudes*, 77: 161–7.

Guattari, F. (1995) *Chaosmosis: An Ethico-Aesthetic Paradigm*, trans P. Bains and J. Pefanis, Bloomington, IN: Indiana University Press.

Guattari, F. (2005) *The Three Ecologies*, trans I. Pindar and P. Sutton, London: Continuum.

James, W. (1950) *The Principles of Psychology*, Vol 1, Mineola, MN: Dover Publications.

James, W. (2003) *Essays in Radical Empiricism*, Mineola, MN: Dover Publications.

Kant, I. (1987) *Critique of Judgement*, trans W.S. Pluhar, Indianapolis, IN and Cambridge: Hackett Publishing.

Lorimer, J. (2007) 'NonHuman charisma', *Environment and Planning D: Society and Space* 25(5): 911–32.

Massumi, B. (2017) 'Virtual ecology and the question of value', in E. Hörl and J. Burton (eds), *General Ecology: The New Ecological Paradigm*, London: Bloomsbury.

Meneley, A. (2021) 'Hope in the ruins: Seeds, plants, and possibilities of regeneration', *Environment and Planning E: Nature and Space*, 4(1): 158–72.

Mirzoeff, N. (2014) 'Visualizing the Anthropocene', *Public Culture*, 26(2): 213–32.

Nietzsche, F. (1996) *On the Genealogy of Morals*, trans. D. Smith, Oxford: Oxford University Press.

Savransky, M. (2019) 'The bat revolt in values: A parable for living in academic ruins', *Social Text*, 37(2): 135–46.

Savransky, M. (2021a) 'Counter-apocalyptic beginnings: Cosmoecology for the end of the world', *Tapuya: Latin American Science, Technology & Society*, 4(1). https://doi.org/10.1080/25729861.2021.1914423

Savransky, M. (2021b) 'After progress: Notes for an ecology of perhaps', *Ephemera: Theory & Politics in Organisation*, 21(1): 267–81.

Savransky, M. (2021c) *Around the Day in Eighty Worlds: Politics of the Pluriverse*, Durham, NC and London: Duke University Press.

Savransky, M. (2022) 'The cosmoecological workshop: Or, how to philosophise with a hammer', in D. Papadopoulos, M. Puig de la Bellacasa, and M. Tachetti (eds), *Ecological Reparation: Repair, Reparation and Resurgence in Social and Environmental Conflict*, Bristol: Bristol University Press.

Sehgal, M. (2018) 'Aesthetic concerns, philosophical fabulations: The importance of a new aesthetic paradigm', *SubStance*, 47(1): 112–29.

Vidalou, J.-B. (2017) *Être forêts*, Paris: La Découverte.

Whitehead, A.N. (2004) *The Concept of Nature*, Mineola, MN: Dover Publications.

Yusoff, K. (2010) 'Biopolitical economies and the political aesthetics of climate change', *Theory, Culture & Society*, 27(2–3): 73–99.

7

Variations on the Great Refusal via Dante and Whitehead

Cécile Malaspina

For some people there's a day
when they have to come out with the great Yes
or the great No. It's clear at once
who has the Yes ready in him; and saying it,
he goes on to find honor, strong in his conviction.
He who refuses never repents. Asked again,
he'd still say no. Yet that no – the right answer –
defeats him the whole of his life.

C.P. Cavafy, *Che Fece ... Il Gran Rifiuto* (1972)

The ambivalence of the great refusal

In the third canto of Dante's *Inferno*, Virgil leads the poet into the antechamber to hell. 'What are these noises I hear?' he asks Virgil. It is the 'repulsive choir', answers Virgil, of the angels who remained undecided in neutrality when Lucifer turned against God, and the sad souls who lived a life but lived it with no blame and with no praise. Dante then sees the shadow of 'the coward who made the great refusal' (Dante, 1997 [1472], Canto III, verse 50). The nameless figure has long been associated with pope Celestine V, whose abdication precipitated a political calamity as well as Dante's exile and destitution. The trope of the great refusal thereby enters the canon of Western literature as a searing indictment of the cowardice of those who live a life without blame and without praise, and whose greatness lies only in the historic consequences of their pusillanimity. The contemporary relevance of the great refusal could hardly be overstated in light of the widespread refusal to acknowledge the catastrophes wrought by anthropogenic global warming while the horizon of a liveable future collapses. As seasonal records of temperature, fires and floodings are broken, the rich and powerful, together with the middle classes, seem to prefer a life with no blame and with no praise.

However, the aesthetic achievement of Dante's *Divine Comedy* pivots on the inward contemplation of this cowardliness (*viltade*), which Dante first ascribes to his fictional self, as a 'nullifying unease' that voids his undertaking of journeying through hell and heaven, and which one may interpret as the doubt befalling the exiled poet upon embarking on the writing of the *Divine Comedy*, 'like one who unchooses his own choice and thinking again undoes what he has started' (Dante, 1997 [1472], Canto II, verses 25–28).

This chapter will unfold some of the resonances between the aesthetic achievement that resonates through Dante's great refusal and the revival of this phrase by the early 20th-century philosopher Alfred North Whitehead. (Whitehead, 1948; Stengers, 2011). The latter uses it to shine an unforgiving light on the 'prosperous middle classes ... who placed an excessive value upon placidity of existence [refusing] to face the necessities for social [and] for intellectual reform' in his 1925 Lowell lectures, later published as *Science and the Modern World* (1948: 208). However, just as the fictional Dante overcomes his cowardliness to write the *Divine Comedy* by refusing the cowardly refusal, so does Whitehead turn the refusal on its heels, such that it flips from the 'great refusal of rationality to assert its rights' to becoming the primary characteristic of the 'vital truth' of an aesthetic achievement (1948: 94). The great refusal thus becomes the hallmark of the philosopher and of the artist's audacity.

The great refusal is now mostly known through Herbert Marcuse's (1966) *Eros and Civilization* as a rallying cry for principled opposition to injustice and repression. Leaving the detailed analysis of Marcuse's *Eros and Civilization* to another occasion, my attention will be tuned to the elucidation of Marcuse's enigmatic quotation of Whitehead and on the difference, which is lost in Marcuse's quotation, between the refusal as cowardice and as audacity. This difference, I will argue with recourse to Dante, rests on the torment of self-doubt. Only if we insist on this moment of utmost anxiety and indecision can we truly grasp the tipping point by which the great refusal can either be the stigma of self-serving cowardice or the mark of distinction of aesthetic achievement. To underline the crucial importance of this pivoting moment and its contemporary socio-political ramifications, I will accentuate Dante's refusal in light of Mark Fisher's article 'Good for nothing' (Fisher, 2014). Making the ambivalence of the refusal at once personal, aesthetic and political, I will then proceed to analyse it in terms of the difficulty to commit to a 'vital truth' that becomes the vector of emancipation. At stake, however, is not an emancipation of feeling from reason but one that insists that reason must recover its aesthetic dimension. The contemporary relevance of this emancipation must be read against the wider metaphysical adventure that starts with the refusal, to say it with Isabelle Stengers (2011: 41), 'to make nature bifurcate between percepts, on the one hand, and a reality that is essentially spatio-temporal and functional on the other'.

'Abandon all hope, you who enter here': from Dante to Mark Fisher

These words are inscribed in a dark colour over the portal leading into the antechamber to hell in Dante's *Divine Comedy*.[1] 'The sighs, groans and laments at first were so loud, resounding through starless air, I began to weep' cries Dante, asking his guide, Virgil: 'what is this I hear?' To which Virgil replies, 'This is the sorrowful state of souls unsure, whose lives earned neither honour nor bad fame. And they are mingled with angels ... who, neither rebellious to God nor faithful to Him, chose neither side, but kept themselves apart – now heaven expels them, not to mar its splendour, and hell rejects them, lest the wicked of heart take glory over them' (Dante, 1997 [1472], Canto III, verses 19–42).

Hurrying after the whirling banner of conformity, they form 'a train of souls, so long that I would not have thought Death had undone so many' (Dante, 1997 [1472], Canto III, verses 40–8). It is among this 'dreary guild repellent both to God and His enemies' that Dante 'saw and recognized the shadow of the coward who made the Great Refusal' [*vidi e conobbi l'ombra di colui che fece per viltade il gran rifiuto*] (Dante, 1997 [1472], Canto III, verse 50/60).[2] The shade of the great refusal is a figure deliberately left unnamed. There is no great deed to remember. The one who made the great refusal is condemned to oblivion: 'To all memory of them, the world is deaf' (Dante, 1997 [1472], Canto II, verse 43). Interpreters have nevertheless sought to associate the 'shadow of the great refusal' with Pope Celestine V, a Benedictine hermit elected pope in 1294, who served for only five months before abdicating to return to a placid life of prayer. In this line of interpretation, Celestine's excessive humility inadvertently catalyses the unprecedented political power of the church amassed by his successor, Boniface VIII, as well determining Dante's personal destitution and forced exile.[3]

However, the shadow in the vestibule to hell remains purposely unidentified by Dante. In fact, he directly ascribes the invective of *viltà* to only one other figure in the *Divine Comedy*, and this is none other than his fictional self in the first canto, where he invites the reader onto a journey through hell with this searing and universally relatable acknowledgement of our fallibility: 'Midway on our life's journey, I found myself in dark woods, the right road lost' (Dante, 1997 [1472], Canto I, verse 1–2). Dante's path out of the thicket and towards the hill crest is blocked by the allegorical figures of the leopard, the lion and the haggard wolf, (symbolizing desire, pride and avarice). The 'grim she-wolf ... put such heaviness into my spirit, I lost hope of the crest. Like someone eager to win, who tested by loss surrenders to gloom and weeps, so did that beast ... force me back toward where the sun is lost' (Dante, 1997 [1472], Canto I, verses 38–45).

This evocation of the wolf coincides with the appearance of Virgil, who offers to guide Dante through hell and heaven. However, as soon as the second canto, Dante is overcome by self-doubt. A 'nullifying unease' now voids the undertaking, 'like one who unchooses his own choice and thinking again undoes what he has started'. Who am I to undertake this journey? Dante asks himself. 'I am no Aeneas or Paul: not I nor others think me of such worth, and therefore I have my fears of playing the fool to embark on such a venture' (Dante, 1997 [1472], Canto II, verses 25–8). Virgil compares Dante to a child mistaking a shadow for a beast. It is this most common illusion that may so easily 'twist a man away from the noblest enterprise' (Dante, 1997 [1472], Canto II, verses 37–9). And once more, after Virgil has beseeched Dante, with the help of Beatrice, he asks, 'Why, why stay, why is your heart by so much cowardice swayed, where is your ardour and candour?' [*perché, perché restai, perché tanta viltà nel core allette, perché ardire e franchezza non hai?*] (Dante, 1997 [1472], Canto II, verses 98–9, 121–3, my emphasis).[4]

May we infer that it is not plain cowardice or selfishness that Dante resented in the abdicating hermit pope, but rather his surrendering to the torment of excessive humility and his concession to those who, like Boniface, feel entitled to rule? By beginning his *Divine Comedy* with the dramatization of his own *viltade,* Dante points to a truth that is difficult to acknowledge, not only because it touches our own pusillanimity but also because it does not offer a heroic individual as an alternative: so heart drenching is his own self-doubt that it can only be overcome with the help of Virgil and Beatrice. That is, the inner torment that makes those shirk who don't feel entitled can only be overcome collectively. To bring this back to the critical junction at which our own historical moment places us with regards to the climate crisis, it is not enough to point the finger at the cowards and the greedy.

What weight must we accord to what Mark Fisher so aptly called the 'sneering "inner" voice' that turns us into 'a shirker', described in his article 'Good for nothing' (Fisher, 2014)? In Fisher's analysis this voice makes those afflicted by it concede their place to 'the calm confidence of one born to the role'. What Fisher's text attunes us to, when read in light of Dante's refusal, is the magnitude of historical consequences that comes from the surrender to self-doubt by those who thereby concede the space of decision to the entitled.

Mark Fisher brings a Marxist perspective to Dante's acknowledgement of a collective rather than individual emancipation. Far from the intimacy of an inner voice, the sneering self-doubt is but 'the internalised expression of actual social forces', afflicting anyone who belongs to an oppressed group, such that they will feel that they are 'not the kind of person who can fulfil roles which are earmarked for the dominant group'. Those who dare are in fact in danger of 'being overcome by feelings of vertigo, panic and horror', and, quoting Smail's *The Origins of Unhappiness*, of being 'isolated, cut off, surrounded by hostile space, [you are] suddenly without connections, without stability, with nothing to hold you upright or in place': 'a dizzying, sickening unreality takes possession of you; you are threatened by a complete loss of identity, a sense of utter fraudulence; you have no right to be here, now, inhabiting this body, dressed in this way; you are a nothing, and "nothing" is quite literally what you feel you are about to become' (Smail, 1993, in Fisher, 2014).

Fisher argues, with Smail, that there is a flipside of this structural form of depression, namely a form of magical voluntarism, 'the belief that it is within every individual's power to make themselves whatever they want to be'. This voluntarism may indeed inform possible misreadings of Dante's refusal, namely that it is enough not to be a selfish coward: the moralizing lesson that we will become a shadow of ourselves if we do not stand up valiantly. Dante, the historical figure, embarks on writing the *Divine Comedy* with the trepidation of one who is expropriated and exiled and who in this moment of utmost vulnerability is about to tell the most powerful men of his time to go to hell. Each step that his fictional self takes in his traversal of hell corresponds to a page written by the historical Dante in the excruciating circumstances of exile and destitution. The legacy of the *Divine Comedy* is its existence despite Dante's witheringly dramatized self-doubt: the very act of writing the *Divine Comedy* is testament to the virtue of overcoming his *viltade* ('*who am I to ...*'). However, the fictional poet's reliance on the figures of Virgil and Beatrice, and of powerful protectors in real life, also invalidates the interpretation of a 'magical voluntarism', which we must instead unmask, with Fisher, as a foundational lie of contemporary capitalist society.

I would like to argue that the refusing to succumb to self-doubt is great because it is a collective virtue that opens onto the emancipatory refusal of oppression we find in Marcuse: it is the collective refusal to succumb to the lure of abdication, or the refusal of the refusal. It is the purpose of the next section to elucidate Marcuse's reference to Alfred North Whitehead, and therefore to open a novel perspective on Dante's twofold refusal, one that is of vital importance for the recovery of a speculative horizon; in other words, for the recovery of our future from the purported absence of an alternative to the capitalist principle of reality.

Whitehead: from *viltade* to virtue

It is in *Science and the Modern World* that we find Whitehead's expression 'the great refusal', which Hebert Marcuse will bring to greater fame in

Eros and Civilization, from where it will radiate throughout 20th- and 21st-century grassroots movements of emancipation.[5] However, this formulation of the great refusal, which Marcuse takes from Whitehead, remains at first forbiddingly enigmatic. At stake is: 'the truth that some proposition respecting an actual occasion is untrue may express the vital truth as to the aesthetic achievement. It expresses the "great refusal" which is its primary characteristic' (Whitehead, 1948: 150, in Marcuse, 1966: 149). Marcuse interprets Whitehead's words through a Freudian lens: the great refusal must be understood as the refusal to resign oneself to separation from the libidinous object (or subject). Marcuse potentiates Whitehead's as-yet enigmatic refusal with another quotation, by placing it alongside a citation of the surrealist André Breton, who refuses to 'forget what can be'.[6] He thereby seeks to rehabilitate the role of the imagination in what becomes the refusal of the limits imposed by the Freudian reality principle: 'in its refusal to forget what can be, lies the critical function of phantasy' (Marcuse, 1966: 149). The imagination becomes a firewall against the Freudian reality principle, whose logic relies on the repressive function of reason.

Much remains to be said of Marcuse's emancipatory aesthetics, but the focus of the remaining argument will be limited to Whitehead's defence of the imagination, precisely not against the repressive function of reason, but against the repression of reason's exertion of its full rights. The full exercise of what by right belongs to reason, for Whitehead — and by extension his reality principle — stands not opposed to the aesthetic dimension but relies on it. This key nuance, differentiating Whitehead from Marcuse in a critical point, will allow me to insist on the emancipatory potential of rationality, which Marcuse seems at times to reduce to the repressive aspect of the Freudian reality principle, and never more so than when 'technological' rationality in particular becomes responsible for the 'mental and behaviorist pattern for productive performance' and the drive to attain 'power over nature' (Marcuse, 1966: 86).

Focussing on the pivoting moment between the two ambivalent uses of the idea of the refusal in Whitehead, which seems lost in Marcuse, will allow us to elucidate the place that Whitehead attributes to the imagination in speculative philosophy, not as anathema to rationality but as a condition *sine qua non* of its emancipation from what he calls 'intolerant abstraction'. This emancipation of reason is crucial to the observation, fleetingly mentioned by Marcuse (1966: 72), that 'the progressive ideas of rationalism can be recaptured only when they are reformulated'. Focussing on the role of the refusal in Whitehead's speculative philosophy will also allow us to foreground a complex and nuanced function of negativity in reason, one that ultimately contradicts Marcuse's (1966: 102) critique of 'the negativity of reason' and, if anything, brings us closer to Adorno's *Negative Dialectics*.[7]

Our first task is to map the ways in which Whitehead uses the expression 'the great refusal', first designating a form of denial that is very much in keeping with Dante's derogative connotation, and later, in a rather contrary sense, as affirming a vital truth. I will refer to these as refusal I and refusal II. The pivoting from the first to second meaning of the refusal presents us with the problem of an implicit double negation: the virtuous refusal of the cowardly refusal, or to make it more explicit, the refusal of the refusal. However, reading Whitehead closely will help us precisely to avoid the trap of a double negation, if we think of this as a *not not ...* , issuing in a simple affirmation. At stake is precisely the constitutive role that Whitehead reserves for negativity in his speculative philosophy. In Whitehead's speculative aesthetics, the (second) refusal in fact expresses a negativity that is both necessary and significant, affording actions their full importance as situated in a halo of alternatives whose non-actualization is relevant to the event. Closer inspection will allow us to think of the great refusal as being traversed by a fault line. This fault line *runs through negation itself rather than opposing negation to affirmation*. It is a fault line that runs through the fabric of reason: rather than opposing reason to the imagination, as Marcuse appears at times to do, this fault line in Whitehead's thought divides the imaginative use of reason from intolerant abstraction. What distinguishes both is the precise role given to negation. Attention to this set of nuances will enable us to critically reload Marcuse through a close reading of Whitehead in such a way as to eschew the opposition between reason and the imagination. As a contemporary corollary, we may also eschew what, in today's reality principle, anaesthetizes us to the climate crisis: that is, the bifurcation of nature into substance and qualities according to a truncated exercise of reason (Whitehead, 1948: 53).

The removal of perplexity: the great refusal I

Whitehead's first reference to the great refusal in *Science and the Modern World* could hardly be more at odds with Marcuse. The great refusal here refers, as Dante did, to a small-mindedness (you could call it an intellectual *viltade*), the precipitation towards summary answers when confronted with perplexity:

> What is the status of the enduring stability of the order of nature? There is the summary answer, which refers nature to some greater reality standing behind it. This reality occurs in the history of thought under many names, The Absolute, Brahma, The Order of Heaven, God. [...] My point is that any summary conclusion jumping [...] to the easy assumption that there is an ultimate reality which, in some unexplained way, is to be appealed to for the removal of perplexity, constitutes the great refusal of rationality to assert its rights. (Whitehead, 1948: 94)

Isabelle Stengers further elucidates this refusal as the avoidance of a difficulty that follows from the framing of a problem. This avoidance takes the form of a submission to the unknowable which, she insists (2011: 145), 'is just as unacceptable for Whitehead as the theory of "psychic additions", it corresponds to "rationality's great refusal to insist on its rights."' The notion of psychic additions here refers to what Whitehead calls the 'bifurcation of nature,' whereby modern science splits reality into, on the one hand, primary qualities, like solidity, extension, and motion, and, on the other hand, *qualia*, or secondary qualities, like the colour green or the smell of a rose, which are attributed to the mind alone.

However, it is not only the mystical evaporations of uncritical thought that Whitehead subsumes under this refusal to grant reason its full rights. His critique encompasses, in equal measure, the 'intolerant use of abstraction' in modern science, which egregiously confines knowledge to 'certain types of facts, abstracted from the complete circumstances in which they occur' (1948: 18). Modern science is in this respect not unlike like theological dogmatism, as it doubles down on the ultimate ideas of a 'fixed scientific cosmology', like that of 'an irreducible brute matter, or material' that is 'spread throughout space in a flux of configurations' but is in itself 'senseless, valueless, purposeless' (1948: 18). The refusal here defines an obstinacy that, according to Whitehead, illegitimately curtails the full spectrum of scientific reason to sterile abstractions that forego the 'more subtle employment of our senses'. This refusal corresponds to the abdication of reason's audacity in its ultimate 'request for meanings and for coherence of thoughts':

> The success of their ultimate ideas confirmed scientists in their refusal to modify them as the result of an enquiry into their rationality. Every philosophy was bound in some way or other to swallow them whole. [...] Thought is abstract; and the intolerant use of abstractions is the major vice of the intellect. (Whitehead, 1948: 19)

Victim of its own success, modern science gives way to an intolerant use of abstractions in appealing to the unquestionable ultimate ideas and established facts. Just like the dogmatic appeal to an ultimate principle – be it God or matter – the appeal to established facts merely serves 'the removal of perplexity'. It offends 'the self-respect of the intellect' which commands it 'to pursue every tangle of thought to its final unravelment' (Whitehead, 1948: 185).

However, it is not only the sensitivity of the poet which is offended by an intolerant abstraction that reduces matter to senseless, valueless extension, but also that of Whitehead, the formidable mathematician and logician who stands at the cusp of the paradigmatic recasting of geometry and physics.

Empiricism, Whitehead notes, first arises as an intellectual emancipation from the labyrinthine speculations of scholastic rationalism, but Newton '[o]f all people in the world' succumbs to an 'unimaginative empiricism' when he dismisses Huyghen's wave theory, preferring to confine himself to the intuitive solution that best suits the observation of rectilinear rays of shadows cast by obstructing objects (Whitehead, 1948: 48). Newton's insistence on the corpuscular theory of light ultimately confines empiricism, which had first emancipated us from dogma and scholastic sterility, to its own dogma. Empiricism thus becomes guilty, in the eyes of Whitehead, of putting an arbitrary stop to inquisitive reason – and nowhere more scandalously so than in the reductive materialism of John Stuart Mill, who inadvertently puts reason in a straitjacket of mechanical necessity:

> It is obvious that [Mill's] doctrine affords no escape from the dilemma presented by thoroughgoing mechanism. [...] Mill's doctrine is generally accepted, especially among scientists, as though in some way it allowed you to accept the extreme doctrine of materialistic mechanism, and yet mitigated its unbelievable consequences. It does nothing of the sort. Either the molecules blindly run, or they do not. If they blindly run, the mental states are irrelevant in discussing bodily actions. (Whitehead, 1948: 79)

To cast a more understanding light on what Whitehead calls Newton's unimaginative empiricism, we could evoke Dante's own trepidations to entertain a possibility because it seems foolish in light of established facts. To this apparent foolishness Whitehead objects the historical evidence that shows that 'almost all really new ideas have a certain aspect of foolishness when they are first produced' (Whitehead, 1948: 49). The refusal to engage with the demands of reason that at first appear foolish eventually leads to 'the dullest stages of thought since the time of the First Crusade' culminating in the last decades of the 19th century, in a period dominated by the 'efficient, dull, and half-hearted' celebrating 'the triumph of the professional man' (1948: 103).

Negativity in its own right: the great refusal II

This is where Whitehead (1948: 9) introduces the aesthetic dimension of a fully emancipated use of reason, referring first to the Romantic poets, who experience a 'moral repulsion' at intolerant abstraction because what it leaves out 'comprises everything that is most important to the poetic rendering of concrete experience'. Whitehead (1948: 87) will now perform a volte-face concerning the great refusal. Now siding with Wordsworth and Shelley to foreground the 'intuitive refusal seriously to accept the abstract materialism of science', he invests it with the emancipatory ethos we later find in Marcuse.

At first, this about turn may suggest a refusal of scientific rationality, such as one may attribute to Marcuse when he casts rationality in the role of the executioner of Freud's repressive reality principle. Upon closer inspection, however, we discover a motivation that aims not at an aesthetic irrationalism but at the emancipation of reason through aesthetics. It will become apparent that this volte-face, this refusal of the great refusal, does not amount to a Romantic refusal of scientific rationality. Nor can it ultimately be reduced to the logic of a double negation if we take this to issue in a straightforward affirmation. As we will see, this second refusal now encompasses a hitherto ignored halo of possibilities, irreducible to established facts, and that is nevertheless both fully within the realm of reason and of the event. In fact, without it, the event would be devoid of both value and signification. The second great refusal thus does imply an affirmation: the affirmation of value. In this respect it certainly goes beyond modern science, if we accept that modern science corresponds to a narrow view of what is given in actuality, thereby excluding large swathes of reality, notably the realm of aesthetic value. Nevertheless, this emancipatory refusal hinges on a negativity that is not resorbed by the affirmation of value. It is this persistence of negativity that now needs to be elucidated. All the difficulty lies in articulating the different aspects of negativity and positivity that encompass the two kinds of refusal.

In the first refusal we had a simplistic negation that was, paradoxically, fixed to a dogged *affirmation* of what is 'given' in empirical reality. This is the sense in which Whitehead critiques three centuries of scientific materialism as an obstinate limitation to an ontology of the given and as the idolatry of the matter of fact. Whitehead is here exercising his critique from the point of view of quantum physics and relativity as much as from the point of view of poetry: there is more to reality than meets the eye. The second refusal, contrary to the first, relies on an understanding of negation, not merely as that which logically enables affirmation, but as more fundamentally co-constitutive of an actual reality. Its speculative remit is one in which not all that is real is given in actuality, yet what is given necessarily also implies what is negated: reality is only actualized in relation to possibilities that participate, of necessity, in actual reality – even *and sometimes especially* as excluded from actualization. This is when the refusal is 'great' in this second, emancipatory sense. In what way, then, is this negativity constitutive of what is given in actuality? Of what nature is the reality of that which is excluded from actualization?

Whitehead clearly endorses the Romantic poets for their 'intuitive refusal' to bow to modern science's rigid abstractions – their refusal of modern science's own refusal to encompass the aesthetic dimension of actuality within scientific rationality. *However, it is not feeling that must emancipate itself from reason; it is reason that must recover its aesthetic dimension.* It is therefore unsurprising that it is in Whitehead's reflections on the nature of abstraction that we encounter the second and most significant mention of the 'great refusal'. This second refusal certainly designates the opposite of the first refusal, that is, the opposite of intolerant abstraction. In this sense it is indeed correct to see the double negation as issuing in an affirmation, namely the affirmation of a more magnanimous spirit of abstraction, understood as the affirmation of reason's full rights. However, this second refusal also signals a slightly different and more complex topology of value than that which issues from the double negation (the refusal of a refusal) into a simple affirmation.

An essential aspect of the great refusal, understood in the second sense, lies in the necessary and constitutive role that negation plays in any rationally coherent affirmation. What is negated thus belongs to the event, not as an actual occurrence but as participating in a realm of possibilities of which only a fraction is actualized. The realm of the possible thus has a foothold in the event, to the extent that it is partially actualized, but also because the full sweep of possibility is co-constitutive of the event. The event, for Whitehead, necessarily partakes in a system of possibility that is more complex than pure affirmation, that exceeds established fact, and that is more complex than a simple binary of affirmation versus negation.

To make Whitehead's sophisticated account of abstraction and concretization more tangible, I will imagine two chess players. At the start of a game, all possible combinations of sequences, given the rules of the game, are extant. Prior to the actual occurrence of the first move, the set of all possible sequences of moves constitutes a realm of alternatives that mutually determine each other. The first move is contingent with respect to the set of all possibilities. By actualizing one possibility, this move determines it as true and all other possible first moves as categorically untrue. The first move thereby partially determines the relation of the event with the realm of possibility: by eliminating all other possible first moves for this game and, for each negated first move also the panoply of their possible subsequent sequences. An entire region in the realm of interconnected alternatives has thereby been demoted to the status of excluded from actualization in the event. We could say of this first move that it brings about 'the truth that some proposition[s] respecting [this] actual occasion [are] untrue' (Whitehead 1948: 159). The player now envisages an evolving set of possibilities, a pattern of possible sequences of moves contrasting true and untrue. Each move produced as true 'vibrates', to say it with Stengers (2011: 219) 'with the "great refusal" of everything that, inseparably, will have been produced as untrue'. Each actual move is thus informed by this evolving complex of possibilities and its shifting pattern of true and untrue propositions. Like a spotlight, it actualizes only one possibility and thereby rearticulates the full sweep of possible sequences – redistributing the status and modality of each position in the constellation of possible moves. The game of chess consists in navigating this changing fugue of possible sequences, respecting and anticipating the evolving hierarchies between actual and possible which, like a kaleidoscope, transform the pattern of true and untrue propositions.

The game thus constitutes an event in which the actual is intrinsically wedded to an ideal realm, a realm of possibilities without which the game could not exist and without which its moves would be devoid of significance. Each move highlights the actual as a limitation of possibility and hence as the negation that this limitation necessarily implies. It is by virtue of this negation that each move may bring forth the value of its game.[8] But what is a 'great' move? A great move is one that is *decisive* in proportion to the importance for it of its untrue propositions. It is one that briefly innervates this realm of possibilities, such that the refused alternatives scintillate with significance. While negation is ubiquitous with regards to the actualization of possibility, a move is great only when the negation it implies highlights the significance of its actualization as an achievement that manifests itself as aesthetic value. We can speak, in this case, of the refusal as giving rise to aesthetic value. As Stengers puts it, the great refusal expresses a vital truth of aesthetic accomplishment, when untrue propositions can 'be *predicated significantly* with regard to an occasion'. Stengers emphasizes here '*the real relevance* of these same untrue propositions, and of their importance *for* the event' (2011: 219, emphasis in original).

In this second sense of the refusal, negation coincides with the emergence of value and the disclosure of the event's aesthetic dimension. The refusal is great in proportion to the significance of a possibility to the event – a moment of inattention, triggering a cascade of moves including the possible victory of the opponent – that has been determined as categorically untrue. The significance of this now untrue proposition 'cannot be dissociated from what the event is in itself by way of achievement' (Whitehead, 1948: 159). The event is thus indissociable from its untrue propositions. The process of its actualization involves a limitation that we can imagine as sheering through the realm of the possible, bifurcating true and untrue propositions. Whitehead tethers the emergence of value and the disclosure of the event's aesthetic dimension to this speculative horizon of possibility that far outstrips both that of established facts – the meagre meal of the 'unimaginative empiricist' – and of the 'intolerant abstractions' of modern science. To understand how dissatisfied Whitehead was with the coarse distinction between established facts and possibilities, let us briefly conclude with his nuanced understanding of abstraction.

Think of the coordinates on the chessboard as 'eternal objects',[9] and the sets of coordinates on the chess board, as well as the functions and variables connecting them via the game's rules, as eternal objects of different degrees of abstraction. Possibility inhabits the full sweep of this realm of eternal objects. It is partially actualized in the event, but it also transcends the actual occasion without therefore being unreal. The possible must therefore be understood as included in the ideal situation, according to its status *as partially excluded* from actualization. In Isabelle Stengers' words, 'The ideal situation corresponds to a complete envisagement of the eternal objects and their relations, that is, just as much to the determination of what is included as "being" as of what is excluded as "not-being"' (2011: 219).

Each eternal object – each coordinate, position or possible sequence of moves – may be actualized to a certain degree in different combinations within the same game, or by other players in other games. The eternal object may enter actual occasions in infinite iterations and combinations, just as the colour red may be actualized in infinite iterations and combinations without losing its eternal quality: 'It haunts time, like a spirit. It comes and it goes. But where it comes, it is the same colour. It neither survives nor does it live' (Whitehead, 1948: 88).

Reason, thus emancipated and in possession of the full sweep of its speculative faculties, therefore also requires that actuality is constituted by both affirmation and negation. This is indeed what any philosophy holding on to rationality has accepted since Plato's *Parmenides*.[10] Whitehead, in turn, recasts the coarse opposition of affirmation and negation in light of a new topology of abstraction, informed by the infinite dimensions of non-Euclidian geometry, the transfinite sets of post-Cantorian axiomatic set theory, and the pluralization of logic. The complexity of modern logic explodes the Aristotelian corset of classification (of universals into genera and species) and provokes a metamorphosis of Porphyry's tree of logic, you could say, into a supernova of abstraction. It is immediately evident, however, that my metaphor of the supernova conveys only the faintest idea of the momentum and scale by which reason discloses new and transfinite realms of abstraction, without being able to convey precisely the *limitation* that the metaphor's reference to the four dimensions of space-time implies, since it designates merely a limited region of what is, for Whitehead, 'the full sweep' of the systematic complex of possibilities.

Also, the example of the game of chess now presents itself as a stark limitation: its unfathomable but finite concept breaks off abruptly from the illimitable complexity of physical reality (which is itself only a limited region of the full sweep of possibility). Take, for instance, the number of possible variations of a game of chess, which is staggering. It is estimated that it broaches the conservative lower bound of the 'game-tree complexity', or Shannon number, of 10^{111} and 10^{123} positions (Shannon, 1950). This is more than the estimated number of atoms in the observable universe. Now imagine the illimitable complexity of the universe as a physical event comparable to a 'chess game', but with a number of 'chessmen' to rival the Shannon number and played by an unknown number of players, according to rules or invariants of which only a limited number is known, and involving aspects of the possible and actual universe that range from dark energy to the aesthetic experience of the red glow of the sunset.

This reformed and ever-expanding understanding of the realm of eternal objects belongs by right to every instance of its partial and singular actualization. Its increasingly complex choreography of the possible and the actual is the playing field for Whitehead's great refusal.

The negativity of limitation indeed intervenes by default in every actualization. It inexorably articulates the dance of possibility and actuality, without which actuality would be devoid of signification. It belongs by right to the halo of possibilities encompassing every actualized situation. But the great refusal is that of a *decisive* negativity. It is great because it implicates the possibilities that it has *unchosen* in a now vital truth: one that renders the untrue propositions regarding the actual occasion significant.

It is the singular merit of Whitehead to have drawn the full speculative and aesthetic consequences of Dante's great refusal. Mark Fisher's attention to the structural conditions affecting the false virtues of both self-entitlement and of excessive self-doubt ('who am I to ... ?'), furthermore attunes us to the collective dimension of the emancipatory refusal. Like Dante, we need friends to embark on the emancipatory adventure of thought. Whitehead needed the Romantic poets to strengthen his conviction in undertaking the apparently foolish reconciliation of reason with aesthetic value. Even Newton risked regressing to an 'unimaginative empiricism' without the synergy of collective intellectual audacity. It is perhaps wise to conclude, in light of the pivoting from the first to the second refusal, that the great refusal always teeters on the edge of a great denial.

Notes

[1] Verse seven of the opening of Canto III: 'Through me you enter into the city of woes, through me you enter into eternal pain, through me you enter the population of loss. ... Abandon all hope, you who enter here'. Dante at first does not understand these words, which he encounters written on a sign upon entering hell's vestibule. Virgil explains: 'All fear must be left here, and cowardice die' (Dante, 1997 [1472]).

[2] I have slightly altered Pinsky's translation here as it sometimes leaves words out. Pinsky's translation says 'Of him who made the Great Refusal, impelled by cowardice'. There does not seem to be a satisfactory translation of *viltade,* which is here imperfectly translated as cowardice. I would like to thank Gregory Van Wagenen for pointing that *viltade* relates to *vilitas, villis*, 'cheaply bought', mean, base, vile, (but distinct from *villain*). It signifies a pusillanimity or lack of virtue rather than merely the lack of courage of someone with noble intentions.

[3] Dante, a Guelph, had first defended papal power against the Ghibellines who sided with the emperor, but he later sided with the White against the Black Guelphs in defence of the autonomy of secular power from papal overreach. Boniface summoned Dante to Rome, allowing the Black Guelphs to expropriate and exile him. This tragic turn of events may indeed be a plausible reason to see the meek hermit in the shadow of the one who committed the great refusal.

[4] I decided to deviate once more from Pinsky's translation: 'What is this? Why, why should you hold back? Why be a coward rather than bolder, freer–'

5. A more recent publication, *The Great Refusal: Herbert Marcuse and Contemporary Social Movements*, links the great refusal to the student protests of the 1960s, to the Asian uprisings of the 1980s and 1990s (Lamas, 2017), the Arab Spring as much as the anti-austerity Occupy Wallstreet movement or the Black Lives Matter movement, without forgetting rural migrant labour resistance in India and China, the Zapatistas and Brazil's landless workers' movement, the women of Kerala and their textile cooperatives and the barter clubs and neighbourhood assemblies in Argentina, Cuba's *organoponicos* and the Quechua concept of *sumac kawsay* (*buen vivir* or good living), as well as community gardens around the world and *degrowth* and *do-it-yourself* movements (Vieta, 2017). Angela Davis directly associates the great refusal with gender diversity, trans and disability movements, and with an aesthetics of 'radical imagination' that in Black music, literature and art that belies the singularity of the predominantly White avant garde (Davis, 2017: viii).
6. 'La seule imagination me rend compte de ce qui peut être' (Breton, 1946, in Marcuse, 1966: 149, note 12). 'To reduce imagination to slavery–even if one's so-called happiness is at stake–means to violate all that one finds in one's inmost self of ultimate justice. Imagination alone tells me what can be' (Breton, 1946: 15, in Marcuse, 1966: 149, note 12).
7. Cf. 'To change this direction of conceptuality, to give it a turn towards nonidentity, is the hinge of negative dialectics' (Adorno, (1990 [1966]: 12).
8. Cf. Whitehead (1948: 174).
9. Whitehead refers to 'eternal objects' to avoid speaking of universals so as to better reform the realm of rational abstraction, dissociating it from the outdated Aristotelian logic (of classification according to genera and species) that remains historically tethered to the idea of universals.
10. Cf. Brassier (2013).

References

Adorno, T. (1990 [1966]) *Negative Dialectics*, London: Routledge.

Brassier, R. (2013) 'That which is not: Of truth and negativity', *Stasis*, 1(1) Politics of Negativity. https://stasisjournal.net/index.php/journal/issue/view/3 (Accessed 14 May 2022).

Breton, A. (1946) *Les Manifestes du Surréalisme*, Paris: Éditions du Sagittaire.

Cavafy, C.P. (1972) *Selected Poems by C.P. Cavafy*, trans. E. Keeley and P. Sherrard, Princeton, NJ: Princeton University Press.

Dante, A. (1997 [1472]) *The Inferno of Dante* (bilingual edition), trans. R. Pinsky, Iowa, IA: Farrar, Straus and Giroux/University of Iowa.

Davis, A. (2017) 'Abolition and refusal', in A.T. Lamas, T. Wolfson and P.N. Funke (eds), *The Great Refusal: Herbert Marcuse and Contemporary Social Movements*, Philadelphia, PA: Temple University Press, pp vii–xi.

Fisher, M. (2014) 'Good for nothing', *The Occupied Times*, 19 March. https://theoccupiedtimes.org/?p=12841 (Accessed 14 May 2022).

Lamas, A.T., Wolfson, T. and Funke, P.N. (eds) (2017) *The Great Refusal: Herbert Marcuse and Contemporary Social Movements*, Philadelphia, PA: Temple University Press.

Marcuse, H. (1955; 1966) *Eros and Civilization: Philosophical Inquiry into Freud*, Boston: Beacon Press.

Shannon, C. (1950) 'XXII. Programming a computer for playing chess', *Philosophical Magazine,* 7, 41(314). https://web.archive.org/web/20200523062243/http:/archive.computerhistory.org/projects/chess/related_materials/text/2-0%20and%202-1.Programming_a_computer_for_playing_chess.shannon/2-0%20and%202-1.Programming_a_computer_for_playing_chess.shannon.062303002.pdf

Smail, D. (2015) *The Origins of Unhappiness,* Abingdon: Routledge.

Stengers, I. (2011) *Thinking with Whitehead,* Cambridge, MA: Harvard University Press.

Vieta, M. (2017) 'Inklings of the great refusal: Echoes of Marcuse's post-technological rationality today', in A.T. Lamas, T. Wolfson and P.N. Funke (eds), *The Great Refusal: Herbert Marcuse and Contemporary Social Movements,* Philadelphia, PA: Temple University Press.

Whitehead, A.N. (1948) *Science and the Modern (World Lowell Lectures 1925),* New York: Pelican Mentor Books.

8

Aesthetic Axiology: Amanda Piña's *Climatic Dances/Danzas Climáticas*

Maximilian Haas

> It has become imperative to recast the axes of values, the fundamental finalities of human relations and productive activity. An ecology of the virtual is thus just as pressing as ecologies of the visible world.
> Félix Guattari, *Chaosmosis: An Ethico-aesthetic Paradigm* (1995: 91)

Opening address

A woman enters the stage from the back, slowly walks across it and stands sideways in front of the audience. Her figure is concealed by loose sports clothing with long fringes hanging from her arms and chest. Her head is masked by a baseball cap and a face cloth. All the fabrics have a similar blue, grey and brown camouflage pattern. She raises her voice, amplified by a microphone, and addresses the audience. The dance performance *Climatic Dances/Danzas Climáticas* is preceded by an introduction, an opening address – the only use of language in the one-hour performance. Amanda Piña, the maker of the piece, speaks about the relationship of the Chilean community where she grew up to the neighbouring Andean mountain Cerro El Plomo or Apu Wamani near Santiago, and the ongoing damage to people and natures perpetrated by an international mining business.

Her approach to this case could not be more direct: she names the company responsible for the exploitation, Anglo American. She reports how this company has historically accumulated the capital that is now funding this resource extraction, including diamond mining in Africa. She directly addresses Anglo American's CEO, Mark Cutifani, and discloses his annual income of 14 million euro. And she describes in detail the geotechnical interventions in the mountain that destroy the living conditions of humans and non-humans alike. Referring to her mother, who is still living in the neighbouring community under increasingly harmful conditions, she links this case directly to her own life and thus also links the geopolitics of extractivism to intergenerational trauma. Consequently, she claims, "This is not an artistic text, it is personal. But is also a voice of a very large collective". And from this she derives an obligation for a specific part of the audience, including me: "If you are a critic today, sitting in the audience, don't write about me, write about this, don't consume it, don't extract it". Later she adds: "Be with it".[1]

I must admit that when I saw the piece in autumn 2021 at a performance festival in Mannheim, Germany, I found this address to be a rather bold attempt to charge the following dance material with unmistakable political undertones. It was only in a long, intensive seminar conversation about the piece that I realized how far-reaching this appeal and its personal as well as geopolitical motivation is: It is, in fact, a challenge to the Western art system as a reception framework for human–environment relations, especially when they come from the realm of so-called Indigenous cosmologies. While the performance certainly makes use of this art system and the associated forms of expression, it problematizes these very forms as techniques to cut the existential obligations that render such a relation politically and personally meaningful. And since the following movement sequences are employed as an approach to, and appreciation of, such obligations, as a "homage to the people who are with mountains" on the level of both individual and collective practices, it cannot do without this problematization of the re/presentational context in which it presents itself. Thus, in fact, the address creates an opening not only for the piece itself but also for the larger field of contemporary performing arts.

Aesthetic practices and the nature–culture divide

In her article 'Aesthetic concerns, philosophical fabulations: The importance of a "new aesthetic paradigm"', philosopher Melanie Sehgal (2018) makes a speculative argument about the role of aesthetics in the historical formation of the modern nature–culture divide, which yields far-reaching conceptual ramifications for the theory and practice of aesthetics in light of cosmopolitical problems such as the one posed by Piña. Sehgal starts from Alfred North Whitehead's diagnosis of a 'bifurcation of nature' at the inception of what was to become modern epistemology (1920: 26–48). Through the cosmological revolution of mechanistic physics, Whitehead argues, nature is divided into bare matter as studied in the natural sciences, where it has no qualities, values and meaning, and nature as perceived by humans, which contains all this but cannot claim full reality according to the modern episteme. In other words, reality is divided into an objective realm of nature 'as it really is' and the subjective realm of human experience – a division that has been so successfully implemented in modern habits of feeling that it eventually appears as a natural condition of reality perceived (1948: 39–56; Sehgal and Wilkie, Chapter 1, this volume).

We can say that this bifurcation of nature resulted in the epistemological, methodological and institutional opposition between the sciences and the humanities, which not only expresses the modern nature–culture divide but continually reinscribes it. As Sehgal (2018) shows, this also plays out in the history of aesthetics. In establishing modern aesthetics, philosophers such as Alexander Gottlieb Baumgarten and Immanuel Kant accepted the rule of modern physics over 'real' nature and limited their project to the accidentals of nature perceived or, outright, exclusively to human affairs. And this not only affirmed this bifurcation of nature but completed it by way of counter-realization. Aesthetics, then, is not only marked by the bifurcation of nature but is an important agent in its establishment to this day, as it is constantly reenacted within institutionalized practices of aesthetic criticism, research and education that actively inherit, rehearse and thus help preserve this modern cosmology.

If this argument holds true for the philosophical discipline of aesthetics, it does so even more for associated aesthetic practices, especially in the performing arts. In a complementary movement to the 'purification' of modern sciences from the qualities, values and politics of human affairs, as diagnosed by Bruno Latour (1993), theatre spaces seal themselves off from their natural surroundings in order to focus on human intersubjectivity as well as, ironically, to artificially produce 'nature' by means of increasingly elaborate stage techniques. This artificial nature, however, appears mostly as a symbolic backdrop for anthropocentric conflicts; material objects, including the human body, appear as attributes of dramatis personae. Thus, they only acquire aesthetic value and meaning when they are manipulated and utilized representationally by artists. In the post-Enlightenment theatre of representation, actual instances of non-human nature such as animals are scandalized and banned from the stage.[2] This, too, is no mere expression of the bifurcation of nature at the heart of the modern episteme (even if it is also that) but is actively involved in its formation. Theatre could even be seen as a school of human–environment relations, which in modernity, however, teaches human exceptionalism and the nature–culture divide, that is, forms of negative or non-relations between humans and environments. The artistic means of modern theatre therefore seem ill-suited to deal with cosmological issues such as those raised by Piña, as they tend to reintroduce these oppositions time and again.

Yet Sehgal proposes another speculative argument, which does not refer to the history of modernity but to its possible futures, and which is concerned less with the limits and pitfalls of aesthetics than with its possibilities. With Isabelle Stengers' concept of an 'ecology of practices', she asks for contemporary aesthetic practices that are not delimited and defined by

Western art institutions and practice a different form of human–environment relation that does not follow 'the habit of letting nature bifurcate' (2018: 113), as she rephrases Whitehead's diagnosis in a pragmatist vein. These are aesthetic practices that are not oriented towards the sovereign creation of self-contained works of art, which present themselves as autonomous. In contrast, with Stengers, she aims to conceive of these practices through the constraints with which they are associated, which she further differentiates into requirements and obligations: requirements are the socio-material conditions for a practice to function (in the intended way), while obligations are the rules that the practice imposes on the recipients.

Stengers (2010) developed her concept of an ecology of practices with regard to the experimental sciences and in response to the science wars of the 1990s in order to sidestep the epistemologically toxic opposition between scientific realism and social constructivism; this concept makes it possible to conceive of scientific practice without resorting to such pre-established, totalizing belief systems. With her underlying understanding of ecology, which she derives from Gilles Deleuze's and Félix Guattari's ethological concept of a value-generating 'entre-capture' between heterogeneous agents, and which aligns with Guattari's later 'axiological creationism', she argues for a pragmatics of mutual relating as an ontologically primary event: an encounter that is neither reducible to systemic conditions nor to respective functions or interests.

In order to specify this more general ecology of values to the relational practices in the experimental sciences, Stengers introduces the concepts of requirements and obligations as enabling constraints for these practices (2010, 42–55). In contrast to 'raw' facts, which she presents as indifferent to their interpretations, Stengers argues that experimental facts are in fact artefacts, which mobilize human and non-human entities towards certain interpretations and thus render such an artefact epistemically valuable. An experimental fact is therefore existentially partial to the way it is perceived – and this partiality is built into its very form and process of realization within (more-than-human) social relations. This relational constitution concerns first the (material) phenomena of which an experimental fact is composed and which must be organized in a certain way in order for it to generate epistemic value; this is what Stengers conceives as its 'requirements'. Second, it pertains to the interpretive demands that this fact imposes on its recipients, which she terms 'obligations'. In short, an experimental fact must be well constructed and construed.

Whether this ecologically immanent approach to the artefact in its existential relations can be applied to artistic practices depends on two aspects. The first is whether they are truly experimental (beyond the inflationary claim of 'experimental art' as a mere genre), in that they enact an artistic wager that may or may not create genuinely new (forms of) aesthetic values, thus challenging the established mechanics of aesthetic valuation in certain artistic fields (including experimental arts). The second aspect is the concept and status of the autonomy/heteronomy of the artwork, since Stengers' ecology of practices presents a provocation to both the sovereignty of artistic production and aesthetic reception. Thus, the translation of this approach to contemporary artistic practices is itself an experimental undertaking that renders some fundamental assumptions (for example, of valuation standards or of freedom and self-determination) in post-enlightenment aesthetics problematic (in the productive Deleuzian sense embraced by Stengers).

Yet, following Sehgal, this undertaking is ethico-politically important, even necessary, especially when aesthetic engagement is organized, in a decolonial way, transversally to heterogeneous cosmologies, as is the case with Piña. For, as Sehgal writes:

> Describing practices in terms of their requirements and obligations rules out any attempt to describe them via external, pre-established values such as 'objectivity', 'truth', the 'good', or 'the beautiful', and it enables one to speak about practices without making use of the structurally polemic distinction between 'modern' and 'non-modern'. Thus, these terms are of critical importance in asking how to think about aesthetic practices beyond modern strictures. (Sehgal, 2018: 124)

Sehgal herself, however, remains ambivalent about how this thinking can actually be applied to aesthetic practices *in the field of art*, where self-referential hermeticism and the operative idea of the genius creator ex nihilo in part still prevail (2018: 116). But she concludes that, if this were possible, thinking in terms of constraints should not be focused here, in an essentially modern way, on either the subject or the object of aesthetic experience or on the production or reception of a work of art, but that one must 'search for it in the world, that is, in feeling, and consider it pragmatically, in view of the experiential effects and consequences of an aesthetic occurrence' (125).

Following this proposition, in this chapter I will discuss *Climatic Dances/Danzas Climáticas* in terms of its requirements and obligations, which in turn directly relate to the modern strictures I have already mentioned, including the distinction between modern and non-modern practices. And I will do so under the rubric of a concept that is central to both the philosophical propositions of Stengers, Whitehead and Guattari and to the aesthetic discourse of performance itself: the concept of value.

Aesthetic axiology

As indicated in the previous section, the opening address of *Climatic Dances/Danzas Climáticas* responds to the chronically complex problems at the intersections of geopolitics and cosmopolitics, and it does so by simplifying these problems for tactical, political reasons. Amanda Piña names the problems, their causes and effects, and those who profit and those who suffer, with an attitude of positioned precision. This aesthetic of disambiguation is also applied to the problem of values. Piña introduces it with an interview quote from CEO Mark Cutifani: "Anglo American creates value for shareholders, stakeholders, and employees". She moreover addresses him directly when she qualifies this form of value production as "stealing". This stealing, however, is not an individual misconduct. It is rather a general geo- and cosmopolitical condition that Piña links to capitalist exploitation – and furthermore to a whole culture of extractivism based on scientific materialism. And she holds the audience responsible for taking part in this culture when she says: "Your words are words of death. H_2O, geology, tourism, natural resource, nature – are words of death" – "First you kill with a word … "

Piña goes even further here. Sitting down cross-legged on the stage floor, she ventures more deeply, and speculatively, into the realm of modern cosmology by deriving this extractivist culture from a notorious religious source of the Western nature–culture divide. She goes back to the 'dominium terrae', the Old Testamentary command of "the god of Anglo American" to fill and subdue the earth, which she reformulates as the obligation of "White men" to "rule over it [the earth], make profit, extract, don't give nothing in return". And consequently, she presents today's resource extraction as a form of sacrifice to this very god: a sacrifice that resonates with the Spanish term *zona de scarificio* (sacrifice zone), which refers to geographic areas subjected to 'locally unwanted land use' by corporate business practices. Thus, as Piña argues with Brazilian Indigenous lands rights activist Ailton Krenak: "Mining accidents are not real accidents, they are incidents produced by a very old form of language".

Against this image of a deeply extractivist cosmology, Piña poses the cosmology of the Indigenous communities around Apu Wamani, for which the mountain is more than 'just' a mountain. As Apu, or 'Lord', the mountain is a spiritual earth being which creates and maintains life, and which communicates with the neighbouring societies, human or other, in various ways.[3] And with reference to the Masewal people of the northern highlands of Puebla, Mexico, whose dances form the reference for the second half of this performance, Piña says that mountains have a heart too, and that this heart is made of precious metals such as the ones extracted by mining businesses. But: "If you extract the heart of the mountain, the mountain would die, nothing would ever grow in it. The spirits would leave – it would be dead earth". And thus, following this cosmological proposition, extractivist practices actually produce nature in the image of scientific materialism, which in turn justifies these very practices. In contrast,

Piña adopts the Masewal view that everything that is, in fact comes from the mountains: "People, crops, water, technology, airplanes, light, electricity – a theatre, a theatre with people inside wearing masks, looking at somebody saying a personal text about mountains. Everything, without exception, is made of earth".

This opening address evidently presents us with a contradiction in terms of value: that between Indigenous practices of relational valuation and capitalist modes of exploitative valorization. How is value thus to be conceived and approached? How can Indigenous value practices contribute to a 'revaluation of value'? (Massumi 2018). Against an abstract translation of all values into the general equivalent of financial capital, these practices affirm and support inherent values for their own sake in more-than-human webs of life. Although one must be careful to compare or equate this with yet another Western theory of value, and thus to evaluate it with an equally extrinsic standard of valuation, this understanding of value shares some significant features with the particular *Essay in Cosmology* that Alfred North Whitehead develops in his later writings (1978, as well as 1948, 1967, 1968). This is because this philosophy of nature entails a theory of value, an axiology, that opposes the extractive-consumptive form of valorization and proposes a conceptual answer to the problem of 'being with', raised by Piña in her address, which is deeply informed by aesthetic valuation. Hence, it could be useful here to think with Whitehead's cosmology and to further provincialize capitalist conceptions of value within Western thought, and thus to complexify the axiological contradiction I have raised here.

Whitehead conceives of an entity as an event that comes into being in realizing its subjective goal. In its teleological ontogenesis, however, the entity is situated among other, already existing entities, which are included as objective data in its process of becoming. An entity for Whitehead thus comprises other entities, which it selects, and abstracts, from its surrounding milieu by way of 'prehension' or 'feeling'. The many enter into the feeling of one, which unifies them as aspects of its own completion and thus adds itself to them. Yet Whitehead ascribes the force by which the entity forms this composition to the entity itself: the entity subjectively synthesizes the objective data 'for its own sake'. It is this generalized power of creativity, abstractive composition and unifying synthesis combined with a radically empiricist ontology in which every entity 'feels' its surrounding milieu that constitutes Whitehead's cosmological aesthetic. And the central operator in this cosmological aesthetic is value. '"Value" is the word', Whitehead defines, 'I use for the intrinsic reality of an event' (1948: 95). When an event is subjectively completed, he argues, when it gains 'satisfaction', that is, full actuality, it forms a value that can be objectively received by other events and included in their ontogenesis. For him, it is thus through value that an event presents itself as important: value is what makes an entity perceptible in the first place – including in the sense of scientific measurability, the dominant quantitative form of engaging with values in modern science. But it is no coincidence, Whitehead continues, that the word value also reminds us of the categories of 'being valuable, of having value, of being an end in itself' that oscillate between ethics and aesthetics. For he proposes to 'transfer to the very texture of realisation in itself that value which we recognize so readily in terms of human life' (1948: 95).

It is important to note that the successive, sequential progression of the process of reality entails that the selection and abstraction of objective data and their inherent values can never completely appropriate or exhaust a previous event. Rather, this event enters into the becoming of a new event through modes of inheritance. In this way, the ontogenetic process resembles the notion of constraint discussed earlier in Stengers' ecology of practices. The objective data of a given event form the requirement for the new event to unfold in its particular way. And after completion, or satisfaction, is achieved, this new event forms an obligation for the unfolding entities to come. However, these requirements and obligations are not to be conceived of as codified, juridical or rational; they function in a purely pragmatic way within the ontogenesis of the real. Whitehead conceives of values as immanent to the things themselves, namely, as operative in their process of realization. And as such, they are erased when evaluated according to external criteria. Even the recognition of values is destructive of the values in this radically empiricist axiology. This raises a difficult epistemological problem – how to account for values as such? – which Whitehead confronts by means of aesthetics.

This is because while aesthetics, as shown in the preceding discussion, is deeply enmeshed in the bifurcation of nature, it also contains some elements that can counteract, disempower or dissolve this bifurcation. Or, as Sehgal and Wilkie argue in Chapter 1 of this volume, it is precisely *because* aesthetics as a discipline is thus relayed to the margins of modern cosmology that levers can be found here to unhinge dominant modes of thought. A corresponding argument can be found in Steven Shaviro's Whiteheadian reading of Kant's *Critique of the Power of Judgment*. In *Without Criteria* (2009), Shaviro claims that the disinterested passion of aesthetic experience, the existential ability to respond to a unique situation, which is inexhaustible through codification, generalization and legislation, gains political value in times of environmental crises and technoscientific solutionism. He thus advances a 'critical aestheticism' based on a term usually considered escapist: beauty. For this concept also entails a particular epistemology for which objects cannot be subsumed under pre-existing categories but 'can only be comprehended through new categories that they themselves create' (Shaviro, 2009: 17). For Shaviro, then, the relation between things and thought organizes itself in an immanent way as an indeterminable process of feeling the singular. And this intuitive process is set in motion by the lure of beauty, which is based on the pleasure of not being able to fully and adequately conceptualize reality – a reality that is somewhat rebellious towards its comprehension, always ahead of it, and keeps its provisional categories in motion. Like Whitehead's cosmology, which methodologically moves beyond the foundation of established concepts as validated by the specialist sciences, aesthetic judgement is thus an 'adventure' of speculation (Whitehead, 1968: 173).

Following Shaviro, I argue that – within the framework of the modern episteme and against the role of aesthetics and aesthetic practices in establishing the nature–culture divide – it is precisely the aesthetic mode of engagement with reality that allows us to account for values in the mode of Whitehead's 'for its own sake'. And this is also why, for Whitehead, aesthetics is 'first philosophy', as Shaviro later concludes (Shaviro, 2014: 13, 42). Aesthetics is indeed bound to judgement from its inception, but to a form of judgement that is, in principle, not predetermined by external standards of evaluation. Thus, aesthetic experience could indeed be conceived as a privileged mode of 'being with' an entity in Piña's sense, given that – and this is certainly the more difficult argument to defend – the values aesthetically conveyed in its process of realization are neither consumed nor extracted. In her performance, Piña proposes two modes of choreographic action that might be understood as corresponding attempts at a 'non-extractive aesthetics', which I would like to discuss in the following sections. One refers to the aesthetic practice of 'dances'; the other to the cosmological practice of 'danzas'.

Dances

The movement sequence after the opening address of *Climatic Dances/Danzas Climáticas* raises the question whether there was any movement at all. And if so, who made the move? Three dancers crouch on the floor, one on the left, one on the right, one in the middle. They turn their backs to the spectators, making it impossible to assign the bodies to the persons. (Besides Piña herself, Lina Venegas and Denise Palmieri performed in the Mannheim version.) The costumes, simpler now, in white and grey camouflage, make the body shapes and identification markers disappear. As the only source of light, a stone desert filmed in bird's eye view is projected on the floor from above, shifting very slowly from right to left. The satellite-like image aesthetic, which is otherwise used to precisely observe object formations on the ground, makes the three bodies appear even more indeterminate. The ultraslow movement of the video image is met by an equally slow movement of the bodies, placing all movement under general suspicion: was it the body that moved, or was it the image? Observation technologies become opacity techniques.

As amorphous lumps of immobile matter, the bodies could actually be stones. But as they remain in the floor position, their faces hidden behind their backs, they slowly unfold through minimal movements. Body parts become recognizable. And people can be distinguished. The rock-like, sheer presence transforms into living organisms that expand and contract, as if in a form of metabolism. While the movements become larger, the bodies rise from the ground and can be perceived in more detail. The movements they make emanate from the centre of the body in terms of both form and volume. The outer parts of the body (the limbs, head etc.) seem to follow these outflowing impulses. This emphasizes the physicality of the bodies as an ontogenetic process that evolves as a series of transformations in flesh and bones.

If this exercise in generic, impersonal stage presence is to be understood as a mode of being with mountains, it is not exemplary of the idea of a dead rock, moved by external forces of geologic formation and decomposition, but as a self-organizing system of endogenous movement. As far as artistic method is concerned, one might think here of Gilles Deleuze's and Félix Guattari's Spinozian idea of a Becoming-Intense (1987: 232–309), which was fleshed out by the authors first and foremost as a Becoming-Animal. And in performance studies, where it has been widely embraced, it has indeed been applied primarily to cases of animal performance. But as a transversal concept that cuts across different ontological domains, it is perhaps even more productive when applied beyond the 'plane of life' (255), for example to mountains.[4]

Deleuze and Guattari famously define the method of Becoming-Intense in contrast to mimetic practices, or outright imitation, on the level of both forms and identities:

> Starting from the forms one has, the subject one is, the organs one has, or the functions one fulfills, becoming is to extract particles between which one establishes the relations of movement and rest, speed and slowness that are *closest* to what one is becoming, and through which one becomes. This is the sense in which becoming is the process of desire. This principle of proximity or approximation is entirely particular and reintroduces no analogy whatsoever. It indicates as rigorously as possible a *zone of proximity* or *copresence* of a particle, the movement into which any particle that enters the zone is drawn. (Deleuze and Guattari, 1987: 272–3)

Thus, on the level of the artistic method, rather than the aesthetic experience, this could indeed be cited as a presentational mode of what Piña calls 'being with'.

Yet, as the performance moves on and the bodies move further into verticality, the mountainous particles shift. While the dancers remain in dynamic relation to the floor position through bent knees, it is primarily Amanda Piña herself, centre stage, who slowly moves to a more upright position. In doing so, she enters into the latently aggressive, or provocative, frontality towards the audience that spatially characterizes most of Piña's recent dance performances. With her eyes focused inward, she moves through a variety of geometrical positions that evoke a presence equally alien to organic forms and human postures. Suddenly looking at the audience, she sticks out her tongue, which is studded with glittering stones. The gaze of the performer and the light reflected from the crust of her tongue create a crack in the performative development of this scene. Another dimension of what was slowly and rather technically approached as the performativity of rocks, presumably related to Cerro El Plomo, breaks into the performance. And this dimension is obviously linked to the values inherent in this mountain. These do shine, but they do not lend themselves for extraction or consumption. Rather, they reveal and conceal themselves according to the will of the quasi-personal face of the mountain, which we might call Apu Wamani.

While the operative concept of Becoming-Intense has certainly inspired many theoretical and artistic approaches to various ontological domains, it remains strangely indifferent to their associated requirements and obligations. The desire to 'become-with' a particle of the real appears unconstrained. The zones of proximity are constructed, not given. Conversely, Stengers is very clear that one cannot choose one's constraints but must work with the constraints in which one finds oneself, and which constitute both the practice and the practitioner as such in the first place (2010: 47). If Deleuze's and Guattari's Becoming-Intense is a method, then it is designed to function in autonomous spaces. And the black box of contemporary dance and performance is intended to provide just that: an autonomous space for the production and reception of performative becomings. It does so, one could argue, through a technical administration of what Whitehead conceives of as positive and negative prehensions, relations of inclusion and exclusion (1978: 41). The stage directs attention in powerful ways and emphasizes the importance of certain things over others. It renders some relations aesthetical and others anaesthetical. The positive prehensions appear as the elements of a performance, while the negative prehensions make their appearance as such possible in the first place. A performance selects and abstracts certain elements of the real and incorporates them into its own composition, articulated towards the synthetical experience of a spectator. Through the administration of prehensions, awareness of some elements is thus enhanced at the expense of others.

On the one hand, this allows the stage to generate new, specific experiences that add to everyday experience. And indeed, the stage has long been claimed as the space of *possible* worlds, where the sense of, or for, the possible is trained. On the other hand, the stage thus positions itself as an alternative reality, accountable to other systems of valuation, and without immediate impact on the concrete production of 'real life'. It is this mode of distancing, inherited from the modern division of experiential faculties, that constitutes the obvious limitations for engaging with diverse arts of living on this planet *in a theatre* – and yet perhaps this also holds some potentials. And it is these potentials that Piña activates here when she approaches mountainous modes of being through the means of contemporary dance, by choreographing extremely subtle movements, executed as slowly as possible, visually amplified and irritated by a projection of rocky patterns. In this way, she carefully constructs an experience that could not have been made elsewhere and otherwise.

With its theory of positive and negative prehensions, Whitehead's cosmology answers to William James' obligation to a radical empiricism: 'To be radical, empiricism must not admit in its constructions any element that is not directly experienced, nor exclude from them any element that is directly experienced. For such a philosophy, [...] any kind of relation experienced must be accounted as "real" as anything else in the system' (1912: 42). Even negative prehensions are felt in a particular way as conditions and constraints of a given event.[5] However, following Whitehead, real situations are in fact encounters of diverse habits of feeling, each of which includes certain relations and excludes others. And, thus, they are bound to be controversial and potentially conflicting. According to Whitehead's ontogenetic axiology, the question is not so much what is considered a value but what is perceived (as such) at all. It is the very givenness of the given – actuality perceived – that is at stake here. As, for example, in the question of what one sees when apprehending Cerro El Plomo or Apu Wamani. And, again, aesthetic practices do not only adopt or represent these conditions but are actively engaged in their production.

Danzas

The Masewal people of the northern highlands of Puebla, Mexico practice various dances that, according to anthropologist Alessandro Questa, do not only visualize or 'remember' complex mountain ecologies as more-than-human societies but are thus also actively involved in their weaving. At the same time, as 'holographic dances', they form 'dynamic models of the spiritual world' which 'involve a profound recognition of shared values between people and their landscape, reminding Masewal people of relations that matter, even if, most of the time, they are not visible' (2019: 143). Because these spiritual worlds, though ancestral, are inextricably interwoven with the present life of the community, these dances provide orientation in a reality that is shaped by capitalist exploitation, neo-colonial extractivism and catastrophic weather events induced by industrial environmental and climate destruction. And in this mess, they form 'lively social devices for communication and bonding between different groups of interrelated people, across generations and between villages', as well as with ecoactivists and non-governmental organizations with whom the Masewal build political alliances (139–40).

In exchange with Questa, Piña adapted two of these dances for her piece: 'Tipekajomeh' and 'Wewentiyo'. In the artist talk after the Mannheim performance, however, she said that these Masewal dances were actually 'quoted', inasmuch as when they are performed in a contemporary (that is, Western) arts festival, they are not only transferred but inherently transformed. Here, they lack not only the social and cosmological but also the ritual context that is required for their very functioning as such. However, they form a ritual in its own right, which places a responsibility upon the audience that transcends mere spectatorship. This is because they are in fact *danzas* and not dances – and therefore a very different kind of socio-material organization: an organization less concerned with the autonomous administration of negative prehensions through which some prehensions are emphasized for aesthetic reception or consumption than with the establishment of relations based on constraints, that is, material requirements and social obligations, through collective actions.

It is at the end of the dance sequence described in the previous section, when the face with the glittering tongue folds back into Piña's physical presence, that an irregularly patterned piece of foil lying on the floor, initially indistinguishable from the projected stone formations, slowly rises. In front of what later becomes recognizable as a mountain (of an eventual height of a human being), the three dancers move together in a line towards the audience, their geometric postures overlapping in a patterned group sequence. And from this first synchronized collective action of the show, the dancers move into a formation, faces turned away from the audience, with single, clean-cut steps. Loud clicking noises cut through the electronic background noise that permeates the entire show and now mixes with the sound of air flowing into the inflatable mountain. They divide the emergent rhythm of the slow movements into a complex yet regular beat. Their continuous development integrates into variations of a repetitive sequence.

The clicking sound comes from castanets that the performers hold and operate, invisibly at first. Starting slowly but then picking up pace, a choreographic sequence of movements develops, organized along a horizontal axis with cross-steps to one side and back. As the speed increases, the clicks form a pulse and the steps a continuous criss-cross of the legs, supported by a shoulder line that rotates with the hips. Suddenly, the performers turn around and move towards the audience and back with a series of steps, turns and kicks. Varying in different directions, this routine now breaks out of the strict orientation along the spatial axes before the dancers come to rest in a squat, observe the audience and let the clicking beat slowly fade out. The inflatable mountain, now at its full size, remains alone on the scene as the performers leave and the projection fades to white.

On their return, they are accompanied by a whole group of people who evenly line up around the mountain. They each hold black cloths in both hands, which they flap in the silent space in sync with rhythmically complex dance movements. The way these movements are performed is much less precise, livelier than the very controlled sequences of the three dancers before. The circle forcefully wobbles around the mountain. The rhythmic slaps with the cloths are now accentuated with short shouts. As the dancers become more and more exhausted, the light slowly fades to black.

Climatic Dances/Danzas Climáticas is the fifth work in the series *Endangered Human Movements* that Piña has been developing since 2014. All these works comprise a variety of instances and formats, including lectures and teaching, interviews and other forms of collaborative research, films and videos, gallery and stage performances. The latter differ more from occasion to occasion, as is common in the iteration of (dance) performances. Performers are exchanged, pieces are further developed after the premiere, depending on the context of presentation. *Endangered Human Movements 5*, developed in exchange with a list of artists, researchers and activists during a two-year artistic research residency at the DAS Graduate School of Amsterdam University of the Arts, is now making social entanglement with the milieu of presentation a material basis for the work presented. Each performance is preceded by a series of workshops with local artists and audience members, in which Piña and her team share the artistic framework and movement routines of the performance. And this includes the second Masewal dance, which the workshop participants will perform at later public shows. In this way, the regular audience in fact forms a secondary audience that observes a mediation process already under way.

And this is by no means a secondary, collateral aspect of the performance itself, but it forms a requirement of its cosmopolitical possibility. For it is indispensable that the *danzas* – ritually embedded in particular cosmologies and bound to specific places that in many ways contradict the presentational conditions of the space in which they are performed here, the realm of contemporary art – are not perceived in purely formal ways, as (merely) aesthetic objects produced by virtuosic, institutionally 'verified' artists. And inasmuch as this realm is defined as a cultural space in a distinctively modern way, as opposed to nature in the image of scientific materialism associated with the forms of valorization and exploitation described in the beginning of the piece, it requires a careful construction of a mediation process that can fail at any time. In its aesthetics of disambiguation and confrontation, the opening address creates a critical awareness of the conditions and limits, the potential pitfalls of this mediation, while the workshop structure creates the social and corporeal conditions under which it might succeed. Between critical distance and guided approximation, *Climatic Dances/Danzas Climáticas* thus explores precisely the slash in this title, between what is experienced as dances or as *danzas*.

But the way Piña involves her audience in the situated realization of the performance is not only a cosmopolitical requirement of her project; it also creates obligations for the perception of the piece, or rather for spectatorial participation. What may have emerged most clearly in the preceding preparatory workshops (in which I was unable to participate) is processed, as it were, in fast-forward for the regular audience. And this may indeed explain why the opening address strikes such clear notes. Quite efficiently, the frontality of the confrontation raises the problems within the cosmopolitical relation to be constructed. Piña's appeal not to consume, not to extract, but to be with the piece problematizes a certain habit of aesthetic and conceptual feeling that is hegemonic in the post-conceptual practices of contemporary (performing) art. And this constraint makes it possible in the first place to perceive both the dances and the danzas if not perhaps on equal ontological footing, then least as an aesthetic experience not already exhaustively formatted by the established rules of the former.

Ends

In his late writings, Félix Guattari inaugurated a 'new aesthetic paradigm' oriented towards a 'transversality with respect to other Universes of value, from which it intensifies, each in its own way, creationist nuclei of autopoietic consistency', thus opposing, or even undoing, the 'autarky and desertification of the Universes of value' under the spell of capitalism and information technologies through ethico-aesthetic deterritorialization (1995: 105). Piña's strategies attest to a more cautious approach to aesthetic transversality, to the means and ends of bridging disparate realities through artistically constructed experiences. By staging the collision of two forms of dance experience that contrast to the point of contradiction or even mutual exclusion within modern cosmology, they render the deterritorializing interchange of modes of valuation impossible. Through this impossibility, however, there emerges a sensibility to the qualitative differences that concern not so much the aesthetic material presented as the modes of presentation themselves. And in this sense of a non-innocent, potentially harmful mixing of environmental conditions, the title aspect of 'climatic' or '*climáticas*' takes on an operative meaning beyond the obvious connections between resource extractivism and climate destruction in the Anthropocene. Thus, aesthetic climates come to bear in a dance performance that, on the level of material, deals with something that is almost antithetical in its sensual qualities, the mountains.

Notes

[1] This quote, like all the following ones by Amanda Piña, is taken from the spoken text of her dance performance *Climatic Dances/Danzas Climaticas*. The piece premiered at DeSingel in Antwerp, Belgium on 24 September 2021 after several work-in-progress presentations. I saw the piece on 9 October 2021 at the Wunder der Prärie festival in Mannheim, Germany.

[2] By scandalizing and banning animals from the stage, dramatic theatre distinguished itself as a high art, separate from popular theatrical forms such as the hippodrama or melodramatic performances with trained dogs, as well as from the circus. A paradigmatic case of such a scandal in the German context revolved around Johann Wolfgang von Goethe, who resigned as director of the Weimar theatre in 1817 because of the controversy surrounding a dog as the protagonist of a performance, a practice that he had already prohibited by decree five years earlier (see Köhring, 2016).

[3] The Indigenous cosmology of earth beings was introduced into contemporary theory by anthropologist Marisol de la Cadena (2015), also with reference to pragmatist philosophy of science and technology, including, prominently, Stengers' ecology of practices.

[4] Indeed, the authors also include cursory mentions of rock or stone in their corresponding chapter (see Deleuze and Guattari, 1987: 280, 295).

[5] For Whitehead, 'each negative prehension has its own subjective form, however trivial and faint. It adds to the emotional complex, though not to the objective data'. Thus, 'the negative prehension of an entity is a positive fact with its emotional subjective form' (1978: 41).

References

de la Cadena, M (2015) *Earth Beings: Ecologies of Practice across Andean Worlds*, Durham, NC: Duke University Press.

Deleuze, G. and Guattari, F. (1987) *A Thousand Plateaus, Capitalism and Schizophrenia*, Minneapolis, MN and London: University of Minnesota Press.

Guattari, F (1995) *Chaosmosis: An Ethico-aesthetic Paradigm*, Bloomington, IN: Indiana University Press.

James, W. (1912) *Essays in Radical Empiricism*, New York, London, Bombay and Calcutta: Longmans, Green and Co.

Köhring, E. (2016) 'Tiere und Theater, Performance, Tanz', in: R. Borgards (ed), *Tiere, Kulturwissenschaftliches Handbuch*, Stuttgart: J.B. Metzler, pp 245–61.

Latour, B. (1993) *We Have Never Been Modern*, Cambridge, MA: Harvard University Press.

Massumi, B. (2018) *99 Theses on the Revaluation of Value: A Postcapitalist Manifesto*, Minneapolis, MN: University of Minnesota Press.

Questa, A. (2019) 'Visible dancers and invisible hunters. Divination and masking among Masewal people in the northern highlands of Puebla, Mexico', in: P. Pitarch and J.A. Kelly (eds), *The Culture of Invention in the Americas, Anthropological Experiments with Roy Wagner*, Canon Pyon: Sean Kingston Publishing, pp 138–57.

Sehgal, M. (2018) 'Aesthetic concerns, philosophical fabulations: The importance of a "new aesthetic paradigm"', *SubStance* 47(1): 145. Isabelle Stengers and the Dramatization of Philosophy, ed M. Savransky: 112–29.

Shaviro, S. (2009) *Without Criteria: Kant, Whitehead, Deleuze, and Aesthetics*, Cambridge, MA and London: MIT Press.

Shaviro, S. (2014) *The Universe of Things: On Speculative Realism*, Minneapolis, MN: University of Minnesota Press.

Stengers, I. (2010) *Cosmopolitics I*, Minneapolis, MN: University of Minnesota Press.

Whitehead, A.N. (1920) *The Concept of Nature*, Cambridge and London: Cambridge University Press.

Whitehead, A.N. (1948) *Science and the Modern World*, New York: Pelican Mentor Books.

Whitehead, A.N. (1967) *Adventures of Ideas*, New York: The Free Press.

Whitehead, A.N. (1968) *Modes of Thought*, New York: The Free Press.

Whitehead, A.N. (1978) *Process and Reality: An Essay in Cosmology*, corrected edn, ed D.R. Griffin and D.W. Sherburne, New York: The Free Press.

PART III

Infecting and Caring

9

To Err is More Than More-Than-Human: Patient Safety and the Aesthetics of a Never Event

Alex Wilkie

Introduction

On Friday 2 November 2018, at 4:47 pm, I was admitted to, registered and triaged at an emergency department (ED) in a South London hospital after sustaining a fall at home earlier that afternoon. My right hip was in extreme pain, but later I learned my body did not exhibit the typical symptoms of a hip fracture, namely a shortened leg due to femoral head displacement. According to clinical records and reports, some five hours after being admitted into the ED, X-rays would reveal that the fracture had caused the head and the neck of my right femur to compact rather than misalign.[1] At 10:20 pm, I was transferred to the major trauma section (majors) after X-rays showed a hip fracture. Attempts to control the immense and unrelenting pain, ruthlessly amplified at increasingly short intervals with intense nerve-induced spasms, were made through the administration of fast-acting liquid oral morphine solution (Oramorph®) and oxycodone hydrochloride injections, but this cocktail of anaesthetics was failing to curtail the pain.[2] The ED clinicians chose to administer an ultrasound-guided fascia iliaca block to anaesthetize my femoral nerve. The block involved an Emergency Registrar (senior doctor) and an anaesthetist using a portable ultrasound device to visually identify the main femoral nerve in my right leg and perform an anaesthetic injection so as to limit the pain signals. During the procedure the Registrar asked the attending nurse for further intravenous (IV) morphine as they were, at this point, and, according to reports, panicking about my distress and pain and keen to ensure I was somewhat calmer as the nerve block required precision. The morphine, prepared in a 5 mm syringe, was administered by way of the cannula that had earlier been inserted into my right forearm.[3] Another three hours later, and after my partner, who was trying to ascertain more painkillers, came across the nurse crying in the aisle, three senior clinicians arrived in my cubicle, one handing me a leaflet while informing me that I'd been the subject of a 'never event'. In short, I had undergone a potentially fatal, but entirely preventable, patient safety incident. As far as I can recall, the leaflet explained how to make a complaint via the Subject Access Team, NHS terminology for patient information services, such as access to health records and imaging.

Although in extreme distress, heavily doped up and delirious with intense pain, the irony of being the subject of a never event was not lost on me, having variously worked on healthcare and Whitehead's concept of the event (for example, Wilkie, 2014). In this case of clinical error, oral morphine, rather than IV morphine, had been accidentally administered via my cannula, which the consultant explained could have fatal consequences, such as an embolism. The senior clinicians believed the immediate danger was in the first one or two hours of the wrong-route administration and were consulting with on-hand drug manuals, Toxbase® (the UK clinical toxicology database of the UK National Poisons Information Service) and the hospital's head pharmacist, as well as attempting to contact the pharmacovigilance practitioners at the Oramorph® manufacturer for clarification. It was around two in the morning, perhaps later. I remember being fatefully but calmly resigned, likely due to morphine-induced recollection, but my partner recalls our fear and anxiety.[4] I was broken, delirious and drugged to the gills. I was told biopsies would be taken to check for bone cancer and, more poignantly, the nerve block was failing to curb the intense thresholds of pain, spasms and agony. How peculiar, I thought, a 'never event'? Later that day, at 2:00 pm, I was operated on. Three DePuySynthes® 7.3 mm cannulated stainless-steel screws were drilled into my hip, reattaching the head of my right femur to the neck.[5] After the operation I was held on the emergency orthopaedic ward for extended observation for five days. As I would come to appreciate over the coming months and years, during gruelling physiotherapy and rehabilitation, this certainly counted as an 'event' in my life as well as my close family's lives, where a distinct before and after could be discerned. Latterly, the never event would be investigated by the NHS as a matter of course and recorded as part of their efforts to render error accountable and reduce its reoccurrence in the healthcare system.

Never events and patient safety

According to a recent NHS never events list (2021) that stipulates guidance to all NHS care-providing organizations on cases of potentially fatal or seriously harmful negligence, the inventory of reported incidents within the

NHS include those occasioned during surgical procedures (such as wrong-site surgery, incorrect placement of an implant or the retention of a foreign object), transfusion or implantation of incompatible blood or organs, the administration of medication (mis-selection of medication, administration via the wrong route, overdoses), equipment and installation failures (for example, incorrect installation of collapsible shower curtains to prevent suicide, inadequacy of restricted windows to prevent falls, entrapments in bed rails), as well as misplaced nasogastric tubes and unintentional connections between patients and air flowmeters rather than oxygen flowmeters. NHS England never event data give an indication of the extent of error in the service, showing that, on average over the past seven years, there were approximately 437 reported never events in England, and an average of 13 reported cases of oral medication given intravenously, suggesting a consistent pattern of wrong-route medication errors.[6] Having said this, data analysis is tricky since NHS frameworks, policy, definitions and data typically undergo revision and change. Furthermore, the data only apply to reported cases within the NHS and not to private healthcare services in the UK.

Such 'events' are defined by the NHS (2018) as 'patient safety incidents that are wholly preventable where guidance and safety recommendations that provide strong systematic protective barriers are available at a national level and have been implemented by healthcare providers'.[7] In other words, never event incidents are those dramas that are known to take place in socio-material clinical practices where systematic measures are already in place to prevent their reoccurrence but the risk of reoccurrence remains. Further, such events are deemed serious as they clearly have the potential to cause serious harm or death.

The NHS also provides guidance and requirements on how healthcare providers must respond to never event incidents, where patients, families and clinicians must be 'meaningfully engaged at the beginning of the process' (NHS, 2018: 8) and throughout investigation. Presumably, then, these requirements help to explain how I found myself being 'engaged' three hours after the wrong-route administration of Oramorph® into my cannula, carried out shortly after the femoral nerve block was delivered. Although being 'informed' while being in an extreme state of pain and anxiety, and experiencing the delirious effects of morphine and hydrochloride, might be contested as 'meaningful' candour, it was meaningful precisely in how it marked a clinical event that served to individuate a particular more-than-human patient safety abstraction. At that precise moment I had been translated from a person receiving urgent medical care into a legal entity involving a new set of clinical obligations and demands, not least precipitating procedures of accountability regarding medical error.

In the context of the application of healthcare policy in the UK, my involuntary involvement with never event reporting and practices of accountability was part of ongoing efforts to improve patient safety, not least in the UK, Europe and the US (Graves, 2005). Since the publication of *To Err Is Human: Building a Safer Health System* (Kohn et al, 2000), the reporting of and response to adverse patient safety events has been transformed through the reconceptualization of healthcare as a sociotechnical system.[8] Crucially, this has involved a shift from placing blame on individual human and clinical error or negligence to attributing and distributing accountability across systems of human caregivers, non-human material technologies and more-than-human factors (Kohn et al, 2000: 52, citing Reason, 1990). In so doing, non-punitive full disclosure of adverse events is seen to reduce medical error as well as cost for the provider. In my case, as I have described, this meant tracing the persons, technologies and practices that contributed to the wrong-route administration of Oramorph® and its aftermath. Systems thinking, however, has a number of downsides for patient outcomes, not least the ways in which healthcare systems are delimited, and effects for patients, such as PTSD, typically extend far beyond their interaction with the providers' 'system' or how 'cultures of safety' disguise interests and practices better associated with risk management and liability. Furthermore, and certainly in my case, patient experience is not figured into the reporting of adverse patient safety events, just those of the attending clinicians as well as the efficacy of the medical technologies. More-than-human clinical systems are thus quite rigid systems with precise roles and capacities attributed to the human and more-than human 'elements'. As I will discuss later, alongside the suppression of feeling taking place in a biomedical sense with the administration of analgesics, the practices of accountability also involve the suppression of feeling and experience where strong mandatory reporting practices include only the clinicians directly involved.

On the one hand, the description of the incident serves to sketch out a background on the nature and prevalence of never events in UK healthcare and how such incidents are managed. On the other hand, it points to how 'events', and 'never events' in particular, are conceptualized in healthcare and clinical practice. Here, A.N. Whitehead's understanding of the 'event', allied with my auto-ethnographic case, is both instructive for examining how NHS never events operate as processes generative of particular abstractions, such as patient-subjects and foreign or mistreated objects, and how these are configured to participate in biopolitical regimes of problem resolution, accountability, liability and care improvement. At the same time, Whitehead's concept of the event also acts as an aesthetic lure to think through potentially fatal and seriously harmful cases of clinical error differently – to break with the habits, conventions and established modes of response-ability towards the problem of avoidable harm in clinical and care settings and consider other becomings and expressions of the problem, as well as perhaps the nature of the problem itself.⁹ Here, I take the never event I experienced as an invitation to consider a 'hard case' of generalized aesthetics, aesthetic experience and aesthetic practice and how aesthetics might be thought differently. That is to say, not as the signature or preserve of 'artistic' endeavour and attendant images of thought, but as a means to open up, investigate and appreciate the non-bifurcated aesthetics at play in fields and domains not typically associated with aesthetics.

Nonetheless, what makes this an interesting investigation for aesthetics, and what can be said about this event that couldn't be said for other events? Indeed, what promise might this hold and what meaningful insights might it yield for understanding clinical never events in aesthetic terms? Moving beyond the superficial resonances between the Whiteheadian concept of 'event' and never events and taking aesthetics as a point of departure for this exercise, it strikes me, here, that there is an opportunity to re-read Whitehead's metaphysics as an aesthetics of the composition of feeling through positive and negative prehensions as a means of conducting an aesthetic analysis of this never event. In so doing, as seems relevant to the case at hand, it is possible to examine the relation between aesthetics and anaesthetics, what is felt and not felt, and what is experienced and what is unrealized potentiality. What positive and negative prehensions offer is a way to analyse the complex relations of the never event that relay the event as a complex of positive and negative feelings, in other words something that sometimes happens or sometimes doesn't happen. In this respect, prehension is a starting point for an aesthetic analysis of feeling, anaesthetics and clinical error – the positive and the negative, the actual and the virtual – staged as complex and mutually constitutive, rather than oppositional. If to think with Whitehead aesthetically is to think of processes of feeling as that which is felt positively and what is felt negatively, then the absence of feeling, or anaesthetics, isn't nothingness but a kind of suppression of feeling or something that is felt negatively. Thus, this is a story of what did not happen as much as a story of what did – a whole sequence of trials related to prehensions and negative prehensions.

Aesthetics, prehensions and negative prehensions

In *Process and Reality*, Whitehead (1978: 19) declares that there are two kinds, or 'species', of prehensions: 'positive prehensions' that stand for feelings and 'negative prehensions' which remove from feeling. Here, the key is 'remove from' or, to directly quote Whitehead, 'eliminate from'. That is to say, rather than eliminate feeling entirely, negative prehensions refer to processes that remove aspects of feelings. Arguably, prehensions, both positive and negative, are also key to understanding or appreciating a Whiteheadian aesthetics as a theory or metaphysics of feeling where feeling is a process of appropriation and individuation necessary to the constitution of all entities (see Halewood's and Savransky's contributions in Chapters 2 and 6, this volume). Thus, and as Didier Debaise (2017: 55) points out, if prehensions characterize operations of capture, then they are vectors of feeling that bring about a passage of becoming from that which exists (as centres of prehension) to a new existence, or reality. Where negative prehension come into play in this schema is a speculative question of how the passage of becoming moves from a flux of feeling and disjunctive diversity to the achievement of certain possibilities, where possibility is understood as the possibility of 'order or unity' (Debaise, 2017: 52). In other words, negative prehension is a concept through which to account for the ways in which certain possibilities are included in an event or downplayed, anaesthetized or excluded: how certain feelings are realized, while others perish. Thus, the compossibility, to borrow a term from Gottfried Wilhelm Leibniz and Gilles Deleuze (2004: 100–1), of a new reality is the interplay of both positive and negative prehensions. Although the notion of prehension is an abstraction – a means of depicting the inter-relations of becoming and actual entities and societies, in the Whiteheadian sense – its emphasis on 'feeling' warrants consideration of becoming as first and foremost an aesthetic process of 'more-than-human experience'. Here, feeling is a technical term that portrays acts of appropriation through positive and negative prehensions at all levels of existence (and granted to any number of enduring entities including humans, hip bones, X-Ray imaging setups, analgesics, cannulated screws, syringes etc), characterizing how processes of becoming take place as a reaching out. For Whitehead (1968: 22), then, bodies, whether human or not, are composed of various centres of experience where the interplay of (positive and negative) prehensions impress on, appropriate and eliminate one another. In this case, and at various moments through intensive care and afterwards, my right hip was variously occasioned as a centre of experience involving the prehensive interplay of femoral fracture, localized nerve excitements and suppression as well as analgesic therapy.

To situate and elaborate on this understanding of prehensions as a way of analysing aesthetics in the case of clinical error, patient safety and never events I am discussing here, the following two aspects of the hip fracture event provide a way to experiment with thinking with prehensions in order to stage an aesthetic analysis of clinical error. The analysis that follows draws on both my auto-ethnographic experience of the hip fracture event as well as the Serious Incident Investigation Report conducted by the ED Consultant and ED Matron at the hospital following the never event incident, as well as the patient records associated with admission and treatment of the hip fracture. I have chosen this episode in part as a way of analysing the aesthetics of trauma and as a trial in extricating aesthetics from the analysis of the arts and placing it at a locus of extreme feeling.

The anaesthetics of a possible embolism

The wrong-route administration of oral morphine, that is, intravenously through the cannula in my right antecubital fossa (elbow pit), according to the report, took place due to a 'misunderstanding' between the Registrar and the nurse in the ED prior to the administration of the femoral block.[10] Having previously been administered oral morphine after being initially triaged, and the administration being logged on the Electronic Prescribing and Medicines Administration (EPMA) system, a verbal request for further IV morphine was made by the Registrar prior to the nerve block for more rapid pain control. Due to the urgency and panic at the time, the request was not made through my Electronic Patient Record (EPR), and another attending doctor failed to write a written order for the morphine in a 'timely fashion'. Without a written order for IV morphine (a controlled drug), the nurse prepared Oramorph® as a temporary solution as the 'PRN' order (meaning, to be taken as needed) for oral morphine was still in effect. At this stage, there remain procedures, policies and preventative material measures in place to avoid wrong-route administration of medication beyond the reporting and logging practices of the clinicians. Here, controlled drugs (CDs) are kept in a locked cupboard in the ED and oral medications are drawn up in purple oral medicine syringes that are incompatible with the standard Luer lock ports of intravenous equipment, supposedly rendering wrong-route administration impossible. However, at the time at which the nurse was preparing the oral morphine, 10 ml purple syringes were out of stock and rather than use a 20 ml purple syringe, which the nurse viewed as an inaccurate means for measuring the amount of oral morphine requested (5 ml), the nurse 'drew the oral morphine up with a more appropriately sized, standard syringe' compatible with the Luer lock. As the nurse reportedly struggled to lock the door of the CD cupboard, the Registrar, tasked with performing the femoral nerve block and keen to administer the drug prior to the procedure, signed for the drug under the impression it was an IV dose. In that time, the nurse was unable to label the syringe, and the Registrar administered the oral morphine via the IV cannula, believing it was IV morphine.[11] The wrong-route administration soon became apparent when the oral morphine dose was recorded on the EPMA and the clinicians realized the mistake, setting off a whole train of procedures and practices for mitigating the incident including immediate cardiac monitoring, close observation, particularly of the injection site as well as extended post-op observation.

Fortunately for all involved, this wrong-route administration of Oramorph® did not yield a potentially fatal embolism or other harmful physical side effects. According to medication safety, there are three main dangers associated with wrong-route administration of oral morphine. First, that doses of oral and intravenous morphine are not equivalent, effectively rendering the oral dose an overdose (approximately twice as much) when injected. Second, morphine sulphate elixir (oral morphine) is not formulated to the same thickness and tonicity of human blood, and its excipients (a substance formulated to stabilize the active drug in particular uses) can result in an embolism. Finally, as oral morphine is not engineered to be administered intravenously, it is not sterile and therefore carries the risk of micro-organisms being injected into the bloodstream, resulting in potentially fatal sepsis.

In this, admittedly partial, opiate-induced account, morphine was being used as an anaesthetic analgesia to suppress the pain and distress I was undergoing prior to the nerve block, which itself was being administered to control the throbbing spasms of pain brought on by femoral nerve dysfunction in my right leg. However, 'partial' strikes me as a somewhat inadequate term here given my narcotized state and the onslaught of novel and intense feelings being produced and suppressed. My positionality was hallucinogenic, messy, unreliable and fraught with faulty recollection. Although the nerve block and morphine worked somewhat to curb the pain I was experiencing, the thresholds of pain proved far too much for the efficacy of the medication.

Suffice to say, then, that the interplay of prehensions in effect in the clinical situation I docilely found myself in were careering towards a vectoring of becoming that were bringing into being the real possibility of a fatal harmony or achievement, most likely in the constitution of an embolism, but sepsis too was being considered as another individuation. This brings into sharp focus how prehensions can render a version of aesthetics unconcerned with harmonious beauty, but rather with a concrescence of orthopaedic trauma and progression, clinical technologies and malfeasance, as well as bodily capacities to become other and become with pharmacological intervention. Although prehensions are typically characterized in the positive singular – this planet, leaf or eye prehends sunlight, or this person prehends this castle, cloud or Cleopatra's Needle – the vignette I have described testifies to the multiplicity of positive and negative prehensions at play, felt and unfelt, contributing to the emergence of a novel prehensive unity in lived reality and possibility: a process of prehensive unification (Whitehead, 1967: 69). The perspective here is that the possibility of the embolism, or sepsis, was clinically and aesthetically perceived in the process and perhaps, by the virtue of negative prehensions, remained for some hours an unrealized existential outcome, though it endures as an imaginative and aesthetic figment (which partly explains why I find myself writing about it). Thus, and somewhat ironically, the administration of an anaesthetic, which would, in part, negatively prehend pain receptors and suppress distress, operated to simultaneously prehend the possibilistic vectoring and concrescence of an embolism or sepsis – which would remain a distinct possibility in the days following the wrongly performed procedure – while precipitating a whole train of positive and negative prehensions for years to come through trauma for instance.

The aesthetics of a more-than-human care system

As mentioned earlier, the disclosure of the wrong-route provision of Oramorph® immediately set in train a whole set of mandatory procedures involving candour of duty, reporting and investigation, including the identification of 'root cause(s)', contributory factors and good practices as well as recommendations for the ED. This culminated in the production of a written Serious Incident Investigation Report, led by the head of the ED and the ED Matron, written one day after the adverse event, followed by a review of the report at the hospital's Risk and Governance Meeting to agree the substantive nature of the never event, clinical and care learnings as well as recommendations and dissemination.

The report sets out a chronology of events and narrates an analysis which identifies the 'root causes' as the 'use of a standard IV syringe in the preparation of an oral drug' and 'inadequate supply of appropriately sized purple syringes for oral drug administration' and contributing to this 'a sequence of errors in communication and documentation, due to haste'. Following this, the report sets out its three recommendations, including calling for a review of existing practices in order to improve safety in the administration of oral and IV drugs; engagement with the clinicians involved to elicit reflection and gain feedback; and an 'education drive' for the entire ED concerning oral and IV administration practices, as set out in the first recommendation. Incidentally, the report states that 12 never events occurred in EDs in the UK in the past two years, five of which match the event reported here, that is, oral morphine administered intravenously.

The following month I met with the ED Consultant at the ED to discuss the never event and to be shown how the recommendations had been implemented. In the main, this involved posters and leaflets placed around the department alerting clinicians to correct usage of Luer lock syringes, drug administration and resupply. What struck me while in conversation with the ED Consultant was the way in which my own accounts of my experience, views and voice had been largely ignored or bracketed out by the clinicians throughout the entire process, despite a key aim of the report being to assess the impact of the incident on me, the patient. Here, the problematic limits and thresholds of the more-than-human system approach to patient safety and accountability becomes apparent through the way it conceives of and consequently involves the elements that comprise a given and situated care system, including the patients themselves. In view of the discussion here, the patient's body, or my body, is not considered a centre of experience involved in ongoing aesthetic processes of concrescence, individuation and becoming, but rather as a given element of a socio-technical system, where the system itself is prioritized over patient safety outcomes.[12] This is, in part, due to the continual occasioning of anaesthetized patient abstractions in healthcare, produced, for instance, by clinical inscription devices (such as EPRs) for reporting and accountability that routinely, and by design, disregard patient experience and feeling.

If, on the other hand, we experiment with an aesthetic version of the patient as an ordered or patterned individuation produced by processes of prehension and negative prehension, we might speculate on the possibilities of imagining alternate more-than-human patient safety systems. That is to say, patient safety procedures predicated on the patient as an aesthetic abstraction rather than a pregiven functional abstraction and voiceless component in risk-management systems. Here, making accountable sensitization to what is felt and what is produced through feeling during patient safety incidents and adverse events could, at the very least, provide a more robust set of practices around assessing the impact of adverse events on patients. The absence of the patient during the investigation, reporting and learning procedures discussed here also act as processes of negative prehension where all kinds of patient experiences are removed or bracketed out of NHS data, though they remain with those that persist in the patient ensembles brought together in clinical care. That is to say, the absence of the patient is also an aesthetic repatterning of the patient via the report, which itself acts to reassure its readership (professional regulators, royal colleges, governance bodies, managers etc) that adverse events are made accountable, learned from, managed, if not entirely removed, and thus serve to act on future conduct.

Conclusion

Provisionally, then, this experiment in the aesthetic analysis of an NHS never event – with positive and negative prehensions – does perhaps have something to say about never events and adverse patient safety incidents as certain kinds of aesthetic events as well as safety incidents as systemic failures. Putting aside NHS terminology for the time being, and to recap, the significance of this episode, in terms of events, is that the never event did and didn't happen, and, yet, for a brief period of time, there was real satisfaction of possibilities, brought about by more-than-human clinical error, that could have realized an embolism or sepsis. This unrealized potentiality was differently felt by those involved and implicated in the incident, not least the attending nurse whose crying betrayed the particular aesthetic strains and stresses of clinical care – an incident witnessed my partner, and one which certainly remains variously 'felt' for me and, most likely, for others too. Speaking for myself, what remains felt of this unrealized possibility often coincides with a multitude of embodied feelings and abstractions, or, echoing Debaise (Chapter 12, this volume) 'scars of existence', not least novel bone and nerve sensations and chronic pain interplaying with flashbacks. The concept of never event might therefore capture those plural virtualities, or possibilities, that coexist alongside one another and events and that themselves are capable of setting off a whole complex web of events. For instance, this may involve adherence to NHS measures to prevent error, including the Serious Incident Investigation Report that sits in front of me, which itself was the centrepiece of the enactment of accountability and risk management. Such an understanding of never events may actually inform NHS never event frameworks and procedures – for example, taking seriously that which didn't happen as encoded into future events and the becoming of the patient who may be able to 'speak' about such experiences to, for instance, ensuing investigations and commissions. Furthermore, the specificity of Whiteheadian terminology on experience, feeling and what is felt allows for an appreciation of aesthetics and unrealized potentiality in healthcare, in contrast to systematic approaches, even if those approaches do acknowledge non-humans. Put bluntly, the more-than-human requires more attention, not simply acknowledgement.

The complex of positive and negative prehensions at play during and after the wrong-route administration of oral morphine also has something to say about aesthetics and clinical error as well as the nature of prehensions. Aesthetics, we might say, stands for a whole set of processes of feeling in which the interplay of positive and negative prehensions produce and eliminate care orderings; in this case positive prehension may be viewed as productive of all manners of pain (constant, throbbing, spasms), while elimination did not entirely remove or curtail this. Thus, pain is a positively produced aesthetic feeling, but something that, at the same time, destroys language, worlds and other aesthetic possibilities, echoing Elaine Scarry (1985), and as such, its elimination is typically desirable. In Whiteheadian terms, pain can be understood as 'feeling' rather than prehension, which requires consistency and order.

Experiences, such as pain or the confrontation with the real and immanent possibility of death through embolism, overdose or sepsis, can be explained away by pain measures, or by 'meaningful' patient engagement procedures, devaluing them or contorting them to the interests of clinical accountability, risk management and service prioritization, as already discussed. Accordingly, patient experience(s) are habitually anaesthetized in evidenced-based medicine, patient safety reporting and accountability processes that are indifferent to aesthetic processes, such as those incidents I have recounted. As I have shown, practices and policies of patient safety are presently unable to meaningfully engage in the medicalized production of experience, not least as an aesthetic process of becoming. This would suggest that not only would more substantive engagements between the knowledge practices of patient experience and patient safety benefit patient outcomes, but, more importantly, that more-than-human healthcare systems could be reimagined as fundamentally aesthetic assemblages involving any manner and patterning of more-than-human feeling and experience.

Finally, this description recounts precisely how, in the patient safety protocols that are meant to care for patients, the violence of aesthetic abstraction was enacted. In the moments where the protocols came into play, I was rendered as an evidence-based figure of patient safety divested of voice, experience and feeling. For Whitehead (1967: 59), a critical task of philosophy is to care for abstractions, and so too is it for healthcare with its own modes of abstraction, not least those that figure patients while striving for improved outcomes.

Acknowledgements

My thanks go to Laura Cuch, Daniel López Gómez, Mike Michael and Melanie Sehgal for their aesthetic concerns, invaluable insights and pragmatisms.

Notes

[1] Here, obtaining X-rays required waiting for a porter to take me on an unhurried journey from ED (and latterly majors) to the General Imaging department where, after a wait outside, and in a large and barely furnished room dedicated to a single imaging system, eight persons were required to lift me from the ED bed to the imaging bed in the centre of the room. To make the lift, I was gently rolled from my back to one side, whereupon a transfer sheet was slid underneath me. I was then rolled back onto the transfer sheet and lifted by the eight onto and positioned on the radiology bed. Any movement caused frightening agony, and I found myself inadvertently expressing unrestrained pain, in further shock and pleading with the staff to take care. Further X-rays and CT scans would be taken that evening to determine the precise nature of the fracture, repeating the harrowing transfer procedure. Morphine, as I became acutely aware, has limits for 'controlling' pain. Needless to say, it is remarkable what a body is capable of enduring.

[2] Oramorph® is a brand of oral morphine produced by German pharmaceutical manufacturer Boehringer Ingelheim.

[3] A cannula is a thin tube inserted into the body for the delivery or removal of fluid or for the gathering of samples.

[4] An anecdote from my stay on the orthopaedic ward here serves to illustrate the side effects of the morphine, perhaps complicating my reliability as a witness to the events recounted here. While in in post-op recovery on the ward, I saw a large spider crawling up the wall beside my bed. I pressed the assistance button, pointed the spider out to the attending nurse, who then gently corrected me: there was nothing there. Nonetheless, during the incident, my partner recalls my presence of mind and lucidity, perhaps as an upshot of the extreme pain, shock and adrenaline.

[5] Cannulated screws, typically used by orthopaedic surgeons for treating fractures, are hollow, allowing them to pass along guidewires.

[6] See NHS England (2023) Never Event data published online.

[7] See Adyanthaya and Patil (2014: 197) for the provenance of the term 'never event' and an overview of the policy in the NHS.
[8] Stefan Timmermans and Marc Berg (2003) discuss the reception of the 'To err is human: Building a safer health system' report on the US healthcare system in relation to evidence-based medicine and the politics of standardization in Western healthcare. They note that the electronic medical record and information technology are crucial for achieving transparency through reporting practices. Andrew Barry (2013: 58–9) provides a discussion of the governmentality of transparency in organizational governance and its role in promoting public accountability and, ironically, in begetting opacity. See Jensen (2008) for a discussion of the transformation of patient safety in Western biomedicine from individual blame and responsibility to the view of healthcare provision as a socio-technical system involving knowledge translation from the social sciences to health policy.
[9] Donna Haraway (2016: 178) contends that 'response-ability requires the risk of being for some worlds rather than others, and helping to compose those worlds with others'. Here, response-ability also involves the therapeutic risk of post-traumatic stress while working to reconceive and recompose how patients are abstracted and safety is understood and practised.
[10] Cousins et al (2005) report on IV therapy as a complex procedure that, despite legislation, professional standards, university curricula and staff training, remains error prone. In the UK, hospitals have adopted the *Manual of Clinical Nursing Procedures* (Mallett and Dougherty, 2000) due to local failures to develop and maintain written procedures. In all cases in their study (824 wards in the UK, Germany and France), Cousins et al (2005: 191) report on a disconnect between taught procedures and local guidance, which is often hospital specific, typically assumed but nevertheless lacking.
[11] Perhaps this deserves more than an endnote, but my partner, present at the time, vividly recalls witnessing very different circumstances at this point: the nurse entered the cubicle and placed the IV-compatible syringe next to the Registrar, all set to perform the nerve block. The nurse promptly and hurriedly left the cubicle without saying a word, failing to explain the switch to the Registrar. Seeing the Luer lock–compatible syringe, the Registrar performed the wrong-route administration. It was later explained to me, by the head of ED, during a visit to discuss the recently completed Serious Incident Investigation Report, that the nurse was crying out of fear for having breached protocols and the professional repercussions of this, not, apparently, for concerns over my welfare. The cold inapt candour of this remains felt and the implications as to the sober veracity of the report presently noted.
[12] This prioritization is disclosed in the terms of reference of the Serious Incident Investigation Report, where the impact of the incident 'on the patient and/or service' was to be assessed.

References

Adyanthaya, S.S. and Patil, V. (2014) 'Never events: An anaesthetic perspective', *Continuing Education in Anaesthesia, Critical Care & Pain*, 14(5): 197–201.

Barry, A. (2013) *Material Politics: Disputes along the Pipeline*, Oxford: Wiley Blackwell.

Cousins, D., Sabatier, B., Begue, D., Schmitt, C. and Hoppe-Tichy, T. (2005) 'Medication errors in intravenous drug preparation and administration: A multicentre audit in the UK, Germany and France', *BMJ Quality & Safety*, 14(3): 190–95.

Debaise, D. (2017) *Speculative Empiricism: Revisiting Whitehead*, Edinburgh: Edinburgh University Press.
Deleuze, G. (2004) *Desert Islands: And Other Texts, 1953--1974,* Los Angeles, CA and New York: Semiotext(e).
Graves, K. (2005) 'Perfusion safety in Europe: Managing risks, learning from mistakes', *Perfusion,* 20(4): 209–15.
Haraway, D.J. (2016) *Staying with the Trouble: Making Kin in the Chthulucene*, Durham, NC: Duke University Press.
Jensen, C.B. (2008) 'Sociology, systems and (patient) safety: Knowledge translations in healthcare policy', *Sociology of Health & Illness,* 30(2): 309–24.
Kohn, L.T., Corrigan, J.M. and Donaldson, M.S. (2000) *To Err Is Human: Building a Safer Health System*, Washington, DC: National Academy Press.
Mallett, J. and Dougherty, L. (2000) *Manual of Clinical Nursing Procedures: Cytotoxic Drugs, Handling and Administration*, 5th edn (The Royal Marsden Hospital), Oxford: Blackwell Science Publishing.
NHS England (2018) *Never Events Policy and Framework*, NHS.
NHS England (2021) *Never Events List 2018 (revised 2021)*, NHS.
NHS England (2023) *Never Events Data*, NHS. https://www.england.nhs.uk/patient-safety/never-events-data/ (Accessed 24 May 2023).
Reason, J. (1990) *Human Error,* New York: Cambridge University Press.
Scarry, E. (1985) *The Body in Pain: The Making and Unmaking of the World,* New York and Oxford: Oxford University Press.
Timmermans, S. and Berg, M. (2003) *The Gold Standard: The Challenge of Evidence-Based Medicine,* Philadelphia, PA: Temple University Press.
Whitehead, A.N. (1967) *Science and the Modern World,* New York: The Free Press.
Whitehead, A.N. (1968) *Modes of Thought,* New York: The Free Press.
Whitehead, A.N. (1978) *Process and Reality: An Essay in Cosmology,* New York: The Free Press.
Wilkie, A. (2014) 'Prototyping as event: Designing the future of obesity', *Journal of Cultural Economy,* 7(4): 476–92.

10

Machinic Highs and Pathic Patchworks of Addicted Systems

Matthew Fuller and Andrew Goffey

Introduction

In a brief essay, 'Défonces machiniques', first published in 1984 and translated as 'Machinic Junkies', the analyst and militant Félix Guattari (2009) argues that 'drugs' and their effects encompass a much broader range of phenomena than is often thought. Machinic *Highs* would have been a better title for that text. Beginning from a stance that views intoxicating highs as central to the *production* of subjectivity in contemporary capitalist societies, Guattari argues for a machinic account of a wide range of activities (rather than substances) that, in procuring drug-like effects, have precise, if difficult to detect, existential ramifications. Machinic highs involve all the 'mechanisms for the production of a subjectivity, everything that works to give the feeling of belonging to something, of being somewhere; and also the feeling of forgetting oneself' (1996: 211). On this count, what is sought in a machinic high is a 'way of making oneself be, of being personally incarnated, whilst the base of one's existential image remains fuzzy' (1996: 212). One can, he argues, 'drug oneself with the noise of rock music, with tiredness, with sleeplessness, like Kafka; or by hitting one's head on the ground like autistic children. With excitation, coldness, repetitive movements, frenzied working, the exertions of sport, fear'. Machinic highs, which generate 'endorphin hits', have 'existential' aspects, albeit ones that cannot be easily detected, and their subjective repercussions must be seen in terms of a broader, overall functioning: a society that cannot manage its machinic highs will, he suggests, lose its 'dynamism', its 'tone'.

The discussion is brief (five pages, in total) and is not presented as a serious clinical study. It is somewhat thin on evidence, and what evidence it does draw on seems impressionistic. Nonetheless, it offers food for thought regarding the critically *clinical* element of the ethico-aesthetic machinic thinking engaged in by Guattari and, more pointedly, the insistently *driven* nature of forms of subjectivity produced in contemporary social and cultural contexts. The machinic high is an ambiguous phenomenon: a priori neither good nor bad. On the one hand, it can, for him, be understood in terms of the repetitions of pinball monomania and video game intoxication, or the 'infantilizing' reading of Manga. On the other hand, the machinic processes that might be in play have a more open-ended, potentially democratizing quality. Clearly, for Guattari, those that spill over into social transformations are the more interesting, and the question of how these machinic highs operate, how they can be turned, diverted, invented, even guided out of black holes and into lines of flight is a matter to be addressed on a case-by-case basis, an issue for an ethico-aesthetic analysis oriented towards praxis.

In the present, when the register of addiction has become a regular feature of casual, diagnostic, and legal discourses around the relationship of users to contemporary digital technologies,[1] drawing addiction into the ethico-aesthetic register of the machinic offers a way of reframing it in more expansively social and political terms, away from a heavily normative obsession with individuals and into a potentially more productive register. And it also offers a helpful starting point for getting a grip on some of the complexities of the technological configurations of what could be called 'user stickiness'. Putatively neuroscientific references frequently suggest the semblance of an explanation for a relationship to digital technology, one recurrently characterized in terms of the language of compulsion: people 'detox' from email, are 'addicted' to games or computers, and so on. Sherry Turkle, for example, argues:

> our neurochemical response to every ping and ring tone seems to be the one elicited by the 'seeking' drive, a deep motivation of the human psyche. Connectivity becomes a craving; when we receive a text or an email, our nervous system responds by giving us a shot of dopamine. We are stimulated by connectivity itself. We learn to require it, even as it depletes us. (2011: 227)

Implicitly, this discourse acknowledges the pharmacological instability (Stengers, 2015: 100) of technological fixes, although it tends to frame it as a problem located in the brain circuitry of demarcated individuals: 'the human psyche', as Turkle puts it. The rhetorically engendered plausibility of these kinds of statements, evoking a ready nod from the typical end user, relentlessly individuated by a host of gadget design tricks, software heuristics and personalizing data filtering strategies, risks clouding the more complex configuration of infrastructural relations that generate the digital environment. Purporting to know where the problem lies (brain chemistry!) is a way of saying 'nothing to see here', a clever bit of prestidigitation that spirits away the complex relations established between humans and machines as such. Hence, a framing of the issue in terms of highs that are specifically *machinic* matters, one that addresses drives in terms of broader and more complex agglomerations of molecular processes constitutive of divergent forms of individuation, transversal to the ready-constituted 'molar' domains of humans, on the one hand, and technologies, on the other, interests us here. It opens up the functioning of the infrastructures of planetary computation – and more specifically the complex textures of experience that take shape at the myriad points where digital technology meets human – to an ethico-aesthetic treatment.

'Meaningful social interactions'

Facilitating or actively encouraging machinic highs seems, intentionally or not, to be an organizational prerequisite of contemporary tech endeavours. Some tech start-ups, utilizing jargon and techniques from among the proliferating subfields of psychology, claim to be able to design for the effects Turkle highlights. They pitch ways of making games, services, apps and other products that would reliably systematize relations to neural and hormonal aspects of user behaviour. Whether or not such 'augmented' behaviours work beyond the sales pitch or are even correctly characterized is largely immaterial from the commercial point of view: it is the technical-scientific promise which enables value to be extracted, because it initially captures and stabilizes not so much the user (there are considerable asymmetries of power in the user's relation to technology) as the organization that is purchasing the technology in the first place. And in any case, who would be in a position to evaluate these claims? It is not as if they have been generated under conditions of rigorous scientific control. Software engineers aren't scientists, and algorithm production is well insulated from the demurs, objections and concerns of end users, for better or (in the kinds of case we have in mind) worse. And once users/venture capitalists/shareholders/advertisers are locked in, who cares? As one proponent of 'behaviour design' says, without much trace of irony '[f]orming habits is imperative for the survival of many products' (Eyal, 2019: 2).

Facebook whistleblower Frances Haugen's October 2021 testimony before a commerce subcommittee of the US Congress, and then later the UK Parliament's Joint Committee on the draft Online Safety Bill offered a glaring and mediatically high-profile example of this kind of issue. Among the concerns her testimony raised, Haugen claimed that Instagram had covered up its own research finding that the app tended to plunge some users into diet/eating disorders. Despite not actually making it into the public domain in any detail, but only as filtered by journalists and parliamentarians, these documents showed an inter-relationship between compulsive engagement within the apparatus of a social media platform and anorexia among teenage girls. This link points up the troubling efficiency of a widely dispersed form of machinic functioning and resonates with claims about the algorithmic tendencies of some social media platforms to draw users to extremes (Tufecki, 2018; Fuller and Weizman, 2021). These suggest that in order to maintain the 'stickiness' of an app, or to maintain 'engagement' (a metric of repeated returns, extended use, and wide sharing of content), users are exposed to increasingly 'extreme' content.

Informal and largely unacknowledged techniques such as these have their origins in Silicon Valley, albeit with connections to broader changes in knowledge production in Cold War America. One conduit for them is The Persuasive Technology Lab at Stanford University. Now rebranded as the Behavior Design Lab, this was once notorious for its embrace of specific kinds of *manipulation* but has more recently been attempting to embrace the growth in the market in what are called 'ethics'. Loudly touted concerns with ethical issues, which are now quite widespread in big tech, should be read in terms of a 'bifurcated' framing of the world in terms of facts and values.[2] References to ethics in this context promote a 'don't ask awkward questions about the basic work that we do' position: we have an ethics committee to address value concerns that stakeholders might have about 'applications'. While such work generally recoils at the view that it indulges in 'manipulation', it also encourages a perception that technology may allow people to be nudged towards being 'their better selves' ('better' here usually meaning more in keeping with some variant of the kind of rational-choice liberalism that originated in the Cold War).[3] Manipulation, then, but optimized, legitimate, guaranteed by experts.[4]

One broad area of technique that is related to behaviour design is gamification. Drawing on behavioural psychology, gamification aims to make processes that may be boring (meetings in the workplace, say) or difficult (such as learning a new language or becoming physically fitter) more enjoyable. It does these by arranging micro-motivations and regularly structured assessments that encourage users to go beyond their existing state by constantly moving on to the next challenge, a bit like PacMan gobbling lines of pills in a maze. Gamification, intrinsic to the design rationale of many apps, uses a set of simple techniques such as: the award of tokens useable for in-game purchases, ratcheted so that there is never enough to complete one process with the gains made in another; a system of uncapped ranking or leagues, so that progress is continuously trumpeted as promotion or threatened by relegation; the use of time compression or speed-ups when, for limited periods, double-level points can be won. To reinforce behaviour or learning, users are often sent back to the beginning of a stage, motivated by loss of status, something also addressed in the use of social sharing of metrics encouraging comparisons between users, often reinforced by notifications. The punitive aspect of gamification is offset by the use of numerous kinds of mini-awards and regular prompting of automated compliments. The gamified production of drives also follows a logic of extremes, as everywhere – workplaces, homelife, education, intimacy and so on – starts to resemble the Las Vegas casinos studied by Naomi Schull but in immersive electronic form.[5]

The capacity to hook moments of boredom, disengagement or the transient need for a confidence boost (Alegre, 2022) in drearily demotivated and increasingly degraded work environments more directly into mechanisms of cash extraction, personal surveillance or training, is not exactly unprecedented in media, any more than are concerned denunciations of manipulation and influence. But such phenomena are more fine-grained, penetrative and ambient, more available and extensive, given the developmental trends of planetary computation, the practically infinite traceability of digital interactions and the governmental ambitions of data science. There is an environmental, even atmospheric quality to this potentially toxic ecology, and anyone, to the extent that they operate within it, is at risk. Our aim here, then, is not so much to evaluate the moral or functional merits or demerits of this condition for the individual user per se – which, as suggested already, is where the debate frequently occurs – but to consider the wider generative complex composed by the interactions of myriad elements within this 'system' in terms of the ethico-aesthetic perception that Guattari seeks to cultivate. How might our perception of the tentacular networks of planetary computation be enhanced if we address them in terms of machinic highs? Guattari proposed, more broadly, a thinking framed in terms of a machinic unconscious that sought to overcome what he referred to as the 'infrastructure complex' (a bifurcated understanding of subjectivity that counterposes culture and its symbols to brute, uniform, biological – or economic – drivers).[6] This approach offers an interesting diagnostic toolbox for addressing contemporary socio-economic structures manifesting addictive obsessions, psychotic deliriums and other complexes in their own right.

Pathic experience: machinic environment

To unpack this, we want first to consider how the machinic environment in which 'connectivity' with its addictive propensities, is formed. To do this, we will take a little detour through psychosis. This will, in turn, shed light on some understudied aspects of the 'ethico-aesthetic paradigm' informing Guattari's conception of the machinic high. The latter's existential emphasis on the ways in which an extravagant proliferation of activities could function as a 'way of making oneself be, of being personally incarnated, whilst the base of one's existential image remains fuzzy' is a conception that itself has a rich background in the field of institutional psychotherapy, which emerged in France in particular in the post-war era and sought to engage imaginatively with the kinds of 'existential catastrophe' characteristic of psychosis in its myriad forms.

For the initiators of institutional psychotherapy, in particular François Tosquelles (2012) and Jean Oury (with whom Guattari worked), the extravagant delusional phenomena manifested in extreme pathologies such as those grouped under the heading schizophrenia (a generic label – it's not one thing at all), while themselves often considered to be 'the illness' – a display of bodily disintegration – were, they argued, to be addressed instead as a creative response to a loss of psychic function. In a continuum with more ordinary normal ('normopathic') existential crises, Oury frames the kind of strangely creative activity to be found in schizophrenic endeavours to engage with the world as a process of *forming,* operating according to a logic also to be found in art. A sort of existential – rather than exclusively biological or neurological – morphogenesis, a self-forming or production of subjectivity, that keeps on breaking down. More or less, mostly less, successful ways of making oneself be, in fact.[7]

Insisting on the creative dimensions of what look very frequently like aberrant, senseless pathologies is not about celebrating madness. Rather more modestly, it is about seeking out emergent potentials that are not a priori negative but, being 'logically anterior to the split between the normal and the pathological',[8] are easily overlooked, crushed, by types of thinking, feeling and acting dominated by the bifurcated categories of 'moderns'. In any case, for Oury and for Guattari (albeit in slightly different ways[9]), what matters here is an attunement to the *pathic* rhythms of sensation and their functioning in troubled relations to the world. Emerging out of phenomenological psychiatry in particular, the concept of the pathic concerns sensory experience, the 'moment' of sensing, of contact with sensory givens, before any, and outside any, reference to a perceived object, almost a sort of pure experience,[10] the existential 'opening' – temporalizing, spatializing – of being. The pathic rhythms of sensation are as much metabolic or visceral as habitual, routine or ritual, and they concern what Viktor von Weizsäcker[11] – on whom both Oury and Guattari draw – would have referred to as the 'commerce' of a living being with its environment, with itself, with others and with the world more broadly. It is the primordial sensations of a living being in its relations to its environment that are perturbed in psychosis, in what Guattari for his part calls 'schizo chaosmosis': not an absence of creative activity but a potential unable to latch on to the myriad rhythms of the environment in which it occurs, caught in the repetitious looping of stasis.[12]

The pathic is not an intellectual thing, and it is not a matter for standardized aesthetic judgement. It is not beautiful or sublime. It entails a more expanded, environmental sense of the aesthetic, a vital datum in the relationship between individual and milieu.[13] If you lack a sense of this pathic dimension, its constantly modulated rising and falling of intensities, the ebb and flow of its rhythms, if you cannot be 'seized' by something in a flow of words, activities, artefacts, the transformative potential of the activity of the schizophrenic will be lost, missed, and the institutional practices that aim to engage with it will effectively generate negative, 'pathoplastic' reactions. Guattari's ethico-aesthetic paradigm frames an engagement with the chaosmic textures of late 20th-century 'integrated world capitalism' precisely in terms of processes of pathic subjectivation and the appeal to a kind of transitive pathic knowledge, attuned to the myriad semiotic-affective vectors plying us, that is closer to existential phenomenology than is usually acknowledged. But more pointedly, engaging with or facilitating the possibilities of existential 'opening' up of a life encircled by the difficulties of connection with one's surroundings – the genesis of a new universe of reference, to use Guattari's jargon – is necessarily also a work on these surroundings, the therapeutic milieu or other environment, and in respect of this, is also necessarily a collective process. There is no empathetic engagement with cranky endeavours of psychosis without the construction of the collective, organizational means for detecting those endeavours and knowing when and how to welcome them in the first place. In the kitchen, perhaps.[14] Or, to put it in a slightly different way: it is difficult, if not impossible, to engage with a milieu with all its ethico-aesthetic, pathic affordances, without a collective practice able to catalyse thinking, feeling and acting.[15]

Modular de-compositions

Of course, an establishment like a psychiatric hospital is nothing like the kind of environment that takes shape around a social media platform, an intranet or the collection of apps on a smartphone.[16] And if we wish to harness some of the interesting speculative potential of Guattari's thinking around machinic highs, we do have to acknowledge that, in spite of the unmistakeably existential flavour of some of his vocabulary, especially with regard to the pathic, it is not in terms of an existential-phenomenological privileging of 'Dasein' or some variant thereof that the ethico-aesthetic thinking practised by Guattari operates.[17] This is, consistent with his work with Deleuze in *A Thousand Plateaus,* more Spinozist, speculative and semiotic, couched in terms of infinite speeds that are not anchored in the ultimately normative coordinates of 'authentic' ek-static temporalities.[18] And it quite specifically proposes a set of conceptual tools that aim to make it possible to work with the aesthetic in the complex configurations of ecologies characterized by accelerated technological development. Yet the machinic environment that the ethico-aesthetic sensitivity towards the pathic discloses for Guattari is not, primarily, a technological environment. It is far more 'animistic',[19] concerned with the forces that compose it and the expressions to which they give rise. From this point of view, as Guattari has it, interfaces, processes, objects, all speak to us in their own way, all participate in the enunciative processes characteristic of the production of subjectivity. There is no clear-cut, hard and fast delineation in such an environment between humans and non-humans, but rather a more encompassing reference to machinic 'alterity'.[20]

In his books *Schizoanalytic Cartographies* and *Chaosmosis,* Guattari insists in this regard on the 'modular' qualities of the forms of semiotization that are part of contemporary, integrated world capitalism, on the ways in which subjectivity is constituted by 'partial enunciators' that extend beyond what conscious, and largely logocentric, experience suggests to us as the limits of individual, individuated being. Ethico-aesthetic thinking thereby endeavours to address processes of the production of subjectivity from a broader, highly 'distributed' point of view, one that extends across ecologies and is capable of exploring the connections between different semiotic regimes (dreams, a sketchy metabolism, the noises of a kitchen, a bureaucratic process and so on) with no necessary cohesiveness or consistency. Indeed, the challenge, from this perspective, is that there is no explicitly or implicitly unitary 'world' to hold myriad processes such as these together. There are multiple semiotics, in multiple material phyla, with different pathic textures and rhythms of sensation, linking to multiple universes of reference. No universe, but a pluriverse, perhaps.[21] The lesson that the experience of working with psychosis offers here is that the consolidation of these processes is precarious, the toing and froing between different elements and the universes of reference they imply, can easily break down, generating the exacerbated and insistent stasis around just a small number of components, 'refrains', that are at risk of turning around on themselves in a loop.

Guattari was writing more or less concurrently with the first flowerings of the internet at the end of the 1980s and start of the 1990s – when it might have been moderately plausible to think (along with Pierre Levy, for instance) that technologies such as hypertext, or even the French State's Minitel service, would facilitate some sort of growing global consciousness – and without much engagement with the details of technology production (for so many political thinkers, science and technology tend to be generic forces, easily encompassed within world historical claims about, say, the state of productive forces and so on). This doesn't mean that his ideas don't offer some useful traction on the industrial-scale production of interfaces between humans and digital-technical machines or that they cannot be brought into a fruitful symbiosis with more technically engaged histories. It is worth underlining here in particular that software production is, and has always been, an intensely *segmented* process. Even before the early days of the emergence of the software industry and the endless discussions among computer scientists and software engineers about how best to understand – and practise – software production, the bureaucratized, Taylorised machinery of State itself adopted the strategy of divide and conquer and the parsing out of computation into analytically decomposed chunks.[22] With the emergence of programming and software production per se, these processes, translated into code, were underpinned – to some extent at least – by quasi-logical formulations of programming as 'structured' programming and by the development of new ways of formalizing relations such as 'systems' analysis.

There's no one-to-one correspondence between the elements of the interfaces that connect humans and digital machines and the semiotic regimes that they key into. Software and the interfaces it involves have developed, historically, from in the middle, as it were, in a constant intercalation of new layers of abstraction between humans and machines, software and interface, that seem to make a greater and greater level of investment in bodies; at least some of their gestures coincide with less and less control over what it is that what those gestures are doing is doing (parse that phrase carefully) and at what scale. We no longer feed punched cards into a machine to program it; we use physical QWERTY keyboards less and less frequently; the mouse and its pointer is now, often, an actual finger, doom-scrolling perhaps, across a touchscreen, and the actions that these gestures accomplish, the affects that they produce, require software located miles away, on other continents, within the Arctic Circle and so on. The successful 'abstracting' of a gesture in this way and its coordination with audio-visual cues are themselves propagated through the complex processes of the endless organizing and reorganizing of practices that happen as software becomes an indispensable component of planet-spanning networks and as the modification of the same can be operated at a distance and often with little control on the part of an end user, who is compelled by endless upgrades to integrate into an ecologically destructive planet-spanning machine

The processes that we are pointing to here – the production of relatively tightly 'coupled' units of human–machine behaviour – emerged as part of a syntax of fairly well-defined, rather limited purposes (when the computer was presented primarily as a business machine) in systems for which one might posit a more or less cohesive 'grammar of action'.[23] More recently – and more notionally – this has extended into a vaguely defined form of digital literacy and a small repertoire of gestures often targeting fingers and, historically, it has been framed in largely behaviouristic-cognitivistic terms, not in terms of the more pathic, semiotic, existential register that ethico-aesthetics offers. Indeed, it is likely that only a behaviourist-cognitivist Frankenstein's monster of experimentally isolated body parts could have facilitated such kinds of abstraction.[24] But that is not at issue here. We think that the processes that

Guattari reads in terms of a modular, pathic semiotics can be used as a way to explore the generation of a constantly modulatable, more or less well integrated semiotization of 'users' articulated around an open, but limited, ensemble of *neuro-sensory-motor refrains* that in turn patch into, correspond to and fritter away larger systemic forces of machinic highs.

A refrain is what a being needs to create (for) itself a territory, what Guattari refers to as an *existential* territory: not so much a territory *in* which to exist but the seed of a more or less precarious territorialization of existence itself. Rocking away in a corner. Walking round and round in circles to find the strength to do or say something. Sneaking a few minutes on Candy Crush or TikTok. Ways of making oneself be, again. Little phrases, recurrent patterns of sounds in music or in the workplace, two or three endlessly repeated gestures is all it takes, and they confer what Guattari refers to as an 'existentialising function' on a specific matter of (semiotic) expression or content. To convey a sense of the potential complexity of refrains, aside from considering animal ethology, birdsong, opera and Marcel Proust's *In Search of Lost Time*, it is to the experience of watching television that Guattari refers:

> when I watch television, I exist at the intersection of: 1. A perceptual fascination provoked by the screen's luminous animation which borders on the hypnotic, 2. A captive relation with the narrative content of the programme, associated with a lateral awareness of surrounding events (water boiling on the stove, a child's cry, the telephone ...), 3. A world of phantasms occupying my daydreams. My feeling of personal identity is thus pulled in different directions. How can I maintain a relative sense of unicity despite the diversity of components of subjectivation that pass through me? (1995: 16)

From the point of view of Guattari's pathic sensibility, the couch potato refrain is far from simple. Located at a nodal point of a crucial technological infrastructure of late 20th-century capitalism, it holds together several different semiotic components, each of which is indexed into a specific universe of reference, with more or less consistency, in a precise territorializing of subjectivity, the unicity of which is not at all a given but what Guattari might call a pathic 'agglomeration'. But if refrains are engaged in processes of territorialization and the repetitive drives associated with the consolidation of a 'there' for existence, they also imply the possibility of an opening up, a transformation. With Deleuze, Guattari evokes Paul Klee's reading of *Gestaltung* as 'cosmogenesis', the generation of a new universe of reference. This, indeed, is what he finds in the work of Marcel Proust. The refrain, in this regard is, he suggests 'a sort of selector of choices, an option machine, for the treatment of the bifurcations around which the degrees of freedom of a system ... will play'.[25]

Don't make me think

The couch potato is a bit like the sticky user nowadays, who is also situated at a crucial nodal point of an albeit different set of infrastructures and interfacing between the multiple universes of digital and non-digital worlds. A focal point for experiments in designing subjectivities with a special investment in the datafication of life, bringing into play different strata of power/knowledge. The information economy, with its cognate terminology, marks a shift in the commodity from the fetish to the function. If we can say that the product design of the 1950s and 1960s was influenced by Freud (Baudrillard, 2006; Colomina et al, 2014) the design of the 'information age' is influenced by cognitive science, itself a complex of psychological approaches, systems thinking and cybernetics. The shift of frameworks generates different target models of subjectivity, new roles to play. Apple's user-friendly machining of the human scale, in contrast to the bureaucratic design codes of IBM, created numerous potential gateways – via devices such as the iPhone – the first smartphone, between the scale of economies – of many kinds – and individual, individuated subjects. The proliferating complexity of these gateways – and this is part of the genius of the Apple design – is rendered manageable through the laying out of everything as *there,* available on-screen, to a user presented as the exclusive, personalized centre of these networks, able to imagine an entire economy as beholden to the slightest gesture captured in millions of pixels of the look and feel of an integrated design language. This is a design aesthetic that is encapsulated very nicely by the 'don't make me think' maxim that user-experience writer Steve Krug (2014) offers as a guide to the 'satisficing' of user experience: thinking, any kind of friction – a hesitation, a doubt, a sense that information might be something needing careful processing – all this should be seen tendentially as an impediment to usability, an expenditure of time and energy that could be, should be smoothed away.[26]

Felix Stalder (2017) describes this as a kind of 'data behaviourism', a process of modularizing human behaviour into discrete highly segmented units of stimulus and reaction. The results of this process are then parlayed in a faceted manner: to users as personalized and efficient services, to data-brokers and others as sources of fresh granular data, to corporations as insightful models and demographic segments, to the designers of such models as convincing means of grappling with the world, and to investors as constructs that can be translated into partially predictable yields. It is possible to read such a structuring of facets as sets of hierarchically ordered permission structures, something operating in a disciplinary mode with defined spaces for certain kinds of roles. Indeed, in a *system,* everyone and everything has to have a defined role.

But behaviourism, in our view, doesn't capture the significant and proliferating indeterminacies generated in the complex intersections between digital and non-digital universes, the peculiar dynamics of the existential refrains that emerge in response to the disassembling and reassembling of so many aspects of everyday life in and by the networks of planetary computation. Data behaviourism performatively models subjectivity rather than objectively describing behaviour. It is not a matter of saying here that we know something that HCI practitioners don't. But we do think that there's something in the everyday experience of the always-on world of the global space of flows that doesn't quite synch with the mooted seamlessness of data flow, that is not 'explained' by objective categories of behaviour, where the models break down. Here, an ethico-aesthetic attunement to all things pathic gives a different angle on the multiple streams of sensual, informatic, signaletic flow (Guattari, 2013: 89). Indeed, the kind of pathic apprehension Guattari flags up as central to ethico-aesthetics does not offer explanations – it is not a matter of playing technoscience at its own game. It is not a matter of referring techniques and practices back to a more encompassing, grounding cause in a sort of ironic movement. Rather, it proposes a humorously pragmatic difference in how we address the machinic environment,[27] pointing us towards an exploration of the clashing dissidence of semiotic vectors, the gaps, spaces or abrupt and unpredictable shifts between processes, scales of action and so on, as scrolling, clicking, swiping fingers are caught up short by an app that hangs, by text predictions unable to grasp the heterogeneity internal to languages. There is far more *alterity* in the machinic environment than technoscientific thinking and its disenchanted critical counterpart allow.[28]

It's not a question here of denying that user engagements in and with digital technologies don't have automatistic qualities. Modelling works, and if 'users' had to think about every single gesture they needed in their technological interactions, nothing much would happen. But insisting on the rights of an autonomous user isn't really a corrective to quasi-behaviourist optimization. One need not become a cyborg to appreciate that the division between the human and the machine breaks down as soon as one starts to explore the concrete assemblages of which digital technologies are a part. And it is especially difficult to address the peculiar affective complexions of machinic existence if we do not look for some way to address those complexions other than in cognitive terms.[29] In addition to engaging with the experience of watching television, Guattari turns to car driving, another experience bound up with the technological infrastructures of everyday life. This time it's a matter of illustrating the composite nature of subjectivity:

> On the road, it is not rare for a state of wakeful dreaming to establish itself on the basis of a pseudo-sleep. In fact [when driving] the subject

is not sleeping; she allows several systems of consciousness to function in parallel, some of which remain on guard whilst others shift to the foreground. This is what happens when a traffic signal, a traffic incident or the yelling of passenger re-establish a sequence of hyper-vigilance. (Guattari, 2013: 22)

Guattari explicitly links these different 'systems' of consciousness to levels of machinic *enslavement*, a term he borrows from cybernetics but which became – in his work with Deleuze – a key element in their conceptualization of capitalism.[30] Driving is a relatively discrete modular – but already highly complex – component of subjectivity. Like others, albeit in different ways, it indissolubly associates subconscious processes with infrastructure.[31] It is of interest here because it points precisely towards some of the complexities of the subjectivities that take shape in machinic environments. Technical systems themselves have an affective dimension to them: escape, road rage, falling asleep at the wheel. The politics of machinic enslavement is no simpler nor more unilateral than are machinic highs (and lows), and the multiplicity of systems in which, through which, it is effected need not be simply passively endured. The psychiatrist and psychoanalyst Léon Chertok, with whom Isabelle Stengers worked closely for some years, offers an anecdote that is particularly interesting in this regard. It concerns long-distance lorry drivers in France who had discovered a way of driving in convoy while also being 'asleep' at the wheel. These truckers, Chertok claims, would 'decide which of them was going to lead the convoy, [that driver] would fill up on coffee and the others, sleeping, would follow, automatically maintaining the distances between themselves'.[32] They discovered that this would only work if the lorries maintained a distance between each other of no more than 15 metres. But it's not machinic enslavement that Chertok refers to here, nor does he characterize this kind of teamwork in pathic terms: he prefers instead to talk in terms of a veritable hypnotic technique invented specifically by the drivers, one that works with some of the affordances of this kind of subconscious affective complexion, a bit like migrating birds flying in formation or the disciplinary regimentation of army drills.

The more general point that we want to make here is that in an ethico-aesthetic reading, even the mundane, now heavily sedimented, routinized, instrumentalized gestural syntax of human–machine interaction, generally considered from the point of view of more or less rational, goal-oriented action (with or without grammar), can be considered a propitious domain for the chaosmic affectivity of the pathic. But not in terms of all-encompassing cybernetic systems or individuated subjects: the refrains that index into the affectively complex territories eked out of the machinic environment also offer 'degrees of freedom' that facilitate the process of creating divergent functionings, dissident vectors. Indeed, in an increasingly complex online environment there cannot but be play in and between systems and the neuro-sensory-motor, gestural refrains through which users establish themselves within it.

Conclusion: addicted systems

The point of view sketched out in this text, and the last couple of paragraphs in particular, suggests that the systemic enrolment of millions of fingers, feelings, people, routines, gadgets, networks and systems in planetary-scale flows of information is perhaps not quite as disenchanted as some critical doomscrollers think. But nor is it quite as fulfilling of personal creativity and expressiveness as enthusiastic proponents of participatory culture have suggested. It is, of course, true that the translation processes through which the hulking militaro-scientifico-business machines of the Cold War have become ubiquitous and gained an ever more extensive and intensive reach allow for both extraordinary scalability on the one hand and finer granularity of actions at a distance on the other. It is true also that digital infrastructures are centrally implicated in a kind of governmentality that Foucault (2007), for his part, never envisaged. Millions of users, billions even, can now be addressed with essentially the same service architecture, at the same time as a cluster of users bearing related traces of possibly thousands of different kinds can be addressed as a set, as counting for one, a kind of belonging generated as a specific kind of performative construct (online propaganda, production of population divisions and so on). Techniques for gathering thousands of dimensions of data, but also working with them through probabilistic methods of reduction – and moving backwards and forwards between these positions – are not only abundant now but a key driver of the demand for ever more capacity, ever more speed. But at the same time, these data populations testify to an immense capacity for the catalysing, ordering and amplifying of pathic atmospheres, with unstable and unpredictable mood swings, addictive or quasi-addictive machinic highs and lows.

Silicon Valley likes to boast about the capacity of its technologies for working 'at scale'. The claim is that the same system – for instance a platform for trading in a certain kind of goods or service – is able to leap, essentially unchanged, from use by a few users to many millions, preserving the logic of its operation, the purity of its function in the process, thereby rendering it predictably quantifiable at the planetary level. We would argue that this principle is susceptible of a different reading. To scale a technological system up in this way inevitably amplifies operative asymmetries, overlooked design assumptions, inconsistencies in offline environments: many network effects are sought after or considered desirable, but not all. It's far easier to optimize the technical processes of uploading 'content' than it is to check it, for example. And one should not forget that the history of digital technological development has from the outset been characterized by crisis, as wildly optimistic assumptions about the difficulty of a particular design challenge generate paralysis, failure or collapse. In the 1950s and 1960s it was machine translation and artificial intelligence (AI). In the 2020s it is driverless cars and AI (still). Cryptocurrencies seemed like a good idea at the time but are probably only the tip of the iceberg regarding the ecological footprint of the fully connected, 24/7 world of the internet of everything. Our point here is that we have no easy or definitive way to distinguish between the normal and the pathological functioning of the machinic environment. The pathic, affective 'mass' into which planetary networks tap is far from being a known quantity. A hallucinatory episode of pathological delusion can, at any moment, scale up just as easily as what might count as normal practice in a technological trajectory in which the one can easily flip into the other, with no one really being any the wiser. It is standard practice nowadays to responsibilize individuals for their boring, crazy, addicted behaviour, but in a world saturated by digital technology, machinic highs operate transversally to conventional distinctions of scale – individual and collective, biological and technological – demanding a politics more attuned to the caprices of their crazy pathic rhythms and a recognition that it is the more or less momentary machinic formations that pass for systems which experience the craziest highs.

Notes

[1] This term is, we recognize, problematic. We retain it here as part of the habitual, tacitly bifurcated, discourse of modern technology.
[2] See the discussion of the bifurcation of nature in the editors' Chapter 1, this volume.
[3] On the latter, see, for example, Amadae (2003), which explicitly addresses the Rand Corporation.
[4] See in this regard the discussions of the A/B testing of colours conducted by Microsoft and by Google for search engine result hyperlinks. For example, 'Google has been A/B testing link colors (again) and this light blue didn't pass', *GoodUI*, 22 July 2019, https://goodui.org/leaks/google-has-been-a-b-testing-link-colors-again-and-this-light-blue-didnt-pass/ and Paul Ray, 'Designing Bing with heart and science', MIX10 conference presentation https://www.youtube.com/watch?v=mNRKHImteiI. Microsoft research into what shade of blue was best for its search links was reputedly worth $80 million per annum more for them in conversions than the previous shade of blue.
[5] On the complex apparatus of the casino in a control society, see Schull (2012). For a brief discussion linking to social media, see Busby (2018).
[6] The institutionally heavily sedimented distinction between 'technical infrastructure' and 'symbolic culture' is a perfect exemplification of the 'operative' characteristic of bifurcated thinking discussed in Chapter 1 of this volume.
[7] The term he uses – taken from Hans Prinzhorn – is *Gestaltung*: not in its more usual acceptance as 'design' but as a complex multifaceted drive to creative expression that Prinzhorn detected and analysed in the work of what would later be called 'outsider art'.

8. Oury (1989: 152). Oury, alongside whom Guattari worked for many years, is an unfamiliar figure in Anglophone scholarship, as is François Tosquelles. Oury and Faugeras (2013) offer an excellent introduction to some of the issues raised here.
9. For his part, Guattari (1995, chapter 4) talks about a 'chaosmic' existential 'stasis'.
10. A detailed account of the pathic is beyond the scope of this chapter. The reader is referred here to Goffey (2022) for an exploration of this concept and its reworking by institutional psychotherapy and specifically by Guattari. It is important, though, to note that a pathic, rhythmic conception of sensation, engaging precisely, but critically, with phenomenology is central to Gilles Deleuze's reading of the paintings of Francis Bacon and to the theorization of art to be found in Deleuze and Guattari's *What Is Philosophy?* (1994).
11. The inventor of 'pathosophy', Von Weizsäcker (2011) is the key reference for Guattari in his appropriation of the notion of the pathic. Interestingly, Michel Foucault translated Von Weizsäcker's key text *Gestaltkreis, as Le Cycle de la Structure* in 1958. See Goffey (2022) for further discussion.
12. On 'schizo chaosmosis', see Guattari (1995, chapter 4), which also refers to 'chaosmic' existential 'stasis'.
13. In this respect, and in respect of the way in which Oury and Guattari engage with it, the pathic invites an appraisal of the aesthetic that brings it into a very specific kind of adventurous, risky relationship with praxis (peoples' lives are sometimes at stake in the way in which hospitals are (re-)organized). This offers an interestingly singular engagement that is very much in tune with the broad approach to the aesthetic elaborated in this volume.
14. Guattari (1995, chapter 3) discusses at length the kitchen at the La Borde clinic where he and Oury worked as a potential locus for these processes of pathic subjectivation, as he calls it.
15. In some ways, institutional psychotherapy and Guattari's divergent inheritance of this as 'schizoanalysis' succeeds in constituting the milieu, the institutional environment, of treating psychosis as something that 'makes it' think in Stengers' sense (2015, 91).
16. And the La Borde clinic where Guattari and Oury worked was in many respects quite unusual for psychiatric establishments also.
17. Emphasizing the pathic and *Gestaltung*, as we have extracted it from the work of Oury, tells us a bit more about the quasi-clinical dimensions of Guattari's later writings on the ethico-aesthetic paradigm and on some of the ways in which his work with Deleuze – in particular, their work on refrains, taps into other engagements with aesthetics. The clinical dimension of his thinking is often overlooked. Much of the discussion of refrains that is to be found in Deleuze and Guattari's *A Thousand Plateaus* (1987), for example, engages with a dimension of aesthetics that was also being explored – by Deleuze's ex-colleague and exponent of Daseinsanalyse Henri Maldiney (2013, 2017) – precisely in terms of the pathic and *Gestaltung* as a sort of creative process of existential forming. The existential-phenomenological account of being 'open' to the world that Maldiney finds in the aesthetic/aesthesiological notion of the pathic is one that he frames, precisely, in terms of the rhythms generative of the spatializing and temporalizing of existence.
18. Peter Pál Pelbart reminds us it is not 'being' in general that the experiences Guattari is interested in disclose, but always a 'signed, dated event'. See Pelbart (2015: 176).
19. References to animism, now quite popular, have to be handled carefully.
20. See Guattari (1995) chapter 2.
21. One interesting approach to the pluriverse, acknowledging James but with a more consistently chaosmic quality perhaps, is offered in Jean-Clet Martin (2010).
22. The first computers, of course, being women, organized in quasi-cybernetic office configurations to crack codes, calculate firing tables and so on. See, for example, Jennifer

S. Light (1999). On the links between the computer and bureaucratic processes of government, see Jon Agar (2003).

[23] The notion of a 'grammar of action' comes from Phil Agre. In relatively closed business systems of the kind in which Agre is interested, the creative, undisciplined possibilities that one might otherwise associate with grammar seem relatively limited. There are only so many ways to 'fulfil an order', say.

[24] Work that theorizes embodied cognition as a way of addressing interface design is a little bit silent about this.

[25] Guattari (2013, 147). The reference to Klee is in Deleuze and Guattari (1987). See also Oury (1989, 180).

[26] It is worth recalling that the notion of 'satisficing' has its origins in Herbert A. Simon's 1947 classic of technocratic thinking, *Administrative Behavior*.

[27] On irony and humour in this sense, see Isabelle Stengers (2000, chapter 4).

[28] A point that Guattari insists on in *Chaomosis*. See especially chapter 2.

[29] Of course it is possible nowadays to say every kind of biological, physiological, neurological or even technological process is 'cognitive', but that is about as helpful as saying that everything is language. What we are concerned about – what the ethico-aesthetic paradigm can help us address – is the singularity, the singularities of machinic existence.

[30] See the discussion in Deleuze and Guattari (1987, plateau 12, 'Apparatuses of Capture'). The concept is also central to Maurizio Lazzarato's theorization of capitalist governmentality. We think that the cybernetic resonances of the concept remain pertinent on condition that we factor technical knowledges into the processes of feedback, amplification and so on that work to produce particular kinds of subjectivity. See in this regard the discussion by Mikkel Borch-Jacobsen (2009, introduction) on the functioning of 'psychiatry in action'.

[31] There is a more complex history of the overlapping of psychic states and infrastructures just waiting to be written. The links between 'trauma' in psychoanalysis, for example, and the physiological impact of railway travel (so-called 'railway spine') deserves much greater attention from this point of view. See Wolfgang Schivelbusch's *The Railway Journey* and also the discussion of trauma in Borch-Jacobsen (2009, chapter 1).

[32] The anecdote, told to Chertok by a historian of mesmerism and animal magnetism, is recounted in Chertok et al (1990: 329).

References

Agar, J. (2003) *The Government Machine. A Revolutionary History of the Computer*, Cambridge, MA: MIT Press

Alegre, S. (2022) *Freedom to Think: The Long Struggle to Liberate Our Minds*, London: Atlantic.

Amadae, S.M. (2003) *Rationalizing Capitalist Democracy: The Cold War Origins of Rational Choice Liberalism*, Chicago, IL: University of Chicago Press.

Baudrillard, J. (2006) *The System of Objects*, trans J. Benedict, London: Verso.

Borch-Jacobsen, M. (2009) *Making Minds and Madness. From Hysteria to Depression*, Cambridge: Cambridge University Press.

Busby, M (2018) 'Social media copies gambling methods "to create psychological cravings"', *The Guardian*, 8 May.

Chertok, L., Gille, D. and Stengers, I. (1990) *Mémoires d'un hérétique*, Paris: La Découverte.

Colomina, B., Brennan, A. and Hookway, B. (eds) (2004) *Cold War Hot Houses: From Cockpit to Playboy*, Princeton, NJ: Princeton Architectural Press.

Deleuze, G. and Guattari, F. (1987) *A Thousand Plateaus: Capitalism and Schizophrenia*, trans B. Massumi, Minneapolis, MN: University of Minnesota Press.

Eyal, N. (2019) *Hooked: How to Build Habit-Forming Products*, London: Penguin.

Foucault, M. (2007) *Security, Territory, Population: Lectures at the Collège De France, 1977–78*, ed A. Davidson, trans G. Burchill, London: Palgrave Macmillan.

Fuller, M. and Weizman, E. (2021) *Investigative Aesthetics: Conflicts and Commons in the Politics of Truth*, London: Verso.

Goffey, A. (2022) 'Pathic subjectivation: Guattari's experiments with contact', *Body and Society*, 28(1–2): 154–79.

Guattari, F. (1995) *Chaosmosis: An Ethico-aesthetic Paradigm*, trans P. Bains and J. Pefanis, Sydney: Power Publications.

Guattari, F. (1996) 'Machinic junkies', in *Soft Subversions*, ed S. Lotringer, trans D.L. Sweet and C. Wiener, New York and Brooklyn, NY: Semiotext(e).

Guattari, F. (2009) 'Défonces machiniques', in *Les Années d'hiver, 1980–1985*, Paris: Les Prairies Ordinaires.

Guattari, F. (2013) *Schizoanalytic Cartographies*, London: Bloomsbury.

Guattari, F. (2015) *Machinic Eros: Writings on Japan*, ed G. Genosko and J. Hetrick, Minneapolis, MN: Univocal.

Krug, S. (2014) *Don't Make Me Think, Revisited, A Common Sense Guide to Web Usability* (3rd edn), San Francisco, CA: New Riders.

Light, J.S. (1999) 'When computers were women', *Technology and Culture*, 40(3): 455–83.

Maldiney, H. (2013) *Regard Parole Espace*, Paris: Cerf.

Maldiney, H. (2017) *Art et existence*, Paris: Klincksieck.

Martin, J.-C. (2010) *Plurivers. Essai sur la fin du monde*, Paris: Presses Universitaires de France.

Oury, J. (1989) *Création et schizophrénie*, Paris: Galilée.

Oury, J. and Faugeras, P. (2013) *Préalables à toute clinique des psychoses*, Paris: Éditions Érès.

Pelbart, P.P. (2015) *Cartography of Exhaustion. Nihilism Inside Out*, trans J. Laudenberger and F. Rebolledo Palazuelos, Minneapolis, MN: University of Minnesota Press.

Schull, N.D. (2012) *Addiction by Design: Machine Gambling in Las Vegas*, Princeton, NJ: Princeton University Press

Stalder, F. (2017) *The Digital Condition*, Cambridge: Polity.

Stengers, I. (2000) *The Invention of Modern Science*, Minneapolis, MN: University of Minnesota Press.

Tosquelles, F. (2012) *Le vécu de la fin du monde dans la folie. Le témoignage de Gérard de Nerval*, Grenoble: Jérôme Millon.

Tufecki, Z. (2018) 'YouTube, the great radicalizer', *The New York Times*, 10 March. https://www.nytimes.com/2018/03/10/opinion/sunday/youtube-politics-radical.html (Accessed 15 November 2023).

Turkle, S. (2011) *Alone Together: Why We Expect More from Technology and Less from Each Other*, New York: Perseus.

Von Weizsäcker, V. (2011) *Pathosophie*, Grenoble: Jérôme Millon.

11

On the Aesthetics of Care/Care of Aesthetics in Social Scientific Research

Mike Michael

Introduction

In this chapter, I explore the doing of social scientific research through the lenses of aesthetics and care. This might seem like an odd conceptual coupling, but as we shall see there is much that is shared when care and aesthetics are both approached in the fullness of their socio-material heterogeneity and the richness of their processuality. In this regard, one of the potential benefits of the present treatment of care and aesthetics (appropriately conceptualized) is to show how they can illuminate each other's operation and together address the dynamics of social scientific research. At the same time, working through the complexities of doing social scientific research, it is also possible to trace some of the mutualities of aesthetics and care.

In this chapter, then, I begin with an account of a case of practice-based research in design. This is because the account crystallizes the aesthetics of two (non-mutually exclusive) phases of doing research: on the one hand, there is the phase of designing a prototype; on the other, there is the phase in which the prototype is implemented, that is, installed with participants (or users) whose responses are subsequently collected. This raises the issue of 'finishing' and how the finish of a prototype entails aesthetics but also care. It also raises issues about the aesthetics and care entailed in the implementation phases in which designers/researchers and users/participants interact in various ways. From here, there is a more detailed explication of how aesthetics and care (and their mutualities) might be grasped in the context of doing research. Out of this emerge a number of points that reframe care, and a series of questions are raised about how we interpellate difference, multiplicity, scale and irony into the Whiteheadian version of aesthetics.

High finish/low finish

Let me begin with an extended quote about what 'highly finished' means for design. Designers Boucher and Gaver (2006) write:

> Our approach to each of these aspects (of design) depended crucially on our initial decision that, instead of developing a prototype useful only for short-term demonstrations, we would aim to produce a robust and highly finished product that could be tested for extended periods in people's homes. We wanted users to suspend their perception of the Drift Table as a research prototype, and instead encourage them to consider the ideas and concepts it embodied in the same way as any consumer product. This implied building the Drift Table to be utterly reliable, easy and unobtrusive to install, and, above all, at a sophisticated level of detail and finish. (24)

> One of the most important lessons we learned in developing the Drift Table was the value of creating a highly finished, robust prototype. This was crucial in allowing users to suspend disbelief and engage fully with the device over long-term trials, and has also meant that the Drift Table can be exhibited for long periods of time without problem. Such attention to detail and finish are perhaps not normally associated with an experiment or prototype, but there are real benefits to be gained by doing so. (27)

To summarize: high finishing is aimed at encouraging – one might say, luring – the user/participant into suspending disbelief, that is to say, treating, and engaging with, the prototype as if it were something pleasing but unexceptional. As an aesthetic object, a prototype would therefore function seamlessly, as it were: there were no seams in its construction or operation. Despite the evident 'oddness' of a prototype – that is, its functional opacity and playfulness – it would be readily domesticated in the sense of integrated into the routines of everyday life. In the case of the Drift Table – a coffee table which presented users with a map of the UK observable through a tabletop viewport and where movement over the map was controlled by the weight of objects that were placed on the table – this 'oddness' took the form of a lack of clarity about the 'function' of the table as a sort of arbitrary map that rendered strange and unexpected routes. The outcome of the 'lure' of the finishing is manifested in the speculative conversations users were able to have about the emergent relations of the household to different parts of the UK (for example, Michael and Gaver, 2009).

Implicit in this account of the 'highly finished' is the contrast to what we might call the 'lowly finished': this latter would, at its extreme, connote unreliability, lack of durability, obtrusiveness. At base it would be un-seamless (seam-ful), that is, 'un-aesthetic', in the sense that it would not be attractive to actual users. However, this contrast can be read in a different way. Rather than a simple contrast between high and low finishing, one can understand this as a phasing of finishing: first, there is the working out of the idea of the prototype, the identification, sourcing, assembling and testing of its key operational components; then there is fine-tuning of the operation of the design (say, the digital interface between design and user) and of the 'enclosure' or the final physical form in which these components are presented to and made 'useable' ('aesthetic', unobtrusive etc) for the users. Needless to say, this is not a strictly linear process: after all, the enclosure must accommodate the 'operational' elements, but the operational elements might also be affected by the limitations imposed, and possibilities offered, by the enclosure.

Here is another way of framing this contrast. 'Finish' is multivalent insofar as it implicates both an initial ending or completion of an event (one might almost say 'satisfaction'), and a second moment of an event's completion where 'polish', as it were, is applied (in the sense that something receives the finishing touches and thus becomes finally or fully or highly finished). The former implies a completion *internal* to an event such that it attains a sort of harmony and cogency. In the second 'moment' of the finishing there is an *external* or outward completion which attracts – lures – a particular, ideally desired, sort of attention or engagement.

We can further unpack the foregoing schema in a way that draws on the terms of Whitehead's vocabulary (1978). The prehensions entailed in the design of the artefact concresce towards a satisfaction (broadly related to the idea of telos towards which the prehensions concresce and therefore events become – see Stronge and Michael, 2012) in which the designers and designed cohere around the function of the prototype (does it work 'technically': in the case of the Drift Table this might include ensuring the sensors function and the connection to Google maps is stable). However, this is another example where the 'great bifurcation' (in which nature and the perception of nature are separated) is put into question. The designers do not just design but are 'designed' too – they emerge from the design process as particular 'superjects' rather than oversee that process as subjects. The skills and shortcomings of the design team concresce with the affordances and limitations of the technologies to yield a 'working prototype' where what counts as working is itself emergent. In the encounter between the Drift Table and its users, there is another concrescence, but here the high finish of the Drift Table is expected to invite the users to 'suspend perception' in order to engage with the ideas incorporated into the Drift Table. Here, satisfaction is comparatively open – it entails a seriousness of engagement (facilitated by the high finish) out of which will potentially emerge a refreshed Drift Table and unexpected users.

This case can be conceptualized as a Whiteheadian aesthetic process. Accordingly, in the first phase of design, a certain cogency (satisfaction) is attained in which there is a harmony between the designers and technologies, even as these 'calibrate' and 'become-with' one another. On this score, we might refer to Shaviro (2014), who emphasizes that for Whitehead 'aesthetics are universal structures, not specifically human ones' (61) and quotes Whitehead's definition of beauty as '"the internal conformation of the various items of experience with each other"' (78). That is to say, prehensions as the items of experience (where experience – and feelings – are understood heterogeneously and as applicable to all entities or prehensions) accommodate to each other within the actual occasion or event. This is the process of concrescence wherein prehensions come together in a 'satisfaction' or what Connolly (2013: 159) calls 'some kind of harmony in the same entity' (or, for that matter, occasion).

As noted, the first finishing (or 'technical' concrescence) is subsequently highly finished to become a prehension that feels, and is felt, in a 'subsequent' actual occasion – that of participant use. Having made this point, there is no guarantee that this second aesthetic moment (mediated by high finish) will attain satisfaction. Given that the prototypes are meant to open up possible or emergent engagements with the 'issues at stake', there is always the prospect that these possibilities will not be realized. In Massumi's (2011) discussion of semblance, the aesthetic engagement with an object such as the prototype ideally should be highly affective, hard to pin down and oriented towards the virtual. Yet, this is not always the case as such aesthetic entities or occasions can in actuality formally shape an audience's (or users' or participants') responses and close down possibilities. Thus, in another design project – the Home Health Monitor (Gaver et al, 2009) – instead of engaging playfully with the prototype's rather ludic outputs, the users focused on the credibility of those outputs. This amounted to a failure of engagement, which the designers put down to the Home Health Monitor failing to be suitably appealing – not being sufficiently finished for its users, as it were. In this regard, we can follow Massumi and suggest that a prototype (or any 'aesthetic' artefact) can fail to yield semblance if it instead generates what he dubs 'action–reaction circuits' – more or less standardized responses to the more or less standardized operation of the prototype. Here, there is no, or very limited, opportunity for the potentiality sought by designers. Moreover, this telos of failure might be driven by the satisfactions of the users or participants who, as Connolly phrases it, 'accede too much to conventional wisdom or power' (Connolly, 2011: 159). The 'unwillingness' or incapacity to open oneself up to the possibilities occasioned by the prototype diffuses any prospect of semblance. On top of this is the irony that designers, in trying to waylay users' unwillingness to engage, place undue stress on the usefulness, as opposed to the semblance, of the prototype. For instance, Wilkie and Michael (2018) have commented on this with regard to the implementation of the Energy Babble (another speculative prototype – see Boucher et al, 2018). In order to encourage engagement, in placing this prototype among members of energy communities, in light of the members' generally utilitarian outlook on energy demand reduction, the speculative dimension of the Babble was downplayed and its utility emphasized. This resulted in a tendency towards more instrumental, rather than speculative, relations with the Babble.

Now, the preceding discussion is grounded in a particular unpacking of a particular set of designerly (sometimes called speculative) forms of making, of finishing. However, I do not see this account as confined to design practices as such (or, more broadly, to practice-based research). Rather, I see this account as a useful means to explore the doing of social science research, which can be disambiguated into a similar phasing of finishing (with the proviso already mentioned). This concerns the initial design of the research instrument or device (for example, the questionnaire schedule or the focus group question sequence that covers all the points relevant to the research question; the choice of ethnographic method in fieldwork sites that best address the research question; and, increasingly, design techniques such as cultural probes), and then the implementation of those instruments. Here, it is the 'social processes' by which those techniques are performed, reflected upon and adapted to the peculiar socio-material circumstances of the research that manifest 'high finishing' in the sense of becoming 'feelable' to the participants in the course of the research. This too is an aesthetic process insofar as it 'lures' participants into the role of respondent, interviewee, focus group member etc so that there is a generation of relevant data. As already discussed, there is no guarantee of success. Participants may well subvert the relations with researchers and reconfigure the very meaning of the research event to the point where it becomes something other (Michael, 2012), and as we shall see, this can be a response to the misplaced high finishing – or caring – embodied by the research device.

In the next section, I want to move on to consider another way of framing this phasing of finishing. This involves a consideration of the aesthetics of finish in terms of the notion of care. After all, the processes of high finishing imply a sort of care for the emergent research event, and not least for the participants. However, this is not straightforward, and in what follows I will explore aspects of the complexity of this relation between the care and the aesthetics of social research.

Matters of care

Let us consider further what it is about the high finish of a speculative prototype that 'lures' its participant users? Is it the aesthetic pleasures it offers: the ease, the robustness and the seamlessness of use, but also the beauty of the packaging of a design? Are these sufficient to overcome its opacity and alienness? Similar questions can be posed of social research instruments – how does, say, a sequence of more or less unfamiliar questions (that is nonetheless internally robust) become attractive: might it be the seriousness and the social performance (the aesthetics?) of the social researcher? In both cases there is, perhaps, something else taking place. There is an evident exercise of 'care': care has been taken with the design, production and implementation of the prototype; care has been taken with the design of the social research device and in the manner of its application. By extension, there has been care for the participant, whose practical and aesthetic 'needs' have been thought about, addressed and realized in the socio-materiality of the prototype and a tool such as a questionnaire *and* their *in situ* operation.

However, as previously hinted at, the way in which this event of engagement unfolds is not predetermined. The Energy Babble prototype was admired for its 'good looks': work and effort had evidently been put into producing such a 'beautiful' artefact, and as such it evinced care and respect for its users. At the same time, the users were from energy communities (communities which competed for funds to support energy demand reduction initiatives), and they voiced their displeasure that funding that they could have used for 'practical purposes' was effectively being diverted into questionable social research. Such 'care' (as embodied in the aesthetics of the Babble) was, therefore, also a signifier of something akin to financial waste. The point is that 'care' is not a straightforward means of luring participants to the 'satisfaction' of the researchers.

To reflect on 'care' a little more, we can go to the works of Maria Puig de la Bellacasa (for example, 2011, 2017). Puig de la Bellacasa elaborates Latour's 'matters of concern'. For Latour (for example, 2004, 2010) scientific, technological or hybrid things – for example, genetically modified animal organs, embryonic stem cells, nanotechnologies of one sort or another – are 'matters of concern'; they are controversial insofar as they are not putative 'matters of fact' but are composed of a heterogeneous array of relations, entities and practices that can be subjected to illumination, to scrutiny. This is not a process of critique in the sense of exposing the ingredients, and thereby the contingencies, undergirding a 'matter of fact'. Rather, it is an opportunity for enabling a broader, cautious and careful collective engagement with these matters. In the case of design, the Energy Babble potentially opens up as a 'matter of concern' what it means to do energy demand reduction and the ways in which information, energy, community and the future feature in this. In the case of social research, the questionnaire and the interview potentially open up the issue at stake (for instance, the supposed facts that inform reassurances about the utility or safety of this or that environmental policy or medical diagnosis or procedure). Puig de la Bellacasa's point is that these encounters need to proceed carefully – they are 'matters of care'.

The form of care that should shape such encounters is, Puig de la Bellacasa advises, 'an affective state, a material vital doing, and an ethico-political obligation' (2011: 90). Accordingly, to operate in regard of 'matters of care' is to affect, and be affected by, the issue at stake and by the other participants (who might well hold to very different understandings to oneself). To care for the issue is also to care for the other participants, even when the views they express diverge significantly from one's own. As Puig de la Bellacasa illustrates, if we as researchers are concerned about the environmental degradations that partly follow in the wake of petrol-hungry sports utility vehicles (SUVs), we also need to be care-ful about those who place their value upon the SUV as affording high status or ensuring a certain sort of safety). In other words, care needs to be exercised not simply in critiquing others' views but in deriving a sense of – an attunement towards – where they are 'coming from' and, additionally, finding common ground that facilitates the continuity of the encounter (that is, also reflects on where one is 'coming from'). After all, a relation between researcher and participant can be complex and multi-stranded, and there will be shared connections or interests (for instance, around the technological innovations incorporated into SUVs or, more broadly, with protecting one's children). For Puig de la Bellacasa, there is, then, an ethico-political obligation entailed in treating social research and design encounters as 'matters of care': it requires the asking of such questions as 'who is doing the caring?', 'who is being harmed or excluded by this caring?' and 'what are the observer's (researcher's) own cares?' (Puig de la Bellacasa, 2011: 91–2). Moreover, as Annemarie Mol's (2008) treatment of care exposes, it is not always easy definitively to identify what precisely care is or entails – the forms taken by practices of care are multiple and recursive, and there is a need to be alert to, and care for, care's limitations and pitfalls. Care can support, excuse, exploit, belittle and moralize as well as open up new possibilities of interaction (one might say, care is instrumental in shaping the form – the how – of concrescence).

In relation to design and social research, to treat the engagement with participants as a matter of care means that the researcher/designer cannot design their 'instrument' in a such a way that it embodies presuppositions about the participant and thus tends towards closing down what can be enacted by the participant. However, as I have already hinted, this is not straightforward, not least because 'care' operates at several levels. For instance, even a highly structured interview in which there is little space for the participant to elaborate or open up (where closed answers are required, such as in multiple choice) can enact care if that questionnaire is part of a research project aimed at evidencing, say, the terrible conditions faced by the group to which participants belong. At the other end of the scale, the evident care taken in the setting up of a focus group, or the design of prototype, can appear condescending (in the sense of being too presumptuous about the participants or users) and precipitate closing down rather than the desired opening up of responses. This also signals the inherent reciprocality of care in these research-oriented events. As Mol (2008) observed, a nurse trying care-fully to treat an elderly patient receives care too: as the patient subtly shifts their body, they care-fully make themselves available to the nurse's care. In a parallel way, participants have to make themselves available to researchers for the research event to remain a research event. Here, we can further note that care as an affective enactment straddles – like affect (see Anderson, 2014) – both the mechanistic and the enunciatory, at once corporeal and linguistic; it is circulatory in that care precipitates responses which are more or less care-ful and takes a variety of modes that range from the formal (as in Mol's logic of choice) to the more diffuse or atmospheric.

This account of care and 'matters of care' echoes the previous discussion of aesthetics (and satisfaction) in that both concern what we might call 'fit' (see also Michael, 2021): what 'goes' with what to bring about a particular conformation or state of affairs (even if that state of affairs is one that is in process, unfolding, possibilistic). In the next section, I attempt to provide a closer analysis of the inter-relations between care and aesthetics, along the way drawing on examples of research events that illustrate the vagaries of 'fit'.

Aesthetics and care: the event of 'fit'

The idea of 'fit' is simply a means of thinking through the ways in which harmony, concrescence and satisfaction are accomplished within a particular event (in the present case, that is a 'research event'). As is well known, an event involves both the inclusion and exclusion of prehensions; the concrescence of those prehensions becomes the prehension for subsequent concrescences or èvents. However, drawing on the notion of 'fit', not least in the context of the complexities of care, we can begin to explore the types of harmony, concrescence, satisfaction and conformation that can emerge, and with that, the borders of the events which they implicate. In the following discussion, I provide three broad and tentative examples of 'fit' within the research event triggered by different enactments of care. These serve as a provisional but hopefully fertile ground on which to examine the complex harmonies that emanate from within the event.

Too much finish, too much care?

High finishing, as noted, can suggest a care for the aesthetics of the prototype (and, by extension, other types of social scientific methodological 'instruments'). This is also a care for potential practitioners/users whose perceived requirements are 'cared for', not least the basic requirement of demonstrating respect: the researcher has worked hard to 'polish' this prototype/instrument for the benefit of the practitioner/user. Yet, again as previously noted, there might be 'too much' polish: finishing might be too high and the care taken in finishing might be directed primarily at – extend feelings mainly towards – the traditions and standards of design/social science. So, for example, the 'finish' of an interview schedule which aims to care for participants by assuming their concerns for large-scale processes of social change might aspire to inclusion but in actuality enact exclusion. Thus, care might be enacted through a presumed common concern for, say, the risks associated with local nuclear installations. However, this can be rejected by participants because that enactment of care misses the point – their concerns lie elsewhere (with poverty, education or the health service). Or one might be care-ful by being transparent about the way that the 'matter of concern' addressed in the research maps onto broader sociological issues (such as globalization); this might be met with discomfort (because it can unintentionally imply ignorance on the part of the participant) or anger at 'ivory tower thinking'.

The point is that research can entail finish that is 'too much' – that is, demonstrates care that 'over-assumes' and 'over-gives' in the sense of showing respect that misses its mark. In other words, the care offered is inappropriate for the participants and their particular concerns, and the hoped-for fit, or harmonization, is dissipated. Of course, this need not be the case. This care about common concerns can be supplemented by, embedded within or entangled with other forms of aesthetic performance (as hinted previously). A gentle joke, a little light teasing, a self-deprecating comment about the research event – these, and many more, let us call them 'micro-mediations' – serve in aestheticizing care in additional ways that might be crucial to the 'satisfaction' of the research event.

More generally, we might say that in the process of the research event there is an ongoing calibration of care (and affect, or 'feeling') among participants. This might or might not lead to a satisfaction in the concrete immediacy of the particular research encounter. However, and this is a point that will be developed in the following sections, there might be a satisfaction of a more 'expansive' research event in which the failing of high finish nevertheless allows for new research insights (as, hopefully, represented by the present text!).

Unreciprocated care?

In some cases, the care enacted in the research event is met with responses that, within the specific setting of an interview or focus group or participatory engagement, are nonsensical. It is not that the participant is caring in an 'inappropriate' or antagonistic way which thereby corrupts 'fit' and dis-harmonizes the research event. Rather, the participant's behaviour (or 'misbehaviour' – see Michael, 2012) simply makes no sense – it occupies a different affective space whose meaning is effectively impenetrable. When participants arrive drunk and promptly fall asleep and snore, or when invitees make utterances that fail to address anything remotely to do with the research event despite the researcher's care-ful conduct, there is a short-circuiting of care and little chance of feelings that harmonize.

One way of describing such a process is through the philosophical figure of the idiot (Stengers, 2005; Michael, 2012). According to Stengers, the idiot 'resists the consensual way in which the situation is presented' (994). The idiot is a figure that refuses (research) events as commonly comprehended. Stengers frames it thus: 'the idiot can neither reply nor discuss the issue ... (the idiot) does not know' (995). Needless to say, researchers are very good at removing the idiot from their accounts, not least by failing to notice their contribution, putting it down to some mishap in the research design or attributing it to a lack of skill in the researcher. However, Stengers suggests that 'the idiot demands that we (in this case the researchers) slow down' (995) and 'bestow efficacy upon the murmurings of the idiot, the "there is something more important" that is so easy to forget because it "cannot be taken into account", because the idiot neither objects nor proposes anything that "counts"' (1001).

In proceeding in this manner, one is enacting a sort of 'meta-care' – caring for the absence of care that allows for a re-delineation of the research event. There is a harmonization that enfolds the alienness of the idiot: as such, the effort of care is directed not to answer the research question that informs the research event, but to open up the research question *per se* and to explore whether more inventive research problems could have emerged (see Fraser, 2010). At base, the research event has been enlarged – new ingredients (the research programme, the relations between researcher and researched) have become relevant and a different aesthetic has become possible.

Other circulations of care?

So far, the presumption has been that the circulation of care within – the aesthetic harmonization of – the research event has been between researcher and researched. However, many research events involve multiple research participants. One of the functions of the researcher is to moderate among participants (indeed, 'moderator' is the title typically given the researcher in a focus group – see, for example, Grønkjær et al, 2011). In this capacity the moderator must take care in enabling as many participant voices as possible to be heard, as well as in ensuring that contributions keep to the topic or matter of concern. As previously noted, though participants can care for the researcher, they can also care for one another. After all, participants, who are more or less unknown to each other, are likely engaged in a process of identification with, and differentiation from, other participants. In the case of members of the public recruited for a series of participant engagement events, there are judgements made about who is a 'good' member of the public and, indeed, what form a 'good public' might take (see Michael, 2009). The point is that in the discussions that take place, care circulating among participants in which there is care-ful engagement with one another does not necessarily sit easily with the care afforded by the researcher.

This, as it were, inter-participant care is not simply a matter of participants supporting one another in order to challenge the substantive assumptions entailed in the researcher's questions. For example, in my own research, 'walkers' questioned my presupposition that the style or aesthetics of walking boots were important: for them, it was insistently *only* about function (Michael, 2000). Care among participants can be rather more transformative, changing the very nature of the research event. Thus, in another focus group with school students who were being asked what sources of information about genetics they deemed most trustworthy, they collectively cycled through a range of sources including textbooks, the internet and GPs. At face value this was an interesting finding at the time, suggesting much more subtle and complex relations of trust to scientific expertise (Michael and Carter, 2001). Subsequently, on reflection, a somewhat different interpretation can be applied to these focus groups. The students were in actuality engaged in a 'game' – competing with one another to present more and more supposedly trusted sources of genetic expertise. The research event had been converted into a competition in which students 'cared' for each other, together sustaining the impression of seriousness (in relation to research) while ironically under-cutting this by coordinating their playfulness (Michael, 2012). In other words, they cared for the moderator by seemingly answering their question while simultaneously undermining that role by caring for each other in the collective playing of a game. At base, there were two co-present research events which, from the perspective of the researchers, were ironicized.

The point here is that there are divergent forms of harmonization and conformation in play: disparate circuits of care are in evidence, and these are, we might say, ironically layered on top of one another. There is a co-emergence of different events. This raises important issues about how we imagine care and aesthetics to inter-relate in the doing of research. In the preceding sections we have discussed the way that 'care' can serve in the disruption, re-categorization, enlargement and ironicization of the aesthetics of a research event. In the concluding section, I draw on these differences to suggest ways in which to continue thinking about the inter-relations of care and aesthetics as they apply to social scientific research more broadly.

Concluding remarks: the aesthetics of care/care of aesthetics

The Whiteheadian model of aesthetics illuminates social method by showing how different ingredients come to fit, to accomplish some sort of satisfaction or harmonization. This is not simply a matter of calibrating researcher and participant perspectives, but of aligning the socio-materialities that are ingredients of the research event. That means that affect and the circulation of affect is central to this process of generating 'social data'. As we have seen, such an aesthetic approach also implicates a phasing of finish – that is, of satisfaction that is internal to the process of the research or prototype design, and then is subsequently 'outward-facing' towards luring users of participants. In the latter phase, we also saw how researcher and researched accomplished 'fit' and 'resolved feelings' as a matter of care. There was, as it were, an aesthetics of care.

However, considering the process of fitting and harmonization through the lens of care added detail. In particular, care, as an affective circulation, exposed the multiplicity of the emerging fit(s) between researcher and researched. As we saw, the conformation of a research event could take several forms: enabled through 'micro-mediations', sustained at a 'meta-care'-ful level or multiplied as co-present or ironicized events. We might call these cases examples of the 'care of aesthetics', though they are neither exhaustive nor mutually exclusive. Nevertheless, they can serve to raise issues about the nature of concrescence, satisfaction and fit as exhibited in the research event. At the very least, they imply the need for a more detailed examination of the types of conformation that can possibly manifest.

In light of all this, we end with a tentative, though hopefully suggestive, series of questions that might alert us to the ways in which research events might concresce. Does the notion of micro-mediations of care suggest mini-harmonizations on which the broader research event is cumulatively based? Does the idea of meta-care suggest that the research event, as a singular encounter, can be harmonized as part of a larger research event? In both these cases, there is a focus on the scale or boundary of a research event: what ingredients can be incorporated into its satisfaction? And how do we warrant this inclusion (or, indeed, exclusion)? Do the variable circulations of care implicate different simultaneous events (or harmonizations) that are (ironically) co-present within the same research event? Is this simply another way of pointing to the messiness and multiplicity entailed in research (for example, Law, 2004), or is there a more dramatic problematic being signalled here, namely that the very notions of concrescence, harmonization and satisfaction need to be queried, not least insofar as they can detract from the mess and multiplicity of the (research) event?

References

Anderson, B. (2014) *Encountering Affect: Capacities, Apparatuses, Conditions*, Farnham: Ashgate.

Boucher, A. and Gaver, W. (2006) 'Developing the drift table', *Interactions*, 13(1): 24–7. https://research.gold.ac.uk/4540/1/p24-boucher.pdf (Accessed 15 November 2023).

Boucher, A., Gaver, W., Kerridge, T., Michael, M., Ovalle, L., Plummer-Fernandez, M. and Wilkie, A. (2018) *Energy Babble: Entangling Design and STS*, Manchester: Mattering Press.

Connolly, W.E. (2013) *The Fragility of Things*, Durham, NC: Duke University Press.

Fraser, M. (2010) 'Facts, ethics and event', in C. Bruun Jensen and K. Rödje (eds), *Deleuzian Intersections in Science, Technology and Anthropology*, New York: Berghahn Press, pp 57–82.

Gaver, W., Bowers, J., Kerridge, T., Boucher, A. and Jarvis, N. (2009) *Anatomy of a failure: How we knew when our design went wrong, and what we learned from it*, Conference on Human Factors in Computing Systems, Boston, MA. 4–9 April 2009. Proceedings of the Special Interest Group on Computer–Human Interaction Conference on Human Factors in Computing Systems.

Grønkjær, M., Curtis, T., de Crespigny, C. and Delmar, C. (2011) 'Analysing group interaction in focus group research: Impact on content and the role of the moderator', *Qualitative Studies*, 2(1): 16–30.

Latour B. (2004) 'Why has critique run out of steam? From matters of fact to matters of concern', *Critical Inquiry*, 30(2): 225-48.

Latour, B. (2010) 'Steps toward the writing of a compositionist manifesto', *New Literary History*, 41: 471–90.

Law, J. (2004) *After Method: Mess in Social Science Research*, London: Routledge.

Massumi, B. (2011) *Semblance and Event*, Cambridge, MA and London: MIT Press.

Michael, M. (2000) *Reconnecting Culture, Technology and Nature: From Society to Heterogeneity*, London: Routledge.

Michael, M. (2009) 'Publics performing publics: Of PiGs, PiPs and politics', *Public Understanding of Science*, 18: 617–31.

Michael, M. (2012) '"What are we busy doing?": Engaging the Idiot', *Science, Technology and Human Values*, 37(5): 528–54.

Michael, M. (2015) 'Ignorance and the eventuation of method', in M. Gross and L. McGoey (eds), *The International Handbook of Ignorance*, London: Routledge, pp 84–91.

Michael M. (2021) *The Research Event: Towards a Prospective Methodology in Sociology*, London: Routledge.

Michael, M. and Carter, S. (2001) 'The facts about fictions and vice versa: Public understanding of human genetics', *Science as Culture*, 10(1): 5–32.

Michael, M. and Gaver, W. (2009) 'Home beyond home: Dwelling with threshold devices', *Space and Culture*, 12: 359–70.

Mol, A. (2008) *The Logic of Care: Health and the Problem of Patient Choice*, Abingdon: Routledge.

Puig de la Bellacasa, M. (2011) 'Matters of care in technoscience: Assembling neglected things', *Social Studies of Science*, 41(1): 85–106.

Puig de la Bellacasa, M. (2017) *Matters of Care*, Minneapolis, MN: University of Minnesota Press.

Shaviro, S. (2014) *The Universe of Things*, Minneapolis, MN: Minnesota University Press.

Stengers, I. (2005) 'The Cosmopolitical Proposal', in B. Latour and P. Webel (eds), *Making Things Public*, Cambridge, MA: MIT Press, pp 994–1003.

Stronge, P. and Michael, M. (2012) 'Suggestion and satisfaction: On the actual occasion of agency', in M. Schillmeier, J. Passoth and B. Peuker (eds), *Agency Without Actors? New Approaches to Collective Action*, London: Routledge, pp 15–30.

Whitehead, A.N. (1978) *Process and Reality: An Essay in Cosmology* (Gifford Lectures of 1927–8), New York: The Free Press.

Wilkie, A. and Michael, M. (2018) 'Designing and doing: Enacting energy-and-community', in N. Marres, M. Guggenheim and A. Wilkie (eds), *Inventing the Social*, Manchester: Mattering Press, pp 125–47.

PART IV

(Un)Learning and Luring

12

An Ethology of Abstractions: Learning How to Cultivate Our Modes of Thought with Stengers

Didier Debaise

Introduction

In her latest book, *Making Sense in Common*, Isabelle Stengers (2023) returns to a requirement that has run through all her work, but which until now had not been the object of any particular attention. It was there, everywhere, animating each book, present in the descriptions of the event represented by Galileo's inclined plane as expressed in *The Invention of Modern Science* (Stengers, 2000); in the requirements proper to the figure of the diplomat as introduced in *Cosmopolitics*; in the predatory powers of soul-capture as developed in *Capitalist Sorcery*; as well as in the status of speculative propositions that animate *Thinking with Whitehead*. This requirement was there, transversal, orienting the problems – but we had to wait for *Making Sense in Common* for it to become entirely explicit and to be at the centre of all the attention. What is it? We will express it by a formula: to take care of our modes of abstraction. This is what animated essentially, but not exclusively, crucial parts of Stengers' work. In its political, speculative and historical dimensions, we find the same underlying care, the same concern, each time local and replaying itself on new scenes. What are the abstractions that govern this or that mode of thought? What dangers are lurking in these modes? How can we take care of them? This attention to modes of abstraction is guided by Whitehead's diagnosis of the modern conception of nature. What moderns call 'nature' would be the end product of a set of gestures, of abstractions, of operations of division, what Whitehead called the 'bifurcation of nature', which he makes the central point of moderns' cosmology. But the problem is broader. It's not just 'nature' that is incomprehensible without an exploration of modes of abstraction; it's all the concepts that form the compasses of modern world.[1] All modern thought seems to revolve around a fallacious vision of abstractions that leads us to oppose what in experience is intertwined: the concrete and the abstract, the real and the apparent, facts and values. And it is undoubtedly in the status of aesthetic experience that these oppositions touch most deeply on the absurd: from our ability to extract all the aesthetic dimensions from nature, we come to believe that nature is devoid of them. So, as Whitehead put it in *Science and the Modern World*, we reduce nature to a reality that is 'soundless, scentless, colourless; merely the hurrying of material, endlessly, meaninglessly' (Whitehead, 1948: 56) and wonder where the aesthetic values we see in it come from. Unable to find them where we had taken them from, in nature itself, we end up attributing them solely to human experience, and in so doing, we are merely displacing ad infinitum the false problems we construct on all sides to make sense of the separations we have produced. What if all this stems from a misunderstanding of the status, place, necessities and effects of our modes of abstraction? Isn't it time to question the place of human and non-human modes of abstraction in nature? This, in any case, is the thrust of Stengers' call to return to Whitehead's last book, *Modes of Thought*, and to the function Whitehead ascribes to philosophy in it:

> Philosophy is the criticism of abstractions which govern special modes of thought. It follows that philosophy, in any proper sense of the term, cannot be proved. For proof is based upon abstraction. Philosophy is either self-evident, or it is not philosophy. The attempt of any philosophic discourse should be to produce self-evidence. (Whitehead, 1938: 48–9)

To the term 'criticism' that Whitehead uses in the passage I have just quoted – a term that must be taken, not in the sense of an opposition or a negation of abstraction, but in the sense of a characterization of the latter – Stengers prefers, in *Making Sense in Common*, verbs such as to cultivate (2023: 20), to be vigilant (2023: 93), to take care of, or to civilize (2023: 27) our modes of abstraction.[2] This allows her to reiterate the function that Whitehead attributed to philosophy, but by giving it a new inclination: 'In every era, writes Whitehead, a crucial task of philosophy is to cultivate vigilance toward the modes of abstraction that equip the thought of that era' (Stengers, 2023: 20).

The reprise differs from the original in two ways that I would like to focus on. First of all, it is important to underline the almost dramatic tone Stengers uses when speaking of a crucial task, as if the absence of care, vigilance or culture could lead to disaster, as if abstraction deprived of these attentions could be the site of profound dangers. In what way, one should ask, could something apparently so innocent, so often reduced to a simple cognitive capacity, be the source of an almost existential danger? What do we risk when neglecting our modes of abstraction? We already understand, by the way Stengers takes up the question, that the dangers proper to abstraction are by no means reducible to simple errors of knowledge, description or generalization of what is given in the experience, but that they concern existential, collective and political dimensions. The question of abstractions could well become the central element of an exploration on an epoch, the dangers which threaten it and the specific forces which accompany it. These dimensions of abstraction are certainly present in Whitehead's work as a background line, implicit and insistent, but Stengers explores them for themselves and gives them new dimensions. Through this gesture, she installs Whiteheadian thought on a ground where speculative, cosmological and ontological questions become directly collective and political, rendering these aspects of abstraction inseparable.

Secondly, Stengers calls for the capacity to 'cultivate' our modes of abstraction and does not hesitate to speak of an actual 'culture of abstraction'. Culture is to be understood in its double etymological sense (cultus): both as the 'action of celebrating' or 'paying homage' on the one hand, and of 'cultivating the earth' on the other. By what may appear as a simple lexical choice – the passage from 'criticism' to 'culture' – as the search for the most accurate expression to characterize the requirements that Whitehead posed for a thought of abstractions, Stengers engages him again towards questions that he had left unanswered or that he could not consider: how is a collective culture of abstraction created? Through which practices, through which devices (*dispositif*), can the invention of an environment of attention to the abstractions that govern our modes of experience be constituted? It is a whole activist dimension of a thought of abstractions and a culture of environments that now takes centre stage. Far from simply evoking it, Stengers poses it by basing her reflections on and by associating herself to the diversity of the ways of producing a 'common sense' through devices (*dispositif*) that she names 'generative'.

The diversity of modes of abstraction

One could object to such a call for a culture of abstraction that it was at the heart of all the attention of the moderns. Is not their history fundamentally tied to the invention of absolutely new modes of abstraction? Didn't they unceasingly celebrate it, by the invention of formalisms of all kinds, by their overvaluation of formal thought, by the construction of multiple axiomatics, at all levels of their experience? Hasn't modern thought been the place of innumerable explorations on the powers and limits of abstraction; hasn't modernity exhausted all the possibilities of considering them; hasn't it left us with nothing more to say as to the subject of abstractions? Wouldn't the slightest retrospective look at the modern experience make us see the endless controversies, debates and pretensions that have crystallized around the question of abstractions? Consequently, wouldn't a radical interrogation of the pretensions of abstraction have to be at the heart of any criticism of hegemonic forms of modern thought today? How, then, does Stengers' call for a 'culture of abstraction' differ from what moderns have developed as the power of 'abstract thought' (Stengers, 2023: 20)? From the very first occurrences of abstraction in *Making Sense in Common*, one understands that such a culture must in no way be reduced to a faculty of knowledge, to a mode of intelligence, to our capacity to simplify, to unify, through thought, the diversities of experience. The gesture, which seems to me so fundamental in the way Stengers inherits from Whitehead, on the contrary consists in widening the meaning of abstraction and giving it a new extension. Thus, beginning by broadening the meaning of abstraction to thought in general, and not to a particular domain of it, she writes: 'Whitehead is not interested in abstract thought, but neither does he attribute concrete thought to children. Thought without abstraction does not exist for him. Thought presupposes abstraction' (Stengers, 2023: 20). This is a first level of amplification of the domain of abstraction. Let us give this point its full importance. Whitehead does not say that abstraction is a mode of thought that governs all other forms of thought; on the contrary, he says that thought requires abstraction, that is, it presupposes it. How can we understand that thought can require abstraction without founding it, implement it without being reducible to it; how can it presuppose it without being its origin? It is here that we must continue to widen the meaning of abstraction a little more, by extending it beyond the level of the activity of thought. Pursuing this movement, Stengers writes: 'the capacity to abstract is not the mark of a particular sort of privilege. For Whitehead, perception is in itself a triumph of abstraction; it is selective and partial, oriented by the needs of action' (Stengers, 2023: 19). By placing it at the level of perception, Whitehead, if we follow Stengers, not only attributes abstraction to modalities of experience (perception, the senses, the power to be affected) to which it had hitherto been only loosely linked, but by the same token he generalizes its scope. Any being insofar as it manifests perceptive behaviours, however small, would implement regimes of abstraction. When abstraction is no longer linked to the activity of symbolic intelligence, to abstract forms of thought, to the capacity to simplify and formalize by the power of thought, however, nothing justifies limiting it to humans and to a single aspect of their existence anymore. If the simplest perception is already, as Stengers affirms, the triumph of abstraction, then all living beings, in the diversity of the modes of perception that characterize them, demonstrate an activity of abstraction. It is a whole new field of exploration on the diversity of the modes of abstraction of living beings that Whitehead's thought opens according to Stengers. Each time, for each being, we would have to ask what activity of abstraction it implements, by what way of abstracting elements of its environment it constitutes itself and maintains its own existence.

But once this enlargement has been made, which we will see is not yet sufficient, the question persists: what is abstraction according to Whitehead? Certainly, we can widen the space of the application of the activity of abstraction, placing it at all levels, human and non-human, of existence. But we must somehow characterize this activity, specify it and distinguish it from other dimensions of experience. In a word, what link could exist between the ways of articulating schemes of thought, of creating 'abstractions', in the usual sense of the term, that is to say entities abstracted from any content, and more or less ephemeral perceptions of the environments of existence of the living, ways of perceiving and of feeling the fluctuations of an environment?

Let us take up again the way in which Stengers links 'perception' and 'abstraction'. She writes that perception 'is selective and partial, oriented by the needs of action' (Stengers, 2023: 19) and that it is the 'triumph of abstraction'. We have three types of the activity of abstraction according to Whitehead. To abstract is first of all to extract particular elements from a medium, from an environment. In its first sense, *ab-strahere*, it designates the concrete act by which one subtracts, pulls, removes, snatches something, which will later give the capacity to 'remove by thought'; then, to abstract is indeed a 'partial' activity in the sense that it is a matter of choosing, of erecting such and such a thing rather than such and such other thing, of emphasizing a part of an environment or of a dimension of an experience; and finally, this partial selection is unthinkable without referring it to the conditions of an action. A predator looking for prey in its environment will be attentive to certain signs (traces left on a path, sounds and smells indicating the passage of a potential prey etc). The way to focus attention on certain elements at the expense of others, to dismiss as relatively insignificant other parts of the visual, olfactory or sensory experience, is unthinkable without the predatory activity of abstraction itself. Abstraction thus defines modes of relations of beings to their environment. No being passively inserts itself in an environment, but from the most inchoate forms of existence to the most elaborated, we find innumerable activities of captures, transformations, appropriations and selections. It is a universe of captures, where beings constitute themselves by integrating, in ways that differ each time, the elements of their environment. What defines a being is its mode of capture, its way of prehending others, of feeling them in a unique modality which defines its existence. Thus, abstraction can be understood as one of the deepest modalities of the aesthetic. In the same way that we should stop situating abstraction in a particular faculty, so often exclusively human, we should stop making aesthetics a way of projecting in nature appreciations, tastes, attachments and enjoyments of which things would be otherwise deprived. There is still a heritage of the bifurcation of the nature which leads us to unfortunately separate the real things from the apparent ones, the facts and the values, the existence and the aesthetic. Against the bifurcation of nature,[3] we have to say that abstraction is everywhere present because the beings define themselves by the captures (prehensions) that they operate on their environment of other beings and that the aesthetic is therefore at the heart of existence because no being can be separated from its modalities of existence, from its manners of being and feeling, from its appreciations, even if they were imperceptible. The Whiteheadian theory of abstraction opens us to what I would call a *universal mannerism*,[4] in which ontology and aesthetics, action and abstraction become indistinguishable.

Possibles haunting beings

Every being is defined by activities of abstraction. From bacterial realities to elaborated forms of organization of the biological body, while passing by acts as diverse as to move, to feel, to perceive, to think, we find a similar activity, which, although it takes varied forms and is each time different, is no less generic, common to all existence. But if we say that a being is defined by the acts of selection, of partiality (decision), which allow it to integrate this aspect of its environment, that existence, that resource to the detriment of those others, what about all that is rejected, put aside and excluded? Is all this reality that beings put aside (of their own constitution; of their existence) simply a pure emptiness that they can indifferently ignore? When, for example, we extract, by the attention linked to an action to be done, an object in our perceptive field, does our attention which selects and chooses send back to nothingness the background of our perceptive field? In short, what about what is rejected? This question is particularly insistent in Whitehead's work and marks a deep originality of his thought. Thus, in *Process and Reality*, Whitehead makes it a fundamental ontological principle:

> An actual entity has a perfectly definite bond with each item in the universe. This determinate bond is its prehension of that item. A negative prehension is the definite exclusion of that item from a positive contribution to the subject's own real internal constitution. This doctrine involves the position that a negative prehension expresses a bond. (Whitehead, 1929: 41)

If we call 'positive prehensions' the acts of capture, of taking or of appropriation by which a being integrates others, we can, writes Whitehead, call 'negative prehensions' the links that it maintains with what it has excluded. These links are as strong, intense and determining as those of the positive prehensions; they mark the beings in their very constitution. Thus:

> A feeling bears on itself the scars of its birth; it recollects as a subjective emotion its struggle for existence; it retains the impress of what it might have been, but is not. It is for this reason that what an actual entity has avoided as a datum for feeling may yet be an important part of its equipment. The actual cannot be reduced to mere matter of fact in divorce from the potential. (Whitehead, 1929: 226–7)

Or yet, as Stengers comments: 'everything that happens might have turned out otherwise than it has' (Stengers, 2023: 135). What the acts of prehension exclude, far from disappearing, from being exterior to the beings, comes to haunt them like so many possibilities that they excluded, like so many trajectories that they could have taken, and which mark them in an indelible way. They are, according to Whitehead's very beautiful expression, the 'scars of existence'. These do not form a secondary surface of the beings, the actions and the events, but they constitute their very fabric. Stengers confirms her re-reading of Whitehead when she proposes that by insisting on the metaphysical importance of 'negative prehensions' that '[i]t is the universe itself, as his metaphysics conceives of it, that gives meaning to the possible, to the insistence on unrealized alternatives, to the link between existence and value, and all of it in a mode that may concern the oyster and tree as much as the human' (Stengers, 2023: 33).

Cultivating possibles

From the interactions of the living to their environments to the reflections on human history, we find at all levels this sense of alternatives, choices and exclusions that define beings. The activities of abstraction are everywhere present, but the attention paid to what they exclude, to the possibilities that accompany them, more or less silently, marks the differences between beings. In two of his main works, *Process and Reality* and *Modes of Thought*, Whitehead went so far as to propose a conception of the differences between beings (the plant, animal and human worlds) according to their respective degrees of attention for the possibilities that accompany them. Rendered negligible with respect to physical realities whose existence is governed by the average – a given that the relevance of 'physical laws' testifies to – this sense is fully activated in living realities. It is in animals that the question becomes intense and vital. Cultivating the sense of what could have been and what could still become is part of the very conditions of existence of the living; their survival depends on it. The relationship that they maintain with their environment, with its fluctuations, with its changes, is entirely marked by this attention to what exceeds the 'simple given of fact', to what Whitehead calls 'feelings', to these vague presences, these forerunners of change, these reminiscences of former situations which insist in their present. The animal on the alert for a possible danger, worried by minimal variations in its environment, attentive to clues and signs referring it to the possible presence of a predator or a prey, all this testifies to a primordial attention to these possibilities anchored in the present fact, in the factuality of a particular moment. The sense of possibility is not present as a secondary attention; it is embedded in the living and characterizes it in the depths of its existence.

Stengers returns to this variable intensity of the sense of possibility in beings. She adds a fundamental element to it in *Making Sense in Common*, namely that this sense also draws differences between knowledge practices that relate to the living. We can always ignore the importance of the choices, of their fragility, and of the insistence of the possibilities that accompany the living in the risky adventures that scandalize their existence. But it is at the price of innumerable reductions of the plurality of the ways of existing of the living, of the setting aside of fundamental aspects of their existence that we do it. It is a whole science of the 'living' that has been established on the basis of this ignorance, the cause of which Whitehead saw in the overvaluation of the physical sciences as a model which impregnates, by its methods, its ambitions, its ways of doing things, the sciences of the living. Thus, in *Modes of Thought*, criticizing the reduction of the life sciences to physical models, he writes (1938: 154): 'Science can find no individual enjoyment in nature; Science can find no aim in nature; Science can find no creativity in nature; it finds mere rules of succession. These negations are true of natural science. They are inherent in its methodology'. Whitehead's criticism of these sciences, which Stengers extends, is that they can only account for the living by denying the importance of what characterizes them; this denial is by no means accidental; it is inscribed in the very depths of their methods, their ambitions and the exigencies of proof they give themselves. Following Deleuze and Guattari, we could call 'royal sciences' or 'majority sciences' those sciences that give illegitimate power to their methods, paradigms and formalisms of all kinds to the detriment of the beings they should try to qualify. Stengers opposes these royal sciences with sciences of another kind: nomadic sciences, which allow themselves to be affected by the possibilities that accompany living beings, which explore the precarious dependencies that make a living being exist only through the various attachments it weaves with others, a science of circulations and alliances, because no discipline can exhaust its meaning. Thus, Stengers writes (2023: 67): 'The biologist must learn from each particular being, because the pathways of deduction are impracticable here. Every relationship between what is achieved and how it holds together must be diagnosed on its own terms, for it might have been otherwise. For biologists, the aura of "what might have been" always hovers over "what is"'. This is how many of them come to experience of [sic] the solemnity of the world'. A knowledge-practice that agrees to be caught up in this 'solemnity of the world', this intense relationship among the living between the importance of the decisions that constitute them and the multiplicity of 'could haves'. Stengers clarifies the meaning of this by taking the work of S. Kauffman as an example:

> Kauffman thus affirms that histories of living beings require us to envisage a world in which the difference between actual and possible, between what is and what might be, is at stake for those beings for whom this difference matters: living beings. And we may characterize events like a becoming relevant, or the emergence of new ways for living beings to count with others and for others, as original in the sense of originating from agents for whom they matter. (Stengers, 2023: 127)

Whereas physical beings, intelligible in terms of statistical averages, undergo the alterations of their environment indifferently – which allows them to be abstracted from this environment and to be subjected to experimental manipulations – this is not the case for living beings. And this difference at the level of beings implies radical differences in the ways of relating to them. As Whitehead writes (1938: 28): 'The impartiality of physical science is the reason of its failure as the sole interpreter of animal behavior'. Whitehead essentially saw this as the cause of failure. By excluding the sense of possibility, by reducing animal experience to physical impartiality, scientists were in danger of falling short of the beings they were dealing with. They were missing that 'living nature' that they sought to interrogate. In a way, Whitehead was trying to understand why modern sciences, so efficient in thinking about 'physical nature', were so impotent in thinking about 'living nature'. Stengers' implementation of a difference between knowledge practices extends, intensifies and reorients Whitehead's observation. Indeed, it is not only a question of understanding the impotence of modern sciences to think about the living, but to diagnose its causes and to follow its effects. The exclusion of the possible and the reduction of the plural dimensions of the living to only one layer considered as explanatory were accompanied and made possible by the exclusion of essential qualities of the living and the disqualification of numerous practices of knowledge. Behind this impotence of modern sciences, which Whitehead associated with the transfer of modes of knowledge from the physical to the living, Stengers draws out a power, but this time of disqualification: 'We live in a veritable cemetery for destroyed practices and collective knowledges' (Stengers, 2015: 98). If Stengers praises those biologists who try to accompany this halo of possibilities of the living,[5] it is not only because they are able to think what characterizes the living in itself, but because, in doing so, they repopulate a world of knowledge, of practices, of feelings, of diverse attachments which had been excluded.

Let us continue this exploration on the varieties of the sense of possibilities in nature. Negligible in physical realities, this sense defines the living. Whitehead considers that with humans a new intensification, a new mode of the possible, finds a favourable space for its deployment. As Stengers remarks:

> In his era, Whitehead must have scandalized those thinkers who defined the human as a thinking being, as *sapiens*. For him, if the Rubicon has been crossed, it is because an 'outrageous novelty is introduced, sometimes beatified, sometimes damned, and sometimes literally patented or protected by copyright', which attests that what might be and yet is not has the power to insist and that the importance of unrealized alternatives has been introduced into the world. Whitehead never ceases to remind us that, without this sense of possibility transfiguring the 'given' or 'datum', there would be no morality, no religion, no technique; nor would there be science (a fact we too often forget). Nor, for that matter, philosophy. There would be no common sense to brood over aspects of existence. After all, if common sense broods, it is because it seeks more than what is given. (Stengers, 2023: 31–2)

I will retain two fundamental elements from this passage. First of all, Stengers gives all its importance here to the singular way in which Whitehead qualifies human experience. She clearly indicates the kind of perplexity that his conception must have produced and continues to produce in those who would seek to define human experience by a remarkable faculty (intelligence, consciousness, reflection), tracing an immeasurable domain, producing a break with other beings. By defining human experience by the sense of possibility, Whitehead begins by inscribing it in an ontological continuity with all living beings and thus opposes any approach that would aim at establishing a form of exceptionalism. Thus, human experience does not involve any quality, any characteristic, which cannot be found in one way or another in other beings; it is indeed a question of highlighting a difference, but this difference is a matter of an intensification of the sense of the possible. The alternative, the unrealized possibility, the sense of what could have been or what could become, acquire a predominant place. Through language, memory, the transmission of adventures from one era to another, the sense of the precariousness of historical events, the ideals that carry them beyond themselves, humans define themselves by the immoderate interest they grant to the potentialities of the situations they deal with; they are interested in 'the infinite variety of specific instances which rest unrealized in the womb of nature' (Whitehead, 1929: 17). They prolong, by intensifying it, this animal dimension of attention to possibilities and cultivate it in its own way.

The influence of this culture of possibilities is particularly felt in the relations that humans maintain with their history, the narratives that constitute historical events, the sometimes dramatic sense of alternatives that accompany the decisive moments of a change of era: 'No fact of history, personal or social, is understood until we know what it has escaped and the narrowness of the escape' (Whitehead, 1938: 89–90). From political events to religious reforms, through the history of science and philosophy, Whitehead has never ceased to interrogate this sense of the possible that is inherent in any event. Thus, as Stengers writes:

> Humans, with their irrational dreams, truly are children of the universe. Faced with the irrevocable partiality of the noncancellable 'thus it will have been decided', the importance they give to unrealized alternatives affirms that what is irrevocable will never have the last word. This does not separate us from a truer, fully immediate relationship to reality. It attests that the fact cannot be separated from the possible. (Stengers, 2023: 78)

In spite of the originality of Whitehead's way of considering human experience and characterizing it, his treatment of it is not without ambiguity. Indeed, one cannot dismiss the feeling that the exacerbated dimension of the sense of possibility also marks a new rupture. Thus, when Whitehead writes in *Modes of Thought* that 'the distinction between men and animals is in one sense only a difference in degree. But the extent of the degree makes all the difference. 'The Rubicon has been crossed' (Whitehead, 1938: 27) or yet, that 'When we come to mankind, nature seems to have burst through another of its boundaries' (Whitehead, 1938: 26), he gives to human experience a place that is perhaps too singular. Certainly, it is in continuity, defined only by a difference of degree, but by seeing in the intensity of this degree a new frontier, doesn't Whitehead reintroduce a new anthropological rupture which, certainly, doesn't pass anymore by a particular faculty but by the new exacerbation of the sense of possibilities?[6] Doesn't the human being designate in him the maximum expression of what in the other beings would be still only in the inchoative, provisional or punctual state? What is the sense of this 'new frontier', of this new crossing of the Rubicon? If one must recognize the importance and the originality in the way of placing the human in a continuity with other beings and of characterizing it by this 'sense of possibilities', one cannot exclude the feeling that Whitehead remains in this respect a child of his time. This is not surprising: to think otherwise would be to make of Whitehead 'a seer or a prophet' (Stengers, 2023: 25). Stengers, in the reprise she proposes, does not in any way spare this question. She writes that Whitehead, on this point as on others (the importance that the notion of civilization has for him, for example), 'belongs to his era, with anxieties that are still our own, and with what may appear to us as blind spots' (Stengers, 2023: 25). How to inherit it today? How can we take up again this concern for the distinction of beings, according to the importance of the attention they give to the possible, without this obliging us to establish ruptures, to draw limits, to draw domains of existence that would make a radical difference between humans and other beings?

To be able to take up this aspect of Whitehead's thought, we need to pose the question of the gradations of the meaning of the possible differently and look for the reasons that led him to establish such distinctions. We see then that each time Whitehead sketches a particular domain of existence (the inert, the living and the human), he never does it in view of characterizing the contours proper to this domain of existence but in order to highlight dangers, singularities or fragilities proper to the status of the possibles that accompany the beings. What interests him is not so much to reveal distinct modes of existence with more or less clear-cut contours as to put in evidence what should imply a particular care required by each form of being. Thus, if at the level of physical existence the sense of the possible is well, according to Whitehead's experience, 'covered by the average', it is on the contrary, as we have seen, central in the existence of the living, requiring the attention of all those who relate to it and who will have to integrate, or otherwise risk missing their existence, the precariousness, the contingency, the hiatus, the sense of the 'could be' which accompanies them. What about humans, then? In what way does the sense of possibility that characterizes them require singular attention? What is so common and so singular about the human experience? To characterize humans as those by whom the sense of possibility is exacerbated then means that they are both carried by a particular adventure and inhabited by dangers of a specific kind. If Whitehead places so much attention in this question of humans, in whom the sense of possibility would be exacerbated, it is not because he intends to sacralize a function that would be latent in others and finally fully deployed in them, but, on the contrary, because he intends to highlight the type of danger inherent to it and the singular prudence it requires.

One can say that one of the great singularities of the recovery proposed by Stengers lies in this attention to the particular dangers that accompany this exacerbation of possibilities. It is a whole new space of investigation that opens up and gives Whitehead's thought a singular form where speculative questions become political and metaphysical categories are transformed into pharmacological resources whose vocation is to problematize this sense of possibility. If humans define themselves by the importance they give to the possible, there is no guarantee in this feature that characterizes them, no value to speak of, and Stengers does not cease in *Making Sense in Common* to highlight this equivocal aspect of the relationship of humans to the possible. The sense of possibility is first of all what allows them to take into account what was neglected in the choices they made, to populate their experience with other dimensions, to imagine new possibilities and to commit themselves to making them exist. It is this dimension, whose list of features is much more extensive than the summary I give here, that Whitehead has most consistently sought to highlight as a particular and singular adventure that characterizes humans in the extension of the multiple histories of the living. But this sense of possibilities also designates what can always become an occasion, a pretext, a justification of the greatest tragedies. How many destructions of practices, of cultures, of attachments, of environments were made in the name of an imagined possibility, a pure abstract entity having to define a destiny, a horizon and a truth which should impose itself against all? And it is sometimes the same sense of possibilities which, at one moment, defines an attention to what could come to enrich a situation, to thicken it, to give it other aspects, and which at another moment, or in another context, can become a predatory power, disqualifying and rejecting everything on its way. It is this equivocality of the meaning of the possible that Stengers focusses on in *Making Sense in Common*:

> As for the foolish enterprises and sensibility for unrealized alternatives of these 'human beings', we cannot and must not forget today that they demand much more than the vigilance of philosophy. Can we, even in a poetic fashion, characterize the human as such in terms that belong first and foremost to our civilization? Let us recall the ominous juridical thesis of terra nullius that defined certain lands as belonging to no one because they were inhabited by 'lazy' people, strangers to the spirit of enterprise, who had not put their lands to work. It designated them as peoples whose 'traditions' should be destroyed, since they stifled the insistence of unrealized alternatives that gives its value to human life. Can we say that it was the human who crossed the Rubicon, if that means separating nature, which is, from culture, which nurtures what might be? Or was it the colonizer, in charge of the 'foolish' mission of civilizing humanity, while animated by the possibility of taking possession of worlds to exploit? (Stengers, 2023: 32)

At every moment, questions arise about the possibilities that can never be decided once and for all, questions that imply attention, a certain anxiety, and that require cultivation and problematization: will these possibilities enrich, intensify, give new perspectives, increase the value of the beings and events to which they are linked, or, on the contrary, will they become instruments of destruction imposing themselves against all odds? The exacerbation of the sense of possibility that characterizes humans is at the same time the problem they always have to deal with, without solutions, without guarantees, and which requires attention and vigilance, a whole 'art of possibilities'.

Conclusion

We can now return to the strange function that Stengers attributes to philosophy: to cultivate a vigilance towards the abstractions that equip the thought of an era. Nothing is more foreign to this proposal than the calls for a thought that would finally be rid of the abstractions that would disguise its meaning, or the search for a pure experience that would precede the mediations of ideas and representation. This would simply repeat the bifurcation of nature between the real and the constructed, the world and the multiple ways of referring to it, facts and values – all bifurcations to which Whitehead has consistently opposed a cosmology in which being and feeling, things and their aesthetic dimensions, existence and modes of perception form the multiple and indissociable aspects of a universe being made. The appeal to a concreteness emptied of all interpretation, of all operations of abstraction, is just as disastrous as the overemphasis on abstract thought. Any thought, any act is saturated with abstractions of all kinds, selections, choices, decisions, without which they could not exist. Abstraction, far from removing us from experience, places us fully in it. No longer limited to a cognitive function, to an act of intelligence, abstraction acquires an ontological dimension concerning humans as well as all other beings. This is one of the great novelties of Whiteheadian thought, which Stengers intends to inherit, and which opens up a new field of exploration on the diversity of the modes of abstraction that govern living beings. Each act is a decision that makes this aspect of the world exist rather than another; each perception highlights a more visible focus on a background that has become more or less shapeless; each thought favours certain dimensions of experience over others. It is this constant selection, this partiality of all action, which abstraction designates and which places aesthetics at the heart of abstraction and not in contradistinction of it. It would thus be absurd to establish a critique of it in the classical sense of the term because that would amount to denying existence itself its partial, singular and contingent character. But, as we have seen, each decision keeps the traces of what it has rejected; it carries with it these 'scars of existence' which give it all its consistency; it carries in itself the fact that it could always have been other, that another course of action was possible, that another selection could have taken place. This attention to what abstraction puts aside, to these 'could haves' is one of the most fundamental dimensions of the living, exacerbated in humans. It does not give them any privilege but indicates the dangers that their actions continually confront them with. It is because humans give an inordinate power to their abstractions, regularly transforming them into predatory powers (Stengers, 2023: 23) that a 'culture of abstraction' is necessary; and it is because they can always transform their possibilities into a normative force that must be imposed at all costs that an art of possibilities must constantly be reinvented. A culture of abstraction and an art of possibilities are the matrices of a new function that Whitehead, according to Stengers, gives to philosophy: 'to weld common sense, which is under attack from those who deem it ignorant and impose requirements for abstract definition, and imagination, which enjoys the experimental use of analogies and the exploration of contrasting ways to characterize a situation' (Stengers, 2023: 88–9).

Notes

1. We could treat all the concepts of modern thought (matter, reality, belief, objectivity, autonomy) as entities with devastating effects arising from confusions between heterogeneous modes of abstraction. In his major work, *An Enquiry on the Modes of Existence*, Bruno Latour uses the term 'amalgams' to describe these confusions between the modes of abstraction that make up modern thought. Thus, on the subject of 'matter', he writes:

   > Because of this Bifurcation, or, better, these multiple Bifurcations, we see the emergence of that strange artifact of matter, res extensacogitans, this world of displacements without transformation, of strict linkages of causes and effects, of transports of indisputable necessities. The fact that this world is impossible and so opposed to experience will not be held against it; on the contrary, that it is contrary to experience proves its reality. In the grip of such a contradiction, Reason herself cannot help but cry out: 'Credo quia absurdum!' 'I believe because it is absurd'. (Latour, 2013: 116)

2. See on this question, A. Mortiaux, 'Cultiver nos pratiques d'abstraction? Penser le soin des pratiques modernes avec Stengers et Dewey', to be published.
3. On this subject, Melanie Sehgal and Alex Wilkie write in Chapter 1 of this volume:

   > Addressing the place of aesthetics within the cosmology of the moderns does not imply criticising aesthetics at large or suggesting that, by being irredeemably marked by the bifurcation of nature, the realm of the aesthetic has become superfluous. Rather we are insisting on rethinking the very nature of aesthetics and its modes of conceptualisation beyond modern confines.

4. I would like to refer the reader to my book *Nature as Event* (2017) for further developments on this 'universal mannerism'.
5. Isabelle Stengers refers to chemists and biologists as diverse as Lynn Margulis, Scott Gilbert, Pierre Sonigo and Stuart Kauffman. On this subject, I would refer the reader to the article I co-authored with Stengers, in which the relationship between abstractions and biology is discussed at greater length, see (Debaise and Stengers, 2022).
6. See on this topic Sehgal (2009).

References

Debaise, D. (2017) *Nature as Event: The Lure of the Possible*, Durham, NC: Duke University Press.

Debaise, D. and Stengers, I. (2022) 'An ecology of trust? Consenting to a pluralist universe', *The Sociological Review*, 70(2): 402–15.

Latour, B. (2013) *An Inquiry into Modes of Existence. An Anthropology of the Moderns*, London: Harvard University Press.

Pignarre, P. and Stengers, I. (2011) *Capitalist Sorcery: Breaking the Spell*, Basingstoke and New York: Palgrave Macmillan.

Sehgal, M. (2009) 'A Sense of Importance. Zum Begriff der Bedeutsamkeit bei Stanley Cavell und Alfred North Whitehead', in K. Thiele and K. Trüstedt (eds), *Happy Days: Lebenswissen nach Cavell*, München: Fink Verlag, pp 322–6.

Stengers, I. (2010) *Cosmopolitics*, trans R. Bononno, Minneapolis, MN: University of Minnesota Press.

Stengers, I. (2011) *Thinking with Whitehead: A Free and Wild Creation of Concepts,* Cambridge, MA: Harvard University Press.

Stengers, I. (2015) *In Catastrophic Times: Resisting the Coming Barbarism*, London: Open Humanities Press.

Stengers, I. (2023) *Making Sense in Common. A Reading of Whitehead in Times of Collapse*, Minneapolis, MN and London: University of Minnesota Press.

Whitehead, A.N. (1929) *Process and Reality,* New York: Macmillan.

Whitehead, A.N. (1938) *Modes of Thought,* New York: Macmillan.

Whitehead, A.N. (1948) *Science and the Modern World,* New York: Macmillan.

13

Back to the Classroom: What Whitehead Took from Art, and What a New Aesthetic Paradigm Can Take from Whitehead

Nicholas Gaskill

Introduction

Perhaps the most overlooked yet defining feature of pragmatist aesthetics is that its major practitioners tied their thinking about art to their work in education. John Dewey, who made his public name as the founder of the progressive Laboratory School at the University of Chicago, came to write about art through his collaborations with the Barnes Foundation, a museum and school devoted to using the arts as educational tools. Alfred North Whitehead spent several years in university administration and first wrote about art in relation to educational reform. Nelson Goodman, while finishing up *Languages of Art* (1968), established and co-directed Project Zero, an arts education initiative at the Harvard Graduate School of Education. And William James, though not as directly engaged with institutions (or, for that matter, aesthetics proper) presented his thoughts on value and interest in a series of lectures to teachers and students, heavily laced with references to literature. In short, pragmatist thinking about aesthetics often doubles as pragmatist thinking about aesthetic education.[1]

The tradition of aesthetic education is entangled with, yet divergent from, that of aesthetic theory. Where philosophies of aesthetics have traditionally delineated the unique modes of thinking and feeling associated with our encounters with art, calls for aesthetic education have asked how and why aesthetic experience might prove socially salutary. Society, in most accounts of aesthetic education, is ailing, usually from a bad case of rationalism and its attendant maladies: industrialism, capitalism or even philosophy itself. Indeed, there is an emphasis on embodied *practice* in this tradition that helps to explain both why its most famous figures were working authors (the playwright and poet Friedrich Schiller; the poet, critic and school inspector Matthew Arnold) and why it attracted the pragmatists, who tied concepts to consequences, rebelled against narrow accounts of knowledge and approached philosophy itself as a constructive practice.

Yet after recognizing this common thread – after seeing Whitehead as involved in the same questions of 'civilization' that motivated Arnold, or Dewey as joining Schiller in using aesthetic experience to resist industrialism – we must immediately differentiate two ways of invoking art against modernity. The first and most common approach is to define the modern world through its overreliance on rationality; then to remark on the spiritual deadness and insensitivity this produces; and finally to offer the emotional, embodied satisfactions of art as a curative or, in Marxist terms, a 'compensation' for the sacrifices made for 'progress'. Romanticism is sometimes the name for this approach, but its manifestations are many and include the ongoing fault line between those disciplines said to address nature (science and technology) and those that focus on expression, interpretation and emotion (the humanities). In other words, and as Melanie Sehgal and Alex Wilkie detail in Chapter 1 of this volume, aesthetic education in this mode takes for granted what Whitehead called 'the bifurcation of nature' into two incompatible realities: one keyed to the really real stuff of causal nature, and another expressive of our phenomenal experience. Even as it insists on the rights of experience, this first model of aesthetic education leaves modernity's basic division in place.

The second approach, the one exemplified in the pragmatist tradition, takes aim at the bifurcation itself. It rejects the opposition of reality on one side and experience on the other in favour of a redescription of reality *as* experience and of experience *as* reality. Like Arnold or Schiller, Dewey and Whitehead gather resources for this redescription from art and aesthetic experience, but rather than stick to the established practices of the arts, they *generalize* from artistic practices to modify the metaphysical assumptions that guide thought and action. In other words, rather than recommend a healthy dose of literature and painting to combat the drudgery of life under capitalism, they look to the qualities and features of aesthetic experience – its emotional and purposive qualities, its relation to value, its composition and orientation – to break the modern habit of relegating our immediate experiences to the questionable realm of 'appearance' in opposition to an inhuman if sturdy physical 'reality'. The aesthetic education they offer has as much to do with the general way we regard our experience as it does with the specific achievements of the arts.[2]

I believe that the pragmatist approach to aesthetic education offers two important lessons for this volume's project of experimenting with an expanded aesthetic paradigm. First, it offers clear examples of what philosophers have taken from art and aesthetics and thus attunes us to the complicated relations between a *generalized* aesthetic aimed at non-bifurcated thinking and the *specific* practices of the arts. Our goal may be a version of aesthetics that goes beyond the arts to encompass *all* practices of shaping feeling, but without an understanding of what we are generalizing *from* we are likely to miss important aspects and affordances of the paradigm in production. The arts, after all, preceded and extend beyond the aesthetic of the moderns and so are not confined to the philosophical roles prescribed to them in Europe in the 18th century. Second, as shown by the repeated link between art and education, pragmatism reminds us not only that aesthetic experience has something to show us but also that, in order to be consequential, it has to be taught. Aesthetic experience, like everything else in this world, cannot do anything on its own. Its import and effects emerge only through the relations it forms and the networks that support it, especially (though not exclusively) through the practices and institutions of education, of which philosophy is a part.

Put programmatically, a new aesthetic paradigm requires a new paradigm of aesthetic education if it is going to succeed. My aim in what follows is to elaborate what this paradigm looks like in Whitehead's work, starting with his educational writing and moving through his meditations on abstractions and 'aesthetic significance' in *Modes of Thought* (1968, first published 1938). Throughout, I will show how Whitehead turned to aesthetics to combat what he saw as the primary intellectual evil of his age: the problem of disciplinary specialization, which he regarded as the institutional manifestation of the modern habit of letting nature bifurcate. Arguably, this problem is with us more than ever, with the added danger that many disciplines – those that fall short on research-based metrics – are in the process of being cut from the university entirely. Whitehead's notion of aesthetic education, framed to address this threat but made ever harder to grasp because of it, forces us finally to ask: how can we justify and institute modes of thought that fall outside the 'knowledge factory' model of the modern research university?

The art in education: generalizing the aesthetic

Whitehead bemoans the increasing specialization of knowledge throughout his career, but the chapter on 'Requisites for social progress' in *Science and the Modern World* (1967b, first published 1925) marks the first time he links this problem explicitly to his account of abstractions. Earlier in that book he sets out his now-famous account of the 'fallacy of misplaced concreteness', the fallacy that describes the mistaken bifurcation of nature (1967b: 3).

Modern thought, in taking the results of natural scientific investigations as the final realities of nature, has, according to Whitehead, confused the products of abstraction – including the selections and clarifications embodied in technical instruments and employed in experiments – with the concrete, felt-all-together quality of immediate experience. The dreadful consequence has been the demotion of so much of our lives, and so many non-scientific practices that wield different abstractions to intensify other possibilities within reality, to mere appearance or pernicious bunk. Even more, because scientific work assumes a divorce between matter and value, the misapprehension of scientific abstractions as concrete realities (rather than as useful possibilities within experience) has generalized a habit of treating all values as human impositions upon dead matter. Whitehead worried about this habit in particular, as it threatened to drain life from what William James called 'the zest, the tingle, the excitement of reality' – of ' "importance" in the only real and positive sense in which importance ever anywhere can be' (1992: 844).

Much of Whitehead's work seeks to reconfigure the relation between abstraction and importance such that the one no longer precludes the other. In *Science and the Modern World* he pitched this project as a matter of education, starting with a diagnosis of what he called 'the method of training professionals' that equated 'effective knowledge' with 'professionalized knowledge', that is, knowledge geared to the concerns and techniques of particular disciplines (1967b: 196, 197). Whitehead saw this method as a dangerous inheritance from the success of science and technology in the 19th century. That success, so dazzling in its transformations of daily life, threatened to lure intelligent people into thinking that scientific practices, with their attendant division between facts and values, could account for the whole of life, when in fact they are best regarded as testifying to the power of specialized abstractions to clarify an otherwise vague possibility in experience – but at the cost of ignoring other possibilities and the values they promise. Each discipline, Whitehead explained, situates its practitioners within a particular 'groove' carved out through its selective abstractions, and while those selections enable limited progress (progress within the groove), they also 'prevent straying across country, and the abstraction abstracts from something to which no further attention is paid' (1967b: 197). The method of training professionals embedded the fallacy of misplaced concreteness in the operations of education.

To combat this tendency, Whitehead recommended 'art and aesthetic education' (1967b: 199). Where professionalization encourages the 'development of particular abstractions' at the price of 'a contraction of concrete appreciation', aesthetic education cultivates an attunement to the 'variety of vivid values' lurking beyond any specialized groove (1967b: 199, 197). Where specialization promotes the 'twin evils' of modern thought – the separation of the organism from its environment and the evacuation of value from reality – and so places undue emphasis on 'intellectual analysis' and 'formularized information', aesthetic education promises to 'strengthen habits of concrete appreciation ... of the infinite variety of vivid values achieved by an organism in its proper environment' (1967b: 198, 199). Against the method of training professionals, Whitehead offers a mode of education that brings students back to the sense of 'importance' that fades the deeper one falls within a groove. He proposes an educational mode that brings abstractions into the service of enlivening appreciation to break the habits of misplacing concreteness and letting nature bifurcate.

This aim at changing our *habits* of abstraction, rather than casting aspersions on abstractions as such, is what prevents Whitehead's call for aesthetic education from repeating the 'compensation' approach as previously described. It's also what makes this seemingly negligible moment in the final and at-first-blush disconnected chapter of *Science and the Modern World* so crucial for understanding Whitehead's wider work: his entire metaphysical project could rightly be said to offer just this sort of aesthetic training in how to use abstractions, that is, how to think and feel in ways that swerve from the grooves of modern thought. All of Whitehead's philosophy could be regarded as a programme in aesthetic education (see Sehgal, 2018).

We can make that grand claim more precise by noting that Whitehead first develops his ideas about *appreciation*, *vivid values* and *importance*, ideas that are central to his later philosophy, in the essays collected in *The Aims of Education* (1955, first published 1929). There, too, his bugbear is educational specialization, along with its accomplice, the standardized exam. Both present knowledge as a collection of 'inert ideas' that students must cram into their heads without regard for their 'importance' (how they bear on the wider sphere of experience beyond the disciplinary groove) or their 'value' (how they might elucidate immediate experience). As in *Science and the Modern World*, the remedy for inert ideas – for narrow abstractions that parade as concrete – is 'appreciation'. In 'The aims of education' (1916), the earliest of his educational essays, the term is introduced directly in relation to the 'importance' of propositions. Anticipating his comments on propositions in *Process and Reality*, Whitehead insists, contrary to the standard ways of presenting ideas in turn-of-the-20th-century education, that our first reaction to a set of propositions is not to try and prove them but to 'appreciate their importance' (1955: 15). In subsequent essays (again, as in *Process and Reality*), he calls his mode of entertaining propositions *aesthetic* or *imaginative* and links it to the actual arts.[3] What then is the relation of 'appreciation', in the broad sense that Whitehead uses it, to the role of the arts in education?

In 'Technical education and its relation to science and literature' (1917), Whitehead gives an ambiguous answer. He joins the Ruskinian tradition of measuring the damage of industrialism according to its degradation of work into drudgery. Like others in that tradition, including William

Morris and John Dewey, he imagines a utopian ideal in which labour, after being reformulated along aesthetic lines, might become 'play' or, better, art (1955: 53). Art, he concludes, is 'a condition of healthy life', something 'analogous to sunshine in the physical world' (1955: 67). Whitehead then proceeds to recommend the cultivation of 'appreciation' through the traditional arts. As he writes elsewhere, 'it would ... require no very great effort to use our schools to produce a population with some enjoyment of music, some enjoyment of drama, and some joy of the beauty of form and colour' (1955: 52). But like Ruskin and company, Whitehead sees the more urgent (and more difficult) task as that of stimulating the modes of embodied engagement – of those acts of absorbed activity in which our entire being seems quickened – that define aesthetic experience. And he observes that in the tripartite division of education in 'literary, scientific, and technical curricula', it is in *technical* education that 'aesthetic appreciation' is most exercised, even though it remains 'of high importance' in the other two branches (1955: 58). Making work aesthetic means more than lining factories with nice pictures; it requires that the abstractions necessary for any activity – philosophizing no less than ironmongering – be framed such that they exemplify the concrete values they attain (1955: 38).

We can see in these comments on aesthetic education, specifically in how they toggle between a specific recommendation to teach the arts and a broader cultivation of aesthetic appreciation in *all* activities, Whitehead sorting through the available notions of the aesthetic to decide what he needs, both for education and for his philosophy (two aims that, as I have already stated, coincide). We can, in other words, watch him pick out what he wants to *generalize*. The first is a relation to *value*. Whitehead linked aesthetic appreciation with technical education because technical education requires *creating* something through a material medium, and because it exemplifies a process whereby 'ideas gain that reality which comes from seeing the limits of their application' (1955: 63). When we make something, we feel the world push back, whether in the form of wood, metal, paint, ideas or some other force. We realize certain possibilities instead of others. And since, as Whitehead writes in *Science and the Modern World*, 'value is the outcome of a limitation' – and 'value' is the name for 'the intrinsic reality of an event' – technical education cultivates an appreciation of the values able to be realized in experience (1967b: 93, 94). Inert ideas realize no value because they are dead; only when ideas are taken up 'imaginatively' can they become part of a process of realization. And only what is realized can be 'appreciated'.

Whitehead worked within the same tradition of educational reform that, in the United States, Dewey championed. At its heart was the insistence that, as the growing field of developmental psychology demonstrated (and as any parent will attest), children learn best when they are *interested*, and 'inert ideas' don't interest them.[4] The teacher's job is to stimulate attention and interest in the subject matter to be learned. This means *doing*, not just memorizing. To take one of Whitehead's examples, when teaching geography, have the students survey a plot of land rather than complete formal exercises. 'Plane-table surveying should lead pupils to a *vivid apprehension* of the immediate application of geometric truths': it should, in other words, foster an appreciation of the vivid values such knowledge practices afford (1955: 22, emphasis added).

The point here is not simply to replace book-learning and specialization with 'active learning'. Whitehead rarely threw out ideas or practices wholesale; instead, he situated them. In his educational writing he places specialization within a more general 'rhythm of education', one that starts with 'romance' (the quickened attention of the pupil, the natural eagerness to know more about a topic of interest and relevance), moves to 'precision' (when the specialized techniques of particular practices show students how to sharpen their initial interest), and ends in 'generalization' (an ability to see how the precise work of specialization fits within the wider ecology of life and learning).[5] These are phases of an ongoing process, not discrete kinds, and so Whitehead admits that the lines are blurry. But for our purposes we can see *appreciation* concentrating in the first and last stages. With 'romance', students have a full sense of the relevance of a topic; they appreciate it in its immediate connection to their interests. Precision might pull away from this interest, in the way that narrow abstractions pull away from the sense of importance, but the task of the final phase is to reinstate it as an appreciation for how the specialized work relates to all that lies beyond its groove. Whitehead sometimes calls this 'wisdom' or 'understanding', the latter meant in 'the sense in which it is used in the French proverb, "To understand all, is to forgive all"' (1955: 14). Understanding results when the adventures of precision have been situated and the student has learned to appreciate what abstractions realize without mistaking them for the concrete. The specific arts are necessary in the first two stages – Whitehead claims that 'our aesthetic emotions provide us with vivid apprehension of value' and that the most expeditious way to exercise them is through the arts. But it is in the final stage that 'art' and 'aesthetic appreciation' in their general sense – indeed, *as* 'generalization' – gain their enduring significance for Whitehead's thought (1955: 51).

In the final pages of 'The rhythmic claims of freedom and discipline' (1923), Whitehead describes this final stage of education in terms that directly anticipate his discussion in *Science and the Modern World*. 'Education', he writes, 'is the guidance of the individual towards a comprehension of the art of life; and by the art of life I mean the most complete achievement of varied actuality expressing the potentialities of that living creature in the face of its actual environment' (1955: 50). He notes that such completeness 'involves an artistic sense', what he elsewhere calls 'style' or the ability to arrange the possibilities available on that occasion (1955: 24). ('Style', then, is at the root of Whitehead's later account of the 'graded relevance' of eternal objects in the concrescence.) *Art* now means something general for Whitehead, a way of using the abstractions that are necessarily involved in actualization without letting them get out of hand, a way of keeping us ever attentive to the necessary links between a selective abstraction and the values it realizes and of appreciating the myriad actualities in any given situation. It's the rhythm not only of education but of Whitehead's speculative method: the flight of the aeroplane that takes off from specialized experience, soars into the realms of imaginative generalization, and then lands to offer further elucidations of experience (1978: 5).

We know, when we read *Science and the Modern World*, that Whitehead is carrying forward the generalized notion of art he worked out through his educational writing because the sole example he gives of 'aesthetic education' is not a Bach sonata or a Turner landscape but ... a factory:

> A factory, with its machinery, its community of operatives, its social service to the general population, its dependence upon organizing and designing genius, its potentialities as a source of wealth to the holders of its stock is an organism exhibiting a variety of values. What we want is the habit of apprehending such an organism in its completeness. (1967b: 200)

The example seems sure to vex and confuse. There's the sheer oddity of illustrating the benefits of aesthetic appreciation with an object that, at least in the eyes of the Romantic poets Whitehead cites earlier in the book, was besmirching the beauty of the natural world. And there's the easy inclusion of stockholders and wealth alongside the lives of workers, as well as the generous assumption that factories produce a 'social service to the general population' (rather than, say, electronic gadgets destined to titillate for a time and then leach chemicals into the water supply). But Whitehead's aesthetic factory exemplifies his aim of enlisting the modes of perception associated with the arts to resist the ever-growing tendency for value to be defined along a single groove. Even factories exhibit a range of vivid values; part of the problem of modern thought is that it makes it so difficult to see these plural values in situated relation.[6]

Whitehead takes for granted that his readers will have a sense of the general features of art and aesthetic experience that he has in mind. A factory may be different from a painting, but the act of 'appreciating' it in its 'completeness' partakes of the qualities of aesthetic perception that have long been a part of the European discourse around art. Artists, on this familiar account, excel in creating compositional arrangements in which the parts magically become *more* themselves through their relation to the whole. In other words, artworks in the modern tradition have been distinguished in their ability to assemble a range of values that are simultaneously *relational* and *unique*. The red in the painting is the red that it is precisely because of its relation to the colours around it. The quickened attention that marks our engagements with art comes from the way that these internal relations have been maximized. 'Intensity', as an aesthetic quality, names this character of felt relations, and when Whitehead later writes that the cosmos aims at intensity, he has rightly been taken to cast reality's processes in the mould of art (see Jones, 1998). Or, as he puts it in *Adventures of Ideas*, '[a]rt at its highest exemplifies the metaphysical doctrine of the interweaving of absoluteness upon relativity' (1967a: 264).

Similarly, Whitehead turns to art for evidence of a direct experience of a non-subjective value and of a non-intellectual (or at least not-just-intellectual) relation to the world. He makes this clearest in his reading of the Romantic poets in *Science and the Modern World*. What he celebrates in Wordsworth and Shelley is their 'protest against the exclusion of value from the essence of matter of fact' (1967b: 94). And throughout his later work he praises poetry as a model of language that, unlike logic and traditional philosophy, works through the imagination to conjure the felt presence of what lies beyond our specialized discourses. Poets, Whitehead insists, feel their world and, by welding feeling to language, heighten our awareness of our embeddedness in an environment. Wordsworth, for instance, 'dwells on that mysterious presence of surrounding things, which imposes itself on any separate element that we set up as an individual for its own sake' (1967b: 83). At 'the height of his genius', Whitehead continues, the poet 'expresses the concrete facts of our apprehension, facts which are distorted in the scientific analysis' because they are shot through with emotion, purpose, and will (1967b: 84).

But here we must tread carefully, more carefully, in fact, than Whitehead. Because in making his 'appeal ... to naïve experience' by turning to 'the evidence of poetry', Whitehead gives the impression that – as bifurcation thinking has long had it – science deals in matters of fact while poetry trucks in intuitions and emotions (1967b: 89). The 'Romantic reaction', on this account, would be a kind of overreaction, a cry to re-enchant the rainbow that Newton so wantonly unwove. What Whitehead fails to emphasize here is that poets don't simply pour out the unfiltered evidence of concrete sense experience but instead *make specialized abstractions of their own*. The difference between poetry and science is not the difference between the abstract and the concrete but between two contrasting approaches to abstraction. Poetic or artistic abstractions, as we've already suggested, keep their selective-ness in view. The arts are artificial, obviously. And, as we've also noted, they retain a sense of purpose and emotion. We can now add – with the help of Whitehead's student Susanne Langer, who pursued his theory of abstractions into the arts – that the arts have developed techniques for abstracting qualities of togetherness from embodied situations. They abstract through *composition*, where scientific and logical abstractions tend to work by isolating individual elements or relations (see Langer 1953, 1957). Poetry feels like life because it retains that primordial sense of situated relations, even as it misses or transforms other qualities of experience. Those transformations, after all, are what equip poetry, like all the arts, to modify experience to new ends.[7]

Art and aesthetic education, then, address our modes of abstraction. Whitehead generalizes particular aspects of these more specialized practices in order to conduct an ambitious project of cultivating in his readers different habits of thinking and feeling. So far, I have focussed on how Whitehead honed this mission through his educational writing (which, in turn, emerged from his years spent in university administration in the University of London system). And I've hinted at how the themes from those essays reappear in his metaphysical work, including *Process and Reality* and *Adventures of Ideas*, each of which develops an account of philosophical generalization that, paradoxically, uses abstractions to quicken our sense of concrete togetherness. They are 'generalizations' that function like the consummatory or 'generalization' phase of education. I now want to show how these concerns take centre stage in Whitehead's final philosophical work, *Modes of Thought*.

Aesthetic significance in *Modes of Thought*

Modes of Thought returns to the preoccupations of *The Aims of Education* in a different key. The notions of *importance* and *understanding* – now given metaphysical rather than narrowly educational significance – each get their own chapters, and the lectures build to a vision of a 'civilized universe' that draws on those ideas to contrast 'chill abstractions' (those that misplace concreteness) with a 'fortunate use of abstractions' (1968: 123). In *Modes of Thought*, the work of generalization from art and aesthetic education is fully developed. Whitehead's concerns are the same: he still fears that hyper-disciplinarity poses a threat to thought and culture. If anything, he has become more emphatic: he charges that 'learned people have handled the specialization of thought with an incredible lack of precaution' (1968: 55). But rather than recommend particular learning tasks, he offers a vision of a 'civilized' intellectual culture that could reboot the habits of thought that support modern abstractions.[8]

In the chapter on 'Understanding', Whitehead's rehearsal of the 19th-century passion for specialization rouses him to a rare moment of sarcasm. Yes, the Victorian age witnessed an impressive proliferation of knowledge, 'but the moderns had lost the sense of vast alternatives, magnificent or hateful, lurking in the background, and awaiting to overwhelm our safe little traditions' (1968: 45). Safe little traditions! Thirteen years after *Science and the Modern World*, Whitehead is no longer content simply to remind people that their abstractions abstract from something. He instead insists that the 'grooved' way of thinking is not only too timid but also positively damaging to the broader health of the culture. 'If civilization is to survive', he continues, 'the expansion of understanding is a prime necessity' (1968: 45). Understanding differs from knowledge because where knowledge thrives in grooves, understanding keeps abstractions in active contact with what lies beyond them. It involves seeing a thing in its relations and never forgetting that the clarity that comes from our specialized practices – knowledge practices foremost among them – requires and proceeds from a vague and interconnected experience. Once that connection is lost, thought becomes stale and fails to draw on the 'vast alternatives ... lurking in the background'. As James once wrote, 'Experience ... has ways of *boiling over*, and making us correct our present formulas' (1987: 583). When our abstractions lose touch with the boiling, such corrections cease to come.

Once again, Whitehead designates what is missing from the 'chill abstractions' of the moderns as *aesthetic*: abstractions go cold when they are 'divorced from aesthetic content' (1968: 123). 'Aesthetic' here designates the general realm of feeling; it is this sense that Whitehead has in mind when he suggests that after 'the topic of aesthetics has been sufficiently explored, it is doubtful whether there will be anything left over for discussion' (1968: 62). But it also describes a mode of feeling a composition, which Whitehead contrasts with that of 'logic'. In logic, a composition is appreciated first in its parts and only subsequently as a whole. In aesthetics, a composition is felt first as one and only later as many (1968: 60–1). As already noted, the appreciation of the one only adds to the appreciation of the value of the many. In this way, an attachment to aesthetic content not only marks 'understanding' as opposed to knowledge, but also maximizes *importance*, Whitehead's technical term for the sense of oneness and connection that underwrites any act of attention and, thus, abstraction. Any act of selection requires a sense of relevance or importance, an emphasis on this over that, and importance, in turn, bespeaks a world beyond the selection. Chill abstractions, in losing touch with aesthetic content, also lose importance.

How can we make our abstractions aesthetic? How can we specialize without stifling importance? Whitehead's answer, already sketched out in his earlier work, is to keep abstractions in situated relation to their realms of concrete relevance. Don't allow them to roam outside their grooves; make them always declare and describe their environment (1968: 55). Constraining abstractions in this way prevents misplaced concreteness and the exaggerations of modern thought, but it also has this added benefit: in staying close to its environment, an abstraction is more likely to stimulate a renewed attention to particulars, more likely to reconnect to the 'vast possibilities' and relevancies of experience. When this happens, 'the effect of the abstraction stimulates the vividness and depth of the whole experience. It stirs the depths' (1968: 123). A 'fortunate' abstraction churns the felt links to a vague environment, bringing *more* into experience, joining rather than divorcing. Lest this seem like too tall of an order, consider that Whitehead's primary examples are sense perception and consciousness. What we hear, see and feel comes only through the selections of our sense organs, but through those selections we are able to engage in richer and more meaningful commerce with the buzzing world from which the senses abstract. 'The sense experience is an abstraction which illustrates and stimulates the completeness of actuality', Whitehead writes; 'It increases importance' (1968: 113). We make these abstractions all the time. Or rather, *they make us*, for without them it's hard to imagine what being human would be like. Consciousness, too, selects and intensifies in this way – but it can go even more wrong than the senses. Whitehead once defined philosophy as 'the self-correction by consciousness of its own initial excess of subjectivity' (1978: 15). Those excesses are all about us; they're unavoidable. In turning to art and aesthetics, Whitehead doesn't try to overcome such selections; rather, he emphasizes 'the importance of a right adjustment of the process of abstraction' (1968: 123).[9] In seeking that adjustment, Whitehead aims to educate us in *understanding* against the excesses of modern knowledge.

Conclusion

Whitehead's complaint rings out still. Knowledge has only got more and more specialized since the publication of *Modes of Thought*, and despite the vogue for interdisciplinary work, the 'method of training professionals' continues to dominate higher education. Even worse: each discipline is now called to account for itself through frameworks of 'research excellence' that are patently geared to the knowledge practices of the sciences and, because ill-suited to educational practices aimed at appreciation or understanding, threaten to canalize education even more dangerously than in Whitehead's lifetime. Whitehead concludes *Modes of Thought* by describing 'the task of a university' as 'the creation of the future, so far as rational thought, and civilized modes of appreciation, can affect the issue' (1968: 171). Is there still a place for 'appreciation' in the knowledge factory model of the 21st-century research university?

In this chapter I have elaborated how Whitehead moved from the specialized practices of art and aesthetic education into his metaphysical interventions into the modern culture of abstraction. Of course, these are not the only areas of practice he considered; as Isabelle Stengers has detailed at length, he also generalized from his experience as a mathematician and from work in the physical sciences (Stengers, 2011). But it is difficult to understand his approach to metaphysics, and especially his approach to modern abstractions, without acknowledging his debt to aesthetics. As he remarked in 1936, every philosopher 'has to start from some limited section of our experience', and that starting point for generalization always 'taints' the philosophy derived. 'My own belief', he continued, 'is that at present the most fruitful ... starting point is that section of value-theory which we term aesthetics' (1937: 184, 185). As I hope to have shown, Whitehead had been experimenting with this starting point at least since the 1910s, when he first came to appreciate the value of aesthetics in his work on education.

To conclude, I want to bring Whitehead's metaphysical framings back in touch with aesthetic education, as I think that these practices need explicating and defending more than ever. We've seen how Whitehead linked 'aesthetic content' to the feeling of a surrounding environment and how he valued the abstractions of sense perception for their ability to deepen our engagements with that environment. Now, with the task of aesthetic education in mind, I want to dwell on just how emphatically Whitehead links aesthetics to our feelings of reality. As he puts it, 'the sense of external reality – that is to say, the sense of being one actuality in a world of actualities – is the gift of aesthetic significance' (1968: 120–1). This is not a new thought for Whitehead: in fact, in his essay on technical education in 1917, he wrote that '[a]rt exists that we may know the deliverances of our senses as good. It heightens the sense-world' (1955: 57). Art and aesthetic significance are for Whitehead the very means by which we come to believe in the world; without them, we are left only with chill abstractions, which, when taken to their extreme, denude us of so much of our reality that life itself threatens to lose its sense of importance. Art quickens our senses, makes us feel alive. It awakens us to new values and possibilities. Whitehead takes these familiar propositions – ones he would have known from Walter Pater and turn-of-the-20th-century aesthetic discourse more generally – and insists that they apply not only to the high achievements of culture but to the day-to-day abstractions through which we build our world.[10] Art, in the general sense, doesn't just make us *feel* alive; it actually contributes to the ongoing composition of the real.

Readers of Whitehead will recognize how he embeds this idea that 'aesthetic attainment is interwoven in the texture of realization' into his metaphysical description of experience (1967b: 94). My question is: what role might this description assign to the study of the arts? Whitehead once wrote that the most direct contribution of the arts is that 'they give vision' (1955: 68). They teach us to see and feel, not least by drawing from the 'vast possibilities' felt in experience to create abstractions that abstract the very feelings of togetherness, value and possibility that chill abstractions push away. And if the sense of reality is given through aesthetic significance, we can go even further to say that in crafting objects that re-shape our habits of perception, the arts also distort, enlarge and otherwise act upon the feelings of realness that make a world. From this perspective, the *study* of the arts involves at least two things. First, teachers cultivate *appreciation* or the ability to experience the 'vivid values' that are made available through the modes of thinking and feeling offered by artworks. This requires teaching students to pay attention to the particularities of artistic compositions and how they fit within the wider histories of artistic practice. Second, teachers will also encourage students to reflect on the particular techniques that the arts have developed for shaping our sense of reality. How do our abstractions make us? What have they made of us? How have particular artists and writers constructed their worlds, and how might an encounter with those worlds modify how we make our own?

These are questions that the Whiteheadian generalization of aesthetics poses for practitioners of literary, musical and artistic education. They automatically lead us beyond the bifurcation of nature and its relegation of aesthetics to the experiential side of the experience/reality dyad because they emphasize the entanglement of all that the bifurcation keeps separate: self and world, feeling and object, nature and culture. Indeed, though it's easy to think of the humanities as occupying a particular spot within the modern partition of knowledge along the nature/culture divide, it is just as important to recognize – as Simon During has pointed out – that the humanities were never 'modern' even in the superficial sense that the sciences thought they were (During, 2020). That is, insofar as their topics and techniques have kept close to appreciation and importance, the humanities have always maintained an island of non-modern practices within the modern university. As such, the ambition to institute a new aesthetic paradigm has much to learn from the example of aesthetic education, even as it drops aesthetic theory's selective emphasis on the arts. As Whitehead's example reminds us, the goal of reshaping our habits of feeling begins in the classroom.

Notes

[1] I admit to stretching the label *pragmatist* a bit thin by including Goodman. I'm using it here as a shorthand for 20th-century philosophers who took their cues (at least in part) from William James.

[2] I'm grateful to Melanie Sehgal for pushing me to formulate this distinction more precisely. Much of what follows responds to her argument that the speculative philosophy of Whitehead and Isabelle Stengers consists in an attempt to change 'habits of feeling' as a prerequisite to modifying 'habits of thought' (see Sehgal, 2018).

[3] For example (from *Process and Reality*):

> The doctrine here laid down is that, in the realization of propositions, 'judgment' is a very rare component, and so is 'consciousness'. The existence of imaginative literature should have warned logicians that their narrow doctrine is absurd. It is difficult to believe that all logicians as they read Hamlet's speech, 'To be or not to be: ...' commence by judging

whether the initial proposition be true or false, and keep up the task of judgment throughout the whole thirty-five lines. Surely, at some point in the reading, judgment is eclipsed by aesthetic delight. (Whitehead 1978: 184–5)

[4] See Dewey (1899) and James (1925).
[5] See 'The rhythm of education' (1922) and 'The rhythmic claims of freedom and discipline' (1923) in Whitehead (1955).
[6] I've offered a more extended account of this passage – and of the role of art and aesthetics in Whitehead's metaphysics more generally – in Gaskill (2015).
[7] For more on the specific abstractions of the arts, see Gaskill (2016).
[8] 'Civilization' is of course a vexed term, and one of the shortcomings of Whitehead's philosophy is that he didn't grasp the integral relation between modernity and the Western discourse of civilization (part of his larger blindness to the preeminently modern phenomena of racialization and colonialism). I won't defend his use of the term here, only note that he means it in the technical sense developed in Part IV of *Adventures of Ideas*.
[9] In addition to quickening a sense of the vague realms of experience that abstractions emerge from and presuppose, philosophy makes its corrections by reconnecting areas of thought that the specialized disciplines kept separate. This is the 'logical' mode as opposed to the 'aesthetic', and Whitehead calls it 'rationalization': 'rationalization is the partial fulfilment of the ideal to recover concrete reality within the disjunction of abstraction'; it is 'the reverse of abstraction, so far as abstraction can be reversed within the area of consciousness' (Whitehead, 1968: 124).
[10] Pater's assertion that 'art comes to you proposing frankly to give nothing but the highest quality to your moments as they pass, and simply for those moment's sake', expresses the view that aesthetic experience marks a 'quickened sense of life' but at the expense of detaching art from what, for Whitehead, marks its true 'importance'. Nonetheless, Pater's understanding of experience as a 'strange, perpetual weaving and unweaving' of our feelings and the world captures something of the 'aesthetic' qualities of Whitehead's metaphysics (Pater, 1873: 213, 210). See also Kaplický (2010).

References

Dewey, J. (1899) *School and Society*, Chicago, IL: University of Chicago Press.

During, S. (2020) 'Are the humanities modern?', in R. Felski and S. Muecke (eds), *Latour and the Humanities*, Baltimore, MD: Johns Hopkins University Press, pp 225–48.

Gaskill, N. (2015) 'The habit of art: Whitehead, aesthetics, and pragmatism,' in B. Henning, W.T. Meyers and J. John (eds), *Thinking with Whitehead and the American Pragmatists: Experience and Reality*, New York: Lexington Books, pp 179–93.

Gaskill, N. (2016) 'The close and the concrete: Aesthetic formalism in context', *New Literary History*, 47(4): 505–24.

James W. (1925) *Talks to Teachers on Psychology and to Students on Some of Life's Ideals*, New York: Henry Holt and Co.

James, W. (1987) *Writings: 1902–1910*, New York: Library of America.

James, W. (1992) *Writings 1878–1899*, New York: Library of America.

Jones, J. (1998) *Intensity: An Essay in Whiteheadian Ontology*, Nashville, TN: Vanderbilt University Press.

Kaplický, M. (2010) 'Aesthetics in the philosophy of Alfred North Whitehead', *Estetika: The Central European Journal of Aesthetics* XLVII. IV(2): 157–71.

Langer, S. (1953) *Feeling and Form*, New York, Charles Scribner's Sons.

Langer, S. (1957) *Problems of Art*, New York, Charles Scribner's Sons.

Pater, W. (1873) *Studies in the History of the Renaissance*, London: Macmillan.

Sehgal, M. (2018) 'Aesthetic concerns, philosophical fabulations: The importance of a "new aesthetic paradigm"', *SubStance*, 47(1): 112–29.

Stengers, I. (2011) *Thinking with Whitehead: A Free and Wild Creation of Concepts*, Cambridge, MA and London: Harvard University Press.

Whitehead, A.N. (1937) 'Remarks', *The Philosophical Review*, 46(2): 1978–86.

Whitehead, A.N. (1955) *The Aims of Education and Other Essays*, New York: Mentor Books.

Whitehead, A.N. (1967a) *Adventures of Ideas*, New York: The Free Press.

Whitehead, A.N. (1967b) *Science and the Modern World*, New York: The Free Press.

Whitehead, A.N. (1968) *Modes of Thought*, New York: The Free Press.

Whitehead, A.N. (1978) *Process and Reality: An Essay in Cosmology*, New York: The Free Press.

14

Schools of Feeling: Unlearning the Bifurcation of Nature Through Aesthetic Education

Melanie Sehgal

Introduction

Today, in times of unprecedented socio-ecological crises, the destructive consequences of the frame of thought that we, in this volume, have, with Whitehead, called the 'bifurcation of nature' are fully coming into view.[1] It is only when nature is first understood as mechanistic, devoid of values for its own sake and wholly other to the second nature of human valuations, that it can be treated as a resource to be exploited and disposed of when its value has been extracted to exhaustion. Indeed, it is only when people are treated as 'nature' in this very way that they can be exploited without end, their worlds shattered and destroyed.

In the context of contemporary discussions on the Anthropocene, Jason Moore (2015: 2) insists that 'the binary Nature/Society is directly implicated in the colossal violence, inequality, and oppression of the modern world, and that the view of Nature as external is a fundamental condition of capital accumulation'. If we agree with Moore that there is an urgency today, in the midst of ecological turmoil, to let go of the political imaginary implied in the nature–culture or nature–society dichotomy, an important question imposes itself: how did this conceptual dyad take on such power as to organize the modern world? As Moore notes (2015: 17), before the advent of modernity, 'never [...] had a civilization organized around a *praxis* of external nature: a world-praxis in which representations, rationality and empirical investigation found common cause with capital accumulation in creating Nature as external'. For Moore (2015: 9), two crucial questions need to be addressed, questions which run counter to a simple environmentalism inquiring into what severed and disrupted the relations between humanity and nature: 'First, how is humanity *unified* with the rest of nature within the web of life? Second, how is human history a *co-produced* history, through which humans have put nature to work – including other humans – in accumulating wealth and power?'.

However, once these questions have been answered, once we start from the assumption that humanity is and always has been one with the rest of nature, that nature and society are inseparable, a third and very urgent question imposes itself: how did this way of structuring reality become operative and even dominant in the modern world, so dominant as to even inform the very critiques of it? How does it perpetuate itself across time and space so as to become general and generally accepted as *the* 'natural' way of ordering the cosmos? It is only when we come to understand how these habits of thought and feeling operate and take hold, how they infect an entire way of life and normalize it, that we might begin to find ways of unlearning them. It is in this task, I argue, that the philosophy of Whitehead, and his diagnosis of a 'bifurcated' concept of nature within modern cosmology, can be helpful today. Here, in fact a double task presents itself which is at once diagnostic and speculative. In a first step, it consists of developing a narrative on how the bifurcation of nature took hold as a dominant mode of thought. In a second step, it involves unlearning these toxic habits of thought. It is in respect to this second, speculative task that aesthetic education proves to be crucial. Arguably, this was the particular promise that aesthetic education held for Whitehead. In what follows, I therefore ask how aesthetic education could contribute to the task of unlearning modern habits of thought, what forms it might take and how, from a Whiteheadian perspective, we can come to understand aesthetic education in the first place. To this end, I read *The Aims of Education* in tight conjunction with Whitehead's critique of the bifurcation of nature in *Science and the Modern World*.[2] I then think through and with examples of educational practices that can be read as countering these habits of thought. Finally, I return to Whitehead's own proposition for aesthetic education which he locates, somewhat surprisingly, in the realm of religion and spiritual experience.

The machinic workings of the bifurcation of nature

Let's begin by inquiring into the status of the bifurcation of nature in and for modern thought – is it a philosophy, a culture of thought, a structure, a set of beliefs, a cosmology or metaphysics? It is certainly not an explicit philosophy or a set of beliefs that some hold and some don't – in the moment of its exposition its incoherence would come to light, an incoherence that remains hidden as long as the two concepts of nature (apparent nature and nature as such) are treated separately. Rather, the bifurcation of nature could be called 'a culture of thought' (Halewood, 2011), 'the metaphysics of modernity' (Sehgal, 2016) or the 'cosmology of the moderns' (Debaise, 2017), in the sense that it patterns thought, action and feeling in the framework of Western modernity, providing a set of implicit assumptions that pervade its way of ordering the cosmos.

The immense scope and extension of this habit of thought justifies speaking of it in this way, but understanding the bifurcation of nature as a cosmology or metaphysics still begs the question of how such a strange and incoherent way of thought could become so powerful as to define the experience of the moderns. Therefore, in Chapter 1 of this volume and in concert with Debaise (2017), we emphasized the machinic character of the bifurcation of nature, the fact that it is not only a way of thought, a set of specific propositions (a mechanistic notion of materiality, simple location etc) but rather a set of particular *gestures* and *operations* that, time and again, make nature bifurcate. But how do these presuppositions about nature and matter take hold? How are they perpetuated, despite their inconsistency and unlikeliness? Where do these operations take place and how do they work? While adequately answering these questions exceeds the limits of this chapter, I would like to follow some clues as to the origins of this mode of thought in Whitehead's own texts. I then address the main question of this chapter: how can we begin to unlearn this toxic habit of thought? If we can discern points, moments or institutionalized settings that permit the dissemination of this way of thinking and acting in the modern world, these very same instances could provide pointers as to how to unhinge this destructive habit of thought.

For Whitehead (1925/1967: 54), the prime exemplification and locus of the bifurcation of nature is the university: 'Every university in the world organises itself in accordance with it'.[3] The university is the principal example of the bifurcation of nature for two reasons. First, its entire organization into departments and faculties follows the dividing lines of the bifurcation. Second, and more fundamentally, if one reconstructs from Whitehead's writing a speculative story of how the moderns became modern, with the habit of letting nature bifurcate at the centre of their cosmology, we are also led to the university as the place of origin of this defining feature of modernity (and not simply as an exemplary site exhibiting it). Whitehead traces the origins of the bifurcation of nature not only to the invention of modern science in general but, more precisely, to the stronghold of Newtonian physics. In this regard, however, Newtonian physics matters less in terms of its theory (about physical bodies issuing in the laws of movement) than it matters in terms of the kinds of practices it institutes. Physics is *the* first subject of the modern research university, establishing methods and ideals of scientific research that extend far beyond its subject matter and hence even physics itself.[4] Isabelle Stengers (2000) links 'the invention of modern science' to Galileo Galilei's invention of the modern experimental dispositive (Stengers, 2000; Sehgal, 2018: 114f.). For her, it is with Galileo's invention of a particular mode of truth-making, issuing in the conception of a scientific fact, that modern bifurcations set in – between fact and value, fact and fiction, science and belief – and with it the particular valuation, or disqualification, of one side of the equation towards the other.

Although experimental science and scientific knowledge production, as an epistemic format and disposition, might explain, however rudimentary, the genesis of a particular ethos and outlook of the new science, they fail to explain the wide dissemination of its subsequent habits of thought, far beyond the realm of science and its institutions. How might such a specialist mode of attention to things as a bifurcated concept of nature – encased not only in an elitist institution but also in the specific temporal and spatial *dispositif* of experimental science – have spread beyond the confines of its place of origin? Here, it seems crucial to take the development and wide instalment of what Whitehead (1925/1967: 196) calls 'the method of training professionals' in the modern research university into account. In contrast to the extensive, often autodidactic training that pre-modern 'natural philosophers' received, the research university creates 'professionals' that immediately embark on specialized research. The danger of this mode of education, which is made accessible to far more people within modern educational institutions than in their medieval predecessors, Whitehead (1925/1967: 196) notes, lies in the fact that it 'produces minds in a groove', unable to fathom the limitations of their own abstractions. The wide dissemination of the bifurcation of nature seems, then, to stem not only from the formats of scientific research such as the experimental *dispositif* (which are crucial, however, for its primary instalment) but from the educational structures of the modern research university that instructs generations of students in the mindset and practices of scientific materialism. It is the professionalization of scientific research and the method of training professionals that anchors this habit of thought, this way of organizing reality, firmly into the world-making practices of the moderns, spilling well beyond university walls. However, the problem with specialized research and education is not specialization per se – after all, specialization warrants scientific advance, creativity and inventiveness. The problem, if we follow Whitehead, is rather that specialization receives no counterbalance, not only in terms of content and the kinds of abstractions, limited to a special field, that per force come with it, but also in terms of form. It is aesthetic education that Whitehead hopes could provide this counterbalance.

The inversion of aesthetic education

Under the epistemic regime of the modern university, humanistic tropes and aesthetic education were systematically removed from the method of training professionals in view of specialized study. Hence, it may come as no surprise that aesthetic education holds a particular promise for Whitehead, providing a lever in order to unhinge modern modes of thought, action and feeling. However, there is a serious objection that needs to be addressed: do we not inherit a whole tradition of aesthetic theory from Schiller to Kant that insists on the importance of aesthetic education in order to counter the impoverishment that comes with the modern condition? Are we not fully in line with this tradition if we suspect that aesthetic education is necessary in order to correct the vices of modern habits of thought and, further, that it proceeds by schooling the faculties of feeling? This objection can be countered by clarifying what precisely is meant by aesthetic education. Such clarification can be achieved by taking the radical empiricism and the metaphysical notion of feeling that undergirds the pragmatist tradition of thought (which I consider Whitehead to be part of) into account as well as the double movement of generalization and inversion of modern aesthetics that it leads to (see Chapter 1, this volume).

For William James, who anticipates Whitehead's (1978) metaphysical notion of feeling, 'feeling' is a generic and impartial term for that which is given in experience, hence before a subject that feels is constituted. 'Feelings' or 'pure experience' in James' words are placeholders for the radical pluralism of the world. Rather than starting from a human subject, already constituted, and inquiring into the ways in which 'subjective data pass into the appearance of an objective world', the radical empiricism of James and Whitehead inverts this order and lets 'the subject (emerge) from the world' (Whitehead, 1985: 88), which has to be taken as a given, an outside to thought that marks its indispensable starting point (Sehgal, 2016: 70ff.). This inversion pertains not only to aesthetic theory but also to its practice: to aesthetic education. The modern tradition of aesthetic education, prominently articulated by Friedrich Schiller, took on the function of *compensation* in relation to the impoverishment that comes along with modern modes of thought, notably the generalization of scientific materialism (Gaskill, Chapter 13, this volume). However, it left the basic assumption of this form of materialism and the bifurcation of nature untouched in simply *adding* human value to a supposedly valueless world. A generalized aesthetic paradigm in contrast starts from a world as given and finds a plurality of values immanent to it (Savransky, Chapter 6, this volume and Savransky 2019). Its task is in consequence to foster ways of appreciating them. The function of aesthetic education then is not simply to school taste, as Schiller and Kant had it, in the sense of schooling a dimension exclusive to humans in their responses to particular aspects of the world, regarded as aesthetically relevant. Rather, the function of aesthetic education is to create modes of appreciation of the immanent plurality of values in the world that, without it, readily get passed over or lost in a culture that has been captured by predatory modes of abstraction that explain values away rather than celebrating their manifold existences.

As suggested in the preceding discussion, Whitehead's (sparse) reflections on aesthetic education are clearly geared towards the specialists that are produced within the modern research university. Whitehead's main criticism of the professionalized training that students receive there lies in the fact that it is 'far too much occupied with intellectual analysis, and with the acquirement of formularized information' (Whitehead 1925/1967: 198). What needs strengthening, to his mind, are 'habits of concrete appreciation of the individual facts in their full interplay of emergent values' (Whitehead 1925/1967: 198), and these habits, for Whitehead, are explicitly aesthetic: 'What we want is to draw out habits of aesthetic apprehension' (Whitehead 1925/1967: 199). The response to the problematic consequences of excessive specialization, for Whitehead, doesn't lie in juxtaposing specialized knowledge and the thoroughness which it harbours with a general and vaguer kind of knowledge (Whitehead, 1929/1967: 11). Rather, such a counterbalance 'should be of a radically different kind from purely intellectual analytical knowledge' altogether (Whitehead 1925/1967: 199) – it should not simply be 'bookish', purely intellectual or analytical. Its task is to '(elicit) our concrete apprehensions' (Whitehead 1925/1967: 198), that is to develop and occasion modes of aesthetic appreciation of concrete experiences, welding aesthetic education to a radical empiricism. This task was at the heart of Whitehead's philosophy. Put more forcefully: it is aesthetic education that *enables* a radical empiricism, in the sense that it fosters the ability to apprehend that 'big blooming buzzing confusion' (James, 1976: 13) of the world. Furthermore, a counterbalance to excessive specialization should also be created by ensuring that knowledge translates into action and that it does so in the particular environment the student finds herself in. Whitehead therefore sums up the function of aesthetic education as follows:

> The centre of gravity of the other side of training should lie in intuition without an analytical divorce from the total environment. Its object is immediate apprehension with the minimum of eviscerating analysis. The type of generality, which above all is wanted, is the appreciation of variety of value, I mean an aesthetic growth. (Whitehead, 1925/1967: 199)

Schools of feeling

Today, the toxic consequences, literally and metaphorically, of a cosmology marked by the bifurcation of nature have become impossible to ignore. There is thus a desperate need for forms of education that foster an 'appreciation of variety of value', a desperate need to find or invent modes of education that not only refrain from engaging the anaesthetizing dimensions of modern modes of thought – separating first from second nature, extracting values and according them to the human subject, thereby (dis)qualifying them as not 'really real', as 'psychological addition', aesthetic fancy or mere interpretation – but that also help to unlearn these habits of thought. How can we work towards counterbalancing this inherent tendency of modern knowledge production? What forms could education take which do not train students in doing away with large parts of 'a world of pure experience' but rather encourage them to appreciate the full range of experiences and values as in and of the world? Whitehead remains vague on this point, merely providing general outlines, such as the suggestion that engineers should read the classics. He does so, perhaps, in part I suppose, on purpose, as he insists on the situatedness of education. For Whitehead, the school is 'the true educational unit' (Whitehead 1929/1967: 13) and should therefore be the target, the place and the origin of educational reform. Whitehead vehemently opposed practices such as a general curriculum or the 'standardized exam' and argued that every school should be allowed to construct its own curriculum in view of its specific circumstances and student body. The question of how to undo and unlearn toxic habits of thought, such as the habit of letting the concept of nature bifurcate, and of how to counterbalance the one-sidedness of specialized education, can therefore never be answered once and for all. But it can be addressed as a problematic, an insistent question that reverberates differently in different contexts, always in a situated and specific way. Hence, these reverberations can only be relayed through examples and stories, even if they will be speculative insofar as I frame them through my problem, trying to find ways of unlearning the bifurcation of nature.

Let us dream, then, about 'schools of feeling', where feeling is understood in the generic, metaphysical sense of Whitehead's radical empiricism, for which nothing can be left out. How would 'schools' – colleges, universities or any site of learning for that matter – look that foster ways of learning that do not let nature bifurcate and do not perpetuate, time and again, the toxic habits of thought that modernity breeds? What could educational practices look like that cut across modern ways of thinking-feeling-doing? What role would they accord aesthetic education? What would the curriculum, schedule or even buildings of such 'schools of feeling' look like? Who would teach and who would be taught? How would such schools be organized – would they have faculties and departments at all? Can we find elements of already existing 'schools of feeling' – within and beyond higher education, in the present or in the past – that could inspire us in imagining and speculatively constructing such a school that responds to the devastation and extinction of modes of feeling in what has come to be called our epoch, the Anthropocene? As the modern research university is where Whitehead primarily locates the habit of letting nature bifurcate, it is necessary, in dreaming of a school of feeling to come, to look at practices and institutions, not necessarily beyond but at the fringes of the modern educational system, with a particular attention to that which the modern constitution has rejected and excluded from the realms of knowledge proper: Indigenous and feminist modes of knowledge production, and spiritual and artistic ones. In the remainder of this chapter, I draw out some lines of flight for imagining forms of education that might mitigate, or have already mitigated, the toxic habits of thought of Western modernity and, in so doing, I focus on the curriculum. Rather than being best-practice examples or recipes, these vignettes or propositions for educational experimentation with feeling are an invitation to continue to dream and experiment. They are formulated in the hopes that they may invoke other examples and aspects of a school of feeling to come.

Countering over-specialization and the disconnect between disciplines

In the context of higher education, one might think of the *studium generale* as a first example that particularly addresses the problem of over-specialization and the disconnect between the disciplines which Whitehead, a century ago, already grasped as a crucial problem 'which kills the vitality of our modern curriculum' (Whitehead 1929/1967: 7). The *studium generale* has its roots in the medieval faculty of the arts and thus predates educational specialization. It was revived, for instance, in the context of German post-war universities where the goal was crucially, but not only, that of mitigating over-specialization. Such programmes were, for instance, also implemented as part of German re-education efforts by the US, or installed to uphold the unity of science (Casale and Molzenberger, 2018). Before specializing in a specific subject, students undertook this mostly year-long programme that comprised a wide variety of subjects. One might argue, as Rita Casale does, that such programmes should rather kick in *after*, and not before, specialized study has taken place. And one might object that this programme is limited to subjects that are *already* part of the modern curriculum and thereby fail to challenge the basic assumptions by which it is constituted. But as limited as it may be in actual fact, the potential it carries for a school of feeling is the capacity to create connections within a specialized curriculum, opening minds towards and beyond the limits of their own discipline, addressing problems that are transversal to them.[5] Thus, the curriculum of a school of feeling certainly will include science, but not as the sole arbiter of experience, setting the standards for all other ways of knowing.

However, the example of the *studium generale* raises the practical and epistemological question of *how* to put heterogenous modes of knowing on an equal footing. That is to say, how to circumvent the implicit and explicit standards of 'scientificity' and 'objectivity' that come at the price of disqualifying other forms of knowledge and disregarded as 'merely psychological' or 'merely cultural'? How can education confront the imposition of standards and accountability, in the form of external assessments and research metrics now commonplace in the neoliberal university, which stand in stark contrast to Whitehead's pledge that educational reform should not impose general standards but start from the individual school and its specific situation?

Relaying situated knowledges

In negotiating the issue of standardized assessment and insisting on the importance of place and situated knowledges, we turn to an initiative of Native Alaskan communities and the way in which it responded to the imposition of standards pertaining to Western and colonizing modes of education that would further disadvantage the children of their communities. In order to enact educational reform for schools in poor rural areas in the US, the National Science Foundation funded the Rural Systemic Initiative (RSI), which explicitly aimed to bring change to the way maths and science was taught in some of the most underprivileged schools in the US. Interestingly, it was maths and science, subjects at the core of the modern Western curriculum and therefore steeped in the bifurcation of nature, that were the target of this initiative, because it was precisely here that students of these communities most often underachieved according to the standards imposed on them. Native American communities have had a fraught relationship with educational institutions to say the least, resulting in absenteeism, high drop-out rates and low academic achievement of Native American children faced with systemically racist institutions (Boyer, 2006: 2). To alleviate these issues, most attempts at educational reform suggested the 'prepackaged, one-size-fits-all solution' (Boyer, 2006: 3) that Whitehead abhorred: 'a new curriculum, a new approach to classroom management, or expensive new computer technology' (Boyer, 2006: 3). The RSI, however, gave communities the space and freedom to envision their own approaches to school reform, taking local needs and resources into account. Faced with the necessity to respond to the introduction of standards – as part of the process of standardization that higher education today faces everywhere – the Alaskan initiative responded not by rejecting standards altogether (after all, they also bring with them some level of accountability) but by adding and developing them, by making explicit and visible their own standards for what should be part of a good education, based on the knowledge of their elders. As Native American pupils form a significant minority, in some schools even a majority, their voices had to be taken into account.

In this process, Tlingit elder Walter Sobolef wrote down his vision, based on the knowledge of his people, of a good, comprehensive education. This included a wide set of skills: food and food preparation, dances, ceremonies, language. 'It also required members to share a sense of responsibility to orphans, widows, the elderly, and the sick. It incorporated respect for self, others, the natural world' (Boyer 2006: 8). The publication *Alaska Standards for Culturally Responsive Schools* (1998) that resulted from this process formulates more than 100 concrete recommendations for how to include, as it phrases it, culturally based standards into education, intended for students, educators, institutions and the entire community alike. Emphasized throughout this collective effort is the importance of place and the relation of knowledge to place: in other words, 'situated knowledges' (Haraway, 1988).

It might seem frustrating that the inclusion of knowledge from Native American communities into the curriculum of Alaskan schools gets couched in terms of the division between nature (Western schooling, maths and science) and culture. But as the words of Ray Barnhardt, Alaska RSI co-principal investigator, suggest, the use of this vocabulary might have been strategic: 'The cultural standards were an attempt to "co-opt the standard process", Barnhardt freely admits', writes Boyer (2006: 7). If we bear in mind Gilles Deleuze' and Félix Guattari's (1987/2005: 291) definition of minority and majority, simply adding to the standards set by Western modes of thought, then, is not as innocent as it might seem at first glance. It strips these latter of their power to define what gets to set the standard. Western ways of knowing become one of many ways to navigate the 'world of pure experience' – useful, certainly, but, taken as the sole compass, utterly incomplete. 'A culturally responsive curriculum', as the *Alaska Standards* manual puts it, for instance, 'treats local cultural knowledge as a *means* to acquire the conventional curriculum content as outlined in state standards, as well as an end in itself' (Alaska Native Knowledge Network, 1998: Alaska Standards 15, emphasis added). Instead of simply adding 'cultural knowledge' to a curriculum framed by modern science, that is, engaging with 'tradition knowledges' on the basis of a Western concept of knowledge, it is this frame itself that is challenged, inverted so to speak, by using situated knowledges that retain a link to the specific environment, natural as well as cultural, in which the students find themselves, as a means to engage with Western ways of knowing (that are hence not simply curtailed either).[6] This document is interesting precisely in how it carefully navigates the fraught relation between Western ways of knowing and what is here termed 'local cultural knowledge'. Its success, I feel, lies in levering the structurally dismissive narrative embedded in modern ways of knowing: 'Before we believed, now we know' or even: 'They believe, we know'.

The place of the arts

How does art and aesthetic education figure in this? What role might art play in an education that attempts to mitigate the destructive effects of overly specialized education and toxic habits of thought? Would art schools not be the obvious place to search for elements for our school of feeling, maybe already operating as such? Whitehead is adamant about the fact that aesthetic education is not about art, or rather it is about 'art in such a general sense of the term that I hardly like to call it by that name. Art is a special example' (Whitehead, 1925/1967: 199). But even if art is not the blueprint for aesthetic education, it could be one way to foster the kind of attention that might provide an antidote to the anaesthetizing modes of thought that come with specialized knowledge production, even if it is not the only one (for how literary studies could accomplish this, see Gaskill, Chapter 13, this volume). For Whitehead, art could take on an important function in the kind of training of the senses and sensibility that is so desperately needed to counterbalance the 'method of training professionals' (Whitehead, 1925/1967: 196) precisely because '[o]ur aesthetic emotions provide us with vivid apprehensions of value' (Whitehead, 1929/1967: 40). Thus, they foster attention to those parts of experience – values – that are easily explained away by scientific materialism. In this regard, an obvious place to turn for inspiration for our 'school of feeling' is Black Mountain College, founded in 1933 in Asheville, Northern Carolina, and known for the array of famous artists that came out of it and changed contemporary art practices for good.[7] The fact that Black Mountain generated a wealth of artists is in itself interesting because, in contrast to its reception, it actually wasn't conceived of as an art school.[8] Art education was here deployed in the conviction that everyone should train not only the mind but also the senses and that artistic practices could nourish general education well beyond the arts, in order to create 'individuals rather than individualists' (Adamic, 1935). Black Mountain's explicit mission was to educate not only the intellect but the whole person in view of fostering citizens capable of, and desiring, democratic participation. To this end, intellectual training had to be complemented by a training of the senses. Josef Albers' courses on colour particularly exemplify this (Gaskill, 2018: 242ff).

The general structure of education at Black Mountain ranged from physics, chemistry, languages and philosophy to the arts, which were put centre stage. Crucially, the educational programme included contributing to the daily maintenance work of the community and the college, such as working on the college farm, serving meals, maintaining the campus buildings and even building new ones. Next to this general structure, there were specific educational practices that cut across ways of thinking-feeling-doing that have come to be known as modern. Xanti Schawinsky, for instance, developed a practice he called 'spectodrama'. First deployed when teaching at Bauhaus, he continued working with this theatrical *dispositif* at Black Mountain from 1936 to 1938. It was a direct result of the frustration of being trapped within modern disciplinary modes of knowing and the literal lack of space to proceed otherwise: 'Classrooms, workshops, laboratories and lecture rooms architecturally and functionally serve the various specialized branches of learning. But the development of interpenetrating concepts of knowledge is frustrated by the very physical separation of one discipline from another' (Schawinsky, 1969: 283). In contrast to these separated spaces, the stage for Schawinsky became a place in which manifold dimensions of experience and multiple ways of knowing – bodily, spatial, emotional, propositional – could coexist and enter into communication. Over the course of a semester and drawing on input from various disciplines – hence not denying the value of specialized knowledge – a spectodrama would circle around broad topics such as time, starting from small improvisations and using all kinds of dramatic means, such as lighting, masks and costumes.[9] At the end of this process stood what Schawinsky called a 'synthetic expression', a way of knowing that included and synthetized all the different ways to know, think and feel, in this case, time.

Educational practices such as these, as well as the conviction that art education is not for artists alone, spilled beyond the institution of Black Mountain through its students.[10] It disseminated the idea that art education is not only about creating artworks, certainly not for an enclosed art world and art market. It's about sensitizing, about broadening awareness to one's surroundings. It's about training one's capacity to feel and be affected by the world one inhabits and co-creates. This example demonstrates the importance of including artistic practices in general education, of deploying the arts in the curriculum of a school of feeling and, as Schawinsky did, of combining artistic ways of knowing with the specialized knowledges of modern disciplines.

'Our one ground for optimism': religious experience as aesthetic education

Whitehead himself, however, despite pointing to the importance of art and aesthetic education, takes an entirely different route in his quest for finding places and techniques to unlearn modern habits of thought: he turns to religion and spiritual experience. One reason for this lies in the fact that religion, and religious experience in particular, has been a prime victim of modern 'explaining away'. It is therefore minoritarian in the Deleuzian sense, providing, perhaps, a lever to unhinge dominant modes of thought. Whitehead's views on religion are particular, to say the least: for instance, he entirely detaches religious experience from the dogmas of existing religions (which, to him, in their conceptualizations are 'crude and horrible', Whitehead, 1996: 26) as well as from a concept of God. It is the experiential dimension of religion alone that interests him in view of unlearning modern habits of thought, because religion has been engaged, like the realm of the arts but potentially much more thoroughly so, with cultivating modes of feeling and sensing since the infancy of humanity. Whitehead goes so far as to state that, in the face of a civilization marked by the fundamental incoherence of the bifurcation of nature, '(t)he fact of the religious vision, and its history of persistent expansion, is our one ground for optimism' (Whitehead, 1925/1967: 192).[11] It is thus religion understood *as* aesthetic education, one might say, that provides 'our one ground for optimism' in the quest to unlearn modern habits of thought whose toxic consequences we can no longer ignore. I conclude by unpacking this understanding of religious experience as aesthetic education.

In *Religion in the Making* Whitehead tells a rather speculative story of the emergence of religion as it developed out of rituals into rationalized belief systems. In rituals, actions that were originally performed for purposes of survival – hunting, for example – are repeated *for their own sake*. Thereby, not only the action but also the emotion that accompany it are repeated. Rituals thus generate emotion; they are in fact explicitly performed in order to do so. The discovery that emotions can be generated for their own sake marks a major event in the history of mankind, according to Whitehead, because people were thus sensitized. One can discern a Jamesian notion of experience and of emotion at play here, according to which emotions are physical occurrences that in turn effect and form the body. Thus, human experience itself has a history. It widens and deepens over time, beyond immediate necessities. Religious practices are important for Whitehead historically precisely because they play a crucial role in such shaping of experience.

Religion is also 'our one ground of optimism' for Whitehead because it entails a mode of experience and a life practice that encourages thinking, feeling and living beyond one's tribe, beyond accustomed habits of thought and feeling. Religion's import lies in its potential function as a corrective to false and predatory abstractions in that, as a mode of experience, it appeals to both – the universal, that is, to that which is common to all occasions, and to each particular moment (Whitehead, 1996: 32). In this way, religious experience complements the aesthetic appreciation of values, or, rather, it could be said to be one mode of aesthetic experience, a mode which has an extremely long and lasting role in the history of humanity. Religion also matters to Whitehead, despite its actual manifestation, because it is never purely theoretical. It is inherently tied to practice and the everyday. Thus, here we have a technique that is able to translate highly speculative and intuitive insights into habitual, everyday practices. Lastly, religious practices give Whitehead hope because 'wandering', departing from one's own immediate context and its routines, is such a crucial part of them:

> The history of rational religion is full of tales of disengagement from the immediate social routine. If we keep to the Bible: Abraham wandered,

the Jews were carried off to Babylon and after two generations were allowed to return peacefully, St. Paul's conversion was on a journey and his theology was elaborated on a journey. This millennium was an age of travel [...]; everyone travelled and found the world fresh and new. A world-consciousness was produced. (Whitehead, 1996: 40)

However, it is important that individuals not only depart from their tribe but that they also return home, full of stories and encounters, 'and in his person and by his example [he, she] promotes the habit of thinking dispassionately beyond the tribe', (Whitehead, 1996: 40). Thus, with religious experience and practice, for Whitehead a possibility to form *new habits* within a 'tribe' opens up. This is why – thinking of his own peculiar tribe of Western modernity shaped by the scientific outlook and the bifurcation of nature – Whitehead could speak of religion as 'our one ground for optimism'. It gives ground for optimism because of its history and practice of wandering, and 'modern science has imposed on humanity the necessity for wandering' (Whitehead 1925/1967, 207): physical wandering but also adventures of thought and adventures of feeling. In searching for the contours of schools of feeling that could, perhaps, help to develop and train us in other habits of feeling than those instilled by Western modernity, don't we then need to include religious and spiritual practices alongside or even as part of the aesthetic? Could wandering be a mode of transversal research? Could such an itinerant mode of knowledge production stitch together the different domains of experience, within and beyond disciplinary structures, in always situated responses to the problems that force us to think today, in times of unprecedented socio-ecological devastation? And could schools of feeling prepare us for such wanderings, especially as they require forms of accountability that are not wedded to the standardized values of modern cosmology but instead are dedicated to the flourishing of more-than-human futures in the varieties of values they come with?

Notes

[1] Whitehead makes this point explicitly in *Science and the Modern World* (1925/1967: 196) when he states that 'the assumption of the bare valuelessness of mere matter led to a lack of reverence in the treatment of natural or artistic beauty'.

[2] The bifurcation of nature does not feature explicitly in *The Aims of Education* (1929) but it can be construed to matter implicitly in Whitehead's insistent critique of exaggerated specialization.

[3] As Whitehead puts it:

> We must note its [the bifurcation of nature, M.S.] astounding efficiency as a system of concepts for the organisation of scientific research. In this respect, it is fully worthy of the genius of the century which produced it. It has held its own as the guiding principle of scientific studies ever since. It is still reigning. Every university in the world organises itself in accordance with it. No alternative system of organising the pursuit of scientific truth has

been suggested. It is not only reigning, but it is without rival. And yet – it is quite unbelievable. (Whitehead, 1925/1967: 54).

[4] Within the history of science and science and technology studies, there is an important set of literature on the operations by means of which physics establishes itself as a natural science and what modes of valuation these operations establish. See Schaffer et al, 1985; Haraway, 1997; Daston et al, 2007.

[5] For a discussion on the transdisciplinary nature of problems in scientific research, see Maniglier (2019).

[6] See also Alaska Standards, 5:

> By shifting the focus in the curriculum from teaching/learning about cultural heritage as another subject to teaching/learning through the local culture as a foundation for all education, it is intended that all forms of knowledge, ways of knowing and world views be recognized as equally valid, adaptable and complementary to one another in mutually beneficial ways. Alaska Native Knowledge Network (1998)

[7] Black Mountain is also an obvious choice as it had close ties with pragmatism due to John Dewey's membership of its board. Also, it seems that Ted Dreier, the second director of Black Mountain, appreciated Whitehead's ideas on education and tried to implement them in the school (Gaskill, personal communication). On the relation between Black Mountain and pragmatism, see Gaskill (2018: 239ff) and Sehgal (2023).

[8] Interestingly, the artists that made Black Mountain famous, both as teachers and as students – Josef and Anni Albers, John Cage, Buckminster Fuller, Charles Olson, Merce Cunningham or Ruth Asawa, to name but a few – became known for their transdisciplinary practice, that is for cutting across the compartments of modern artistic disciplines and media.

[9] The spectodramas are considered as precursors to the 'happening' for which Black Mountain became famous (Ohl, 2014).

[10] Ruth Asawa, sculptor and an alumna of Black Mountain, for instance, advocated aesthetic education for children and citizens as a means of empowerment and transformation in the Alvarado School Art Workshop in the Bay Area. https://www.sfartsed.org/history/ (Accessed 7 June 2023).

[11] Whitehead wrote *Religion in the Making* in 1926, between *Science and the Modern World* (in which he problematized a culture of thought that lets nature bifurcate) and *Process and Reality*, his attempt, if we follow Isabelle Stengers, to construct a metaphysics, a cosmology, that circumvents such an incoherence. For an analysis on the role of religion to 'civilize' modern habits of thought, see Sehgal (2014).

References

Adamic, L. (1935) 'Education on a mountain', *Harper's Monthly Magazine*, 1 December.

Alaska Native Knowledge Network (1998) Alaska Standards for Culturally Responsive Schools. http://ankn.uaf.edu/publications/culturalstandards.pdf (Accessed 8 June 2020).

Boyer, P. (2006) 'It takes a native community: Educators reform schools in an era of standards', *Tribal College Journal of American Indian Higher Education*, 17(4). https://tribalcollegejournal.org/takes-native-community-educators-reform-schools-era-standards/ (Accessed 28 May 2020).

Casale, R. and Molzberger, G. (2018) 'Studium Generale in der BRD nach 1945. Zu Konstitution und Wandel universitärer Bildungsformate', *Erziehungswissenschaft*, 29(56): 121–32.

Daston, L. and Galison, P. (2007) *Objectivity*, New York: Zone Books.

Debaise, D. (2017) *Nature as Event: The Lure of the Possible*, Durham, NC: Duke University Press.

Deleuze, G. and Guattari, F. (1987) *A Thousand Plateaus, Capitalism and Schizophrenia*, Minneapolis, MN: University of Minnesota Press.

Gaskill, N. (2018) *Chromographia: American Literature and the Modernization of Color*, Minneapolis, MN: University of Minnesota Press.

Halewood, M. (2011) *A.N. Whitehead and Social Theory: Tracing a Culture of Thought*, London: Anthem Press.

Haraway, D.J. (1988) 'Situated knowledges: The science question in feminism and the privilege of partial perspective', *Feminist Studies*, 14: 575–99.

Haraway, D.J. (1997) *Modest_Witness@Second_Millennium. FemaleMan©_Meets_OncoMouseTM: Feminism and Technoscience*, New York: Routledge.

James, W. (1976) *Essays in Radical Empiricism*, Vol 3. The Works of William James. Cambridge, MA and London: Harvard University Press.

Maniglier, P. (2019) 'Problem and structure: Bachelard, Deleuze and transdisciplinarity', *Theory, Culture & Society*, 38(2): 25–45.

Moore, J.W. (2015) *Capitalism in the Web of Life: Ecology and the Accumulation of Capital*, London: Verso.

Ohl, M. (2014) 'Einflüsse der Bauhausbühne auf die Bühne am Black Mountain College', *Black Mountain Research*. https://black-mountain-research.com/about/ (Accessed 17 November 2023).

Savransky, M. (2019) 'The bat revolt in values. A parable for living in academic ruins', *Social Text*, 37(2): 135–46.

Schawinsky, X. (1969) 'Spectodrama: Contemporary studies', *Leonardo*, 2(3): 283–6.

Sehgal, M. (2014) 'Zur Bedeutsamkeit religiöser Erfahrung. Whiteheads zivilisationstheoretische Perspektive auf Religion', in D. Sölch (ed), *Erziehung, Politik, Religion – Beiträge zu A.N. Whiteheads Kulturphilosophie*, Freiburg: Karl Alber.

Sehgal, M. (2016) *Eine situierte Metaphysik. Empirismus und Spekulation bei William James und Alfred North Whitehead*, Konstanz: Konstanz University Press.

Sehgal, M. (2018) 'Aesthetic concerns, philosophical fabulations: The importance of a "new aesthetic paradigm"', *SubStance*, 47(1): 112–29.

Sehgal, M. (2023) 'Socrates and the method of dramatization. Pragmatic dimensions of teaching philosophy at Black Mountain College', in P.M. Meyer and A. Dreyblatt (eds), *Black Mountain as Multiverse*, München: Fink Verlag, ch 11.

Shapin, S. and Schaffer, S. (1985) *Leviathan and the Air-Pump: Hobbes, Boyle, and the Experimental Life*, Princeton, NJ: Princeton University Press.

Stengers, I. (2000) *The Invention of Modern Science*, trans D.W. Smith. Minneapolis, MN: University of Minnesota Press.

Whitehead, A.N. (1929) *The Aims of Education and other Essays*, New York: The Free Press.

Whitehead, A.N. (1967) *Science and the Modern World*, New York: The Free Press.

Whitehead, A.N. (1978) *Process and Reality. An Essay in Cosmology* (corrected edn), New York: The Free Press.

Whitehead, A.N. (1996) *Religion in the Making*, New York: Fordham University Press.

Index

References to endnotes show both the page number and the note number (231n3).

A

Abidi, S. 49
abstraction/s 19, 116, 150, 189–91, 202–3, 207, 208, 209, 212, 213–14, 215–16
  'culture of' 191, 192, 203, 216
  diversity of modes of 191–4
  intolerant 109, 110, 111, 114, 115
  possibles 194–202
  'predatory' 7
actor-network theory (ANT) 15, 20n11, 20n112, 21n13, 21n15
actual entities 9, 33, 34, 72
actual occasions 33, 34, 43, 46–7, 52
Adams, E. 78
addiction, to digital technologies 154
  see also machinic highs
Adorno, T. 109
Aesop 90
aesthesis 18, 91, 92, 94, 96
aesthetic axiology 124–8
aesthetic devastation 17, 91
aesthetic education 19, 205–18
  and the arts 19, 205–18, 230–2
  countering over-specialization and disconnect between disciplines 228–9
  inversion of 224–6
  religious experience as 232–4
  schools of feeling 226–8, 234
  unlearning bifurcation of nature through 19, 221–2, 224–35
aesthetic figures 15–16
aesthetic machines 99–102
aesthetic ontology 14–15
aesthetic supplement 33–4, 35, 36
'aesthetically oriented social theory' 20n9
aesthetics 3–4, 72
  and anaesthetics 143
  as beauty/art 29–30, 31
  empirical manifestations of 10
  generalization of 7, 9, 10, 11, 13, 15, 17, 18, 19, 127, 143, 225

art in aesthetic education 207–14, 216–17, 218
  inversion of 7–8, 10
  'new aesthetic paradigm' 3, 92, 94, 121, 134, 207, 218
  origin and meanings of 5–6, 29–30
  as sense perception 29–30, 32
  specifying and singularizing of 10–15
  transcendental 31, 33, 34
  transversal 3–4, 10, 11, 13, 14
  see also care, and aesthetics in social scientific research
aesthetics of immanence 95–6, 98
aesthetics of the outside 94–5, 98
affect 14, 15
Afro-pessimism 80–1
'age of revolutions', eighteenth century 73
AI (artificial intelligence) 167
air 1, 2, 14
Alaska Standards for Culturally Responsive Schools 230
Albers, J. 231
Alcoff, L. 80
Allan, G. 43
alternative possibilities 48, 53–4
'amalgams' 203n1
Amazon rainforest 58
anaesthetics
  and aesthetics 143
  of possible never-event consequences 145–7
Anglo American 120, 125
animal performance 122, 129
ANT (actor-network theory) 15, 20n11, 20n112, 21n13, 21n15
Anthropocene, the 2, 14, 44, 90, 134, 221, 227
  Anthropocene hypothesis 57, 59–61, 62, 64–8
anthropology 11
anti-racism 75, 77, 78, 80
apparent nature 4, 6
Appiah, K.A. 83n5
Apple 163

238

INDEX

appreciation 209, 210, 211
Apu Wamani, Chile 120, 125, 130, 131
  see also Climatic Dances/Danzas Climáticas (Piña)
Arnold, M. 206
artificial intelligence (AI) 167
artistic practices, ecology of 123–4
art/s 10, 13
  and aesthetic education 19, 205–18, 230–2
  aesthetic figures 15–16
  as a form of work 39
  and values 98–9
Asawa, R. 235n10
Asmat shields, New Guinea 11
Ast, D.G. 50
AWG (Anthropocene Working Group) 17, 57, 59–60, 62, 64, 66–8
axiology
  aesthetic 124–8
  see also values

B

Baldwin, J. 79, 80, 82
'bare nature' 4, 6, 121
Barnhardt, R. 230
Bauhaus 231
Baumgarten, A.G. 5–6, 29, 31, 32, 34, 93, 122
beauty 81–2, 93, 95, 127–8, 175
  and eternal objects 52–3
Becoming-Animal 129
Becoming-Intense 129, 130
Behavior Design Lab, Stanford University 156
bifurcation of nature 4–7, 13, 29–30, 31, 39, 111, 121–2, 123, 127, 174, 189–90, 194, 202, 206, 207–8, 218, 234n2, 234n3
  and aesthetic education 19, 221–2, 224–35
  machinic character of 222–4
Black Arts Movement 77
Black Mountain College, North Carolina 231–2, 235n7
Black power movement 77
Black Studies 17, 74, 76–7, 83n6
Blanchot, M. 98
blue, missing shade of 35–6
Boucher, A. 173
Bourdieu, P. 11
Boyer, P. 229, 230
Breton, A. 109
Brill, M. 49

C

Café de Monk, Japan 100
capitalism 17, 18, 30, 39–40, 89, 97, 165
car driving 164–5
care, and aesthetics in social scientific research 18–19, 172–3, 176, 177–9, 183–4
  'fit' in the research event 179–83
Casale, R. 228
causal nature 4

cement, as indicator of the Anthropocene 62, 64
Centre of PostNatural History, Pittsburgh 96, 97
Cerro El Plomo, Chile 120, 130, 131
  see also Climatic Dances/Danzas Climáticas (Piña)
Césaire, A. 71, 78, 91
Chertok, L. 165
chess game example 114–16
Chicago School 11
chicken bones, as indicators of the Anthropocene 62, 64, 66
circulating reference 58
civilization 73, 78–9, 219n8
Climatic Dances/Danzas Climáticas (Piña) 18, 120–1, 124–6, 134–5
  dances 128–31
  danzas 131–4
Cold War 156, 166
colonialism 18, 73, 74, 75, 78–9, 89, 92, 101
colour
  as an eternal object 43, 44, 47, 48, 51–2, 54
  and values 48–9
conceptual personae 15–16
concrete, as indicator of the Anthropocene 62, 64
Connolly, W.E. 175–6
Conservative Party, UK 78
consumption 10, 11
'contextual aesthetics' 11
cosmology 6, 7, 122, 125, 127, 134, 190, 203n3, 222, 223, 234
  Indigenous cosmologies 121, 125–6
couch potatoes 162, 163
cowardice, and the great refusal 104, 105, 106, 107, 110
creativity 46–7
Critical Race Theory 81, 83n8, 83n9
Crutzen, P.J. 2, 60, 68n1
Cundy, A. 66, 67
Cutifani, M. 120, 125

D

Da Vinci, L. 90
dance, contemporary see Climatic Dances/Danzas Climáticas (Piña)
Darwinism 8
Daston, L. 93
'data behaviourism' 163–4
Davis, H. 2
de la Cadena, M. 135n3
Debaise, D. 6, 7, 45, 144, 149, 223
Decamous, G. 53
Decolonial Thought 76–7
decolonization 14
deep time 60, 65
  deep-time aesthetics 57–9
  see also Anthropocene, the; geology

239

definiteness 47
Deleuze, G. 14, 15–16, 43, 45–6, 98, 123, 124, 129, 130, 144, 159, 162, 165, 196, 230, 232
Demos, T.J. 98–9
design, and STS (science and technology studies) 14
Despret, V. 13, 14
devices *(dispotif)* 191
Dewey, J. 8, 10, 11, 29, 30, 36–40, 205, 206, 210, 235n7
digital technologies 154, 166–7
  'don't make me think' maxim 163–6
  machinic environment 18, 157–9, 160, 164, 165–6, 167
  machinic highs 18, 153–5, 159, 165, 167
  'meaningful social interactions' 155–7
  modular de-compositions 159–62
  pathic experience 157–60, 161, 162, 164, 165, 166, 167
  software production 160–1
  see also machinic highs
dopamine *see* machinic highs
Dreier, T. 235n7
Drift Table prototype 173, 174–5
Du Bois, W.E.B. 76, 80, 81, 82, 83n9
During, S. 218
Duvernoy, R.J. 46, 47, 52

E

Earth
  as geologically dynamic 58
  see also geology
eating disorders, and Instagram 155–6
ecology
  of practices 122, 123, 124, 127
  values in 93–4
  of the virtual 94–5
education 229–30
  countering over-specialization and disconnect between disciplines 228–9
  schools of feeling 226–8, 234
  studium generale model 228–9
  see also aesthetic education; universities
Eibl-Eibesfeldt, I. 50
Eichmann, A. 62, 63
embolisms, risk of 140, 145, 146–7, 148, 149
empiricism 111–12
  radical 131
Endangered Human Movements series (Piña) 133
  see also Climatic Dances/Danzas Climáticas (Piña)
endorphins *see* machinic highs
Energy Babble prototype 176, 177–8
entertain, terminology of 32, 38, 40n3, 209
entities, actual 9, 33, 34, 72
environment 3, 39, 40
epistemology 10
Escobar, A. 14
eternal objects 42–3, 115, 116, 117

nuclear waste final repositories 43–5, 49–54, *50*
  and values 45–9
ethico-aesthetics 154, 157, 159–60, 161, 164
ethics
  and digital technology 156
  values in 93
event, the 140, 142, 143
experience 8–9, 14, 30, 31, 36, 38, 46
  effect of bifurcation of nature on 6–7
  human experience 31, 34, 122, 190, 198–9, 200, 233
  indexing of 14, 15
experimental facts 123
Expert Judgement on Markers to Deter Inadvertent Human Intrusion into the Water Isolation Pilot Plant panel 49, 50, *50*, 51
extractivism 18, 89, 92
  see also Climatic Dances/Danzas Climáticas (Piña)

F

facial expressions 50, *50*
factories 212
Fanon, F. 80
feeling 30, 31–2, 36, 46, 72, 82, 126, 196, 225
  indexing of 14, 15
  and prehensions 144
  schools of 226–8, 234
feminism
  feminist knowledge 228
  feminist studies on technoscience 12, 14
Fisher, M. 105, 107–8, 117
Ford, L.S. 32
Forensic Architecture 14
forensics 65
  forensic aesthetics 17, 65
  forensic science
    geology as 61
    and law 62–3
fossils 59–63, 66
  technofossils 17, 64–8
Foucault, M. 166, 168n11
France, *communitairisme* 80–1
Frankfurt School 11
Freud, S. 163
  Freudian reality principle 109, 113

G

Gaia hypothesis 58
Galileo Galilei 224
Galison, P. 93
gamification 18, 156–7
Gaver, W. 173
Gell, A. 11
gendered language 37
generalization, of aesthetics 7, 9, 10, 11, 13, 15, 17, 18, 19, 127, 143, 225
  art in education 207–14, 216–17, 218

INDEX

Geological Time Scale 57, 59, 60, 66
  see also Anthropocene, the,
    Anthropocene hypothesis
geology 17, 57–9
  fossils and planetary forensics 59–63
  technofossils 17, 64–8
God 54n2
Goethe, J.W. von 135n2
Gomart, E. 21n13
Goodman, N. 205
governmentality 166
great refusal, the 18, 104–8
  and Dante 18, 104, 105, 106–7, 108, 110, 112, 117
  and Whitehead 18, 105, 108–10
    Great Refusal I 110–12, 113–14
    Great Refusal II 112–17
Guattari, F. 3–4, 15–16, 92, 94–5, 97–8, 99, 123, 124, 129, 130, 134, 153–4, 157, 158, 159, 160, 162, 164–5, 196, 230

H

habits of thought 3–4, 19, 45, 214, 218n2, 222, 224, 225, 227–8, 231, 232–3, 235n11
Haiti 81
Halewood, M. 82
Harding, S. 12
Hartman, S. 83n9
Haugen F. 155–6
Hennion, A. 20n11, 21n13
historical events 199
Holocene, the 57
Home Health Monitor prototype 175
Hooper, S.E. 46
human experience 31, 34, 122, 190, 198–9, 200, 233
Human Interface Task Force, US Department of Energy 49, 51
human rights law, and forensic anthropology 63
humans, characteristics of 200–1
Hume, D. 11, 35

I

IBM 163
idiot, the (conceptual persona) 16, 181
immanence, aesthetics of 95–6, 98
immigration 78, 79
importance 208, 209, 215
Indigenous cosmologies 121, 125–6
  see also Climatic Dances/Danzas Climáticas (Piña); Masewal people, Pueblo, Mexico
Indigenous knowledge 228
  Native Alaskan communities 229–30
'inert ideas' 209, 210
infrastructure, as indicator of the Anthropocene 62
ingress 47
Instagram, and eating disorders 155–6

'interest convergence' 83n8
interests 12–13
internet, the, development of 160
  see also digital technologies
intolerant abstraction 109, 110, 111, 114, 115
inversion, of aesthetics 7–8, 10

J

James, W. 8–9, 95, 96, 131, 205, 208, 215, 225, 226, 233
Joyce, R. 51

K

Kant, I. 7, 8, 11, 29, 31, 32, 34, 36, 93, 122, 127, 225
Kauffman, S. 197
Keenan, T. 62–3, 65
King, M.L. Jr. 77
Kircher, A. 65
Kircher, A. 61
Klee, P. 162
knowledge
  and experience 8–9
  feminist 228
  Indigenous 228, 229–30
  situated 229–30
  'traditional' 230
  verification of 65–6
Koselleck, R. 65
Krenak, A. 125
Krug, S. 163

L

Landscape of Thorns concept 49
Langer, S. 213–14
language, gendered 37
Latin America 14
Latour, B. 13, 21n15, 58, 122, 177, 203n1
law, and forensic science 62–3
Levy, P. 160
logic 215
Lorde, A. 82
Lorimer, J. 97
Lovelock, J. 58
Lyell, C. 58, 59

M

machinic enslavement 165
machinic environment 18, 157–9, 160, 164, 165–6, 167
machinic highs 18, 153–5, 159, 165, 167
maize cytogenetics 13
'majority sciences' 196
Mallon, R. 83n5
manipulation, and digital technology 156
Marcuse, H. 105, 109–10, 112–13
Masewal people, Pueblo, Mexico 125–6, 131–4
  see also Climatic Dances/Danzas Climáticas (Piña)

Massumi, B. 54, 175
'matters of concern' 177–8
McClintock, B. 13
Mengele, J. 62–3
meta-care 181, 183
metaphysics
 and aesthetics 30, 31–3, 34, 36, 38, 45
 of more-than-human aesthetics 7–10
micro-mediations of care 180, 183
microplastics, as indicator of the
  Anthropocene 64
Mill, J.S. 75, 112
Mills, C. 79
mining see Climatic Dances/Danzas Climáticas
  (Piña)
Mirzoeff, N. 92
missing shade of blue 35–6
mode of production 39–40
moderator role 182
modernity, sociality in 10–11
modes of ingression 47
modular de-compositions, digital
  technologies 159–62
Mol, A. 178, 179
Moore, J. 221–2
more-than-human aesthetics 2–3, 13–15, 38–9
 metaphysics of 7–10
more-than-human, the
 in geology 59
 in technoscience 12–13
morphine, wrong-route administration
  of 140, 141, 142, 145–6, 147,
  149, 151n11
Morris, W. 109–210
Moynihan Report 75
Munch, E. 42, 45, 49–50, 51–2

N

National Museum for African American
  History and Culture, Washington D.D. 76
Native Alaskan communities 229–30
'natural antiquities' 61
nature
 apparent nature 4, 6
 'bare nature' 4, 6
 bifurcation of 4–7, 13, 29–30, 31, 39,
   111, 121–2, 123, 127, 174, 189–90, 206,
   207–8, 218, 234n2, 234n3, 194202
 and aesthetic education 19, 221–2,
   224–35
 causal nature 4
 'nature as perceived' 4
 nature-culture divide 121–4
negative prehension 18, 130, 131, 132, 143,
  144, 146–7, 148, 149, 195
never events, in the NHS 18, 139–43,
  149–51
 aesthetics of a more-than-human care
   system 147–8

anaesthetics of possible consequences 145–7
prehensions and negative
  prehensions 143–4
'new aesthetic paradigm' 3, 92, 94, 121, 134,
  207, 218
Newton, I. 111–12, 117, 213, 223
NHS see never events, in the NHS
Nietzsche, F. 92, 94
Noah's Ark 61
noise pollution 14
nomadic sciences 196
nostalgia 92
Notre-Dame-des-Landres 99–100
novel materials 64
nuclear semiotics 44, 45, 49, 53, 54
nuclear waste final repositories 43–5, 49–54, 50
nuclear weapons testing fallout, as indicator of
  the Anthropocene 62, 66–7, 68

O

obligations 123, 124
occasions, actual 33, 34, 43, 46–7, 52
ontology 10, 14–15
Osborne, T. 20n9
Oury, J. 158
outside, the aesthetics of 94–5, 98

P

Palestine Heirloom Seed Library (PHSL),
  Battir 100–1
Palmieri, D. 128
Pater, W. 217
pathic experience 157–60, 161, 162, 164,
  165, 166, 167
patient safety see never events, in the NHS
perception 32, 33, 34, 192, 193, 216
 missing shade of blue 35–6
Persuasive Technology Lab, Stanford
  University 156
philosophy 5, 8
 'philosophy of organism' 7, 31
 Philosophy of Race 17, 74, 83n5
PHSL (Palestine Heirloom Seed Library),
  Battir 100–1
physics 5, 223
Piña, A. 18, 120–1, 124–6, 128–35
poet, the (aesthetic figure) 16
poetry 213–14
 Romantic poets 16, 48, 112, 113, 117,
   212, 213
polar bears 96, 97
political economy, values in 93
politics 13, 93
positive prehension 18, 130, 131, 143, 144,
  147, 148, 149, 194–5
post-modernity, sociality in 10–11
Pottage, A. 60
pragmatism 123, 135n3, 205, 206, 207,
  225, 235n7

INDEX

'predatory abstractions' 7
prehension 9, 13, 126, 144, 149, 174, 175
 negative 18, 130, 131, 132, 143, 144, 146–7, 148, 149, 195
 positive 18, 130, 131, 143, 144, 147, 148, 149, 194–5
'pre-individual,' the 42
Prinzhorn, H. 167n7
problematics of freedom 20n9
professionalization 208
prototypes 172
 high and low finishing 173–6, 180
Proust, M. 162
psychosis 157–9, 160
Puig de la Bellacasa, M. 13, 177–8
pure potentials 42, 43

Q

Questa, A. 131, 132

R

race
 fiction(s) of 74–7
 social aesthetics of 17, 71–2, 73–4
  aesthetics problems 74–81
  forms of racial sensibility 79–81
  racial projects as aesthetic projects 77–9
 as a social construct 73
racial eliminativism 73, 74, 83n5
Rancière, J. 21n16
rationalism 109
'rationalization' 219n9
'reflex arc concept' 8
refrains 162, 164, 165
religion
 religious experience, as aesthetic education 232–4
 scripture, as source of knowledge 65–6
requirements 123, 124
research events 176
 'fit,' aesthetics and care in 179–83
 matters of care in 177–9, 183–4
ressentiment 92
Rhine valley 58, 59
rituals 233
Romantic poets 16, 48, 112, 113, 117, 212, 213
Romanticism 206
'royal sciences' 196
RSI (Rural Systemic Initiative) 229–30
Ruskin, J. 209–10
Ruyer, R. 45, 48–9, 53–4

S

sacrifice zone *(zona se scarificio)* 125
Sagan, C. 49
Savransky, M. 13, 225
Scarry, E. 149
'scars of existence' 149, 195, 202

Schawinsky, X. 231–2
Schiller, F. 206, 225
schizophrenia 158, 159
schools of feeling 226–8, 234
Schull, N. 157
science 13, 113, 196–7, 208
 and education 223–4
 experimental facts 123
 'majority' 196
 and nature 5–6, 111–12
 nomadic 196
 'royal' 196
 science wars 7, 11–12, 123
 technoscience 12–13, 97
 values in 93
science and technology studies (STS) 12–13, 14
scientific materialism 5–6, 113, 225, 231
Scream, The (Munch) 42, 45, 49–50, 51
scripture, as source of knowledge 65–6
seed banks 100–1
Segall, M. 72
Sehgal, M. 45, 121, 122–3, 124
self, the 9, 38
self-doubt, and the great refusal 107, 108, 117
semblance 175, 176
semiotics, nuclear 44, 45, 49, 53, 54
sense perception 216
sepsis, risk of 146–7, 148, 149
Sexton, J. 80
Shannon, C. 116
Shaviro, S. 9, 48, 127–8, 175
Shelley, P. 16, 112, 213
Silicon Valley 156, 166
 see also digital technologies
Simondon, G. 42–3, 52–3
situated knowledges 229–30
slavery 73, 75, 78, 81
Sloterdijk, P. 66
Smail, D. 108
Sobolef, W. 229–30
social aesthetics 11, 72–4, 81, 82
 of race 17, 71–2, 73–4
  aesthetics problems 74–81
'social capital' 11
social class 10, 11
social media
 'meaningful social interactions' 155–7
 see also machinic highs
social scientific research, aesthetics and care in 18–19, 172–3, 183–4
 'fit' in the research event 179–83
 high and low finishing 173–6, 180
 matters of care 177–9
sociality, in modernity and post-modernity 10–11
societies, life and death of 72–3
socio-cultural research 10–11, 14

243

socio-ecological crisis 17
'sociological wisdom' 72, 73, 78
software production 160–1
soil science 58
Souriau, E. 13
spectrodrama 231–2
speculative forensics 61, 64–8
speculative geology 60–1, 64
  technofossils 64–8
Stadler, F. 163
Stengers, I. 12–13, 16, 45, 54n2, 106, 111, 114, 115–16, 122, 123, 124, 127, 130, 165, 181, 189, 190–1, 192–3, 195, 196–7, 197–8, 199–201, 202, 203, 216, 218n2, 223–4
Steno, N. 61, 65–6
sticky users 163
Stoermer, E.F. 2, 60
stratigraphy 58–9, 60–2, 66
  technostratigraphy 64–5, 68
'stream of thought' 20n6
STS (science and technology studies) 12–13, 14
studium generale 228–9
style 211–12
subject-object relations 11
superposition 61–2
supplementation 33–4, 35, 36
swan songs 89–91, 92, 101
synthetic fertilizers, as indicator of the Anthropocene 62

T

Tamen, M. 62
Taubira, C. 81
Taylor, P. 74
technical education 210
technofossils 17, 64–8
technological revolutions, nineteenth century 73
technoscience 12–13, 97
technosphere 64
technostratigraphy 64–5, 68
television-watching 162, 163
theatre 122
  see also Climatic Dances/*Danzas Climáticas* (Piña)
ticks 14, 15
time capsules 49, 51
Tohuko, Japan 100
Tosquelles, F. 158
transcendental aesthetics 31, 33, 34
transversality 124, 129, 134, 155, 167, 189, 228, 234
  transversal aesthetics 3–4, 10, 11, 13, 14
tsunami, Japan 100
Turkle, S. 154
Turpin, E. 2

U

Uexküll, J.J. von 14
understanding 211, 214–15

universal mannerism 194
universities 223–5
  countering over-specialization and disconnect between disciplines 228–9
  schools of feeling 226–8
  studium generale model 228–9
urban culture 10, 11
'user stickiness' 154

V

value/values 91–2, 93–4, 95–6, 126–7, 208, 209, 210, 212, 213
  aesthetic axiology 124–8
  and eternal objects 45–9
  immanent 95–6
  value ecology 96, 115
Van Wyck, P. 49–50
Venegas, L. 128
virtual, the 43
Von Weizsäcker, V. 158

W

wandering 233–4
warfare and conflict 1, 2
Washington, B. T. 75
Waters, C.N. 64
Weizman, E. 62–3, 65
Welsch, W. 20n10
'white ambush' 80
'white double consciousness' 80, 81
'White Ignorance' 79
'white innocence' 79, 81
Whitehead, A.N. 3–4, 4–5, 6, 7–8, 9–10, 14–15, 16, 29, 30, 31–7, 38, 39, 42, 43, 44, 45, 47–8, 49, 51–2, 53, 54, 71, 72–4, 76, 78, 81, 82, 93, 121–2, 123, 124, 126–7, 128, 130, 131, 140, 142, 143, 144, 149, 150, 174, 175, 183, 189–90, 191, 192, 193, 194–5, 196, 197, 198–9, 200, 201, 202, 203, 221, 222, 223, 224, 225, 226, 227, 231, 232–4
  art and aesthetic education 205, 206, 207–18
Wilderson, F. 80
Wilkie, A. 176
Wordsworth, W. 16, 48, 112, 213
wrong-route drug administration 140, 141, 142, 145–6, 147, 149, 151n11
Wynter, S. 77, 78, 79, 83n6

Y

Yusoff, K. 96

Z

Zack, N. 83n5
ZAD *(zone à défendre)* 99–100
Zalasiewicz, J. 65
zona se scarificio (sacrifice zone) 125
zones of proximity 129, 130

www.ingramcontent.com/pod-product-compliance
Lightning Source LLC
Chambersburg PA
CBHW051535020426
42333CB00016B/1938